Fighting Editors

THE NAYLOR COMPANY

Fighting Editors

The Story of

Editors Who Faced

Six-Shooters with Pens

and Won

Jo Ann Schmitt

SAN ANTONIO, TEXAS

TO

My Parents

Joe L., Jr. and Helen Schmitt

Pioneers in a modern Arizona

Acknowledgments

A work of this nature is only possible because of the unselfish cooperation of numerous individuals and institutions.

The author is particularly indebted to Walter Seifert, advertising executive, and Maurice Frink, director of the Colorado Historical Society, who gave so many helpful comments while this book was in its formulative stage.

My special thanks go to Barbara Pilliod; Jean Schmitt who worked untold hours in checking research notes; and Laura Becker who helped proof the final manuscript. I appreciate the understanding and encouragement of my parents and friends during the five year period that the book was in preparation.

Numerous persons and libraries helped locate pioneer newspapers and long forgotten personal histories. The author acknowledges these research contributors:

Eleanor B. Sloan, secretary of the Arizona Pioneers' Historical Society; the Library of Congress; A. T. Richardson, editor of the Pomona Progress Bulletin; State Historical Society of Wisconsin; the Los Angeles Public Library; the San Diego Public Library; Mr. Alice B. Good, director of the Department of Library and Archives of the State of Arizona; the Bancroft Library at the University of California; the Sharlot Hall Historical Museum; and Dr. W. R. Manning, grandson of editor Rollin C. Brown.

Contents

Publisher's Note

All material quoted in the text of this book has been reprinted exactly as it appeared in the columns of the early-day newspapers from which it was taken. No attempt was made to correct spelling, punctuation or other errors. The original was left as it appeared so the reader might capture more of the flavor of frontier journalism.

Introduction

This is a regal land. A land where death is king and beauty reigns as queen. A land whose history unfolds with the twang of the bowstring, the staccato bark of the six-gun, and the growl of the pioneer printing press.

The Papago Indians name the royal province "Aleh-zon," but the trapper, explorer, soldier, missionary, miner, settler, and newspaper editor desecrate it by more colorful names — mostly Hell! Five sites will bear that infernal title. Future generations will know it as Arizona.

Nature groans in protest when the first man ruptures the virgin soil and stares in awe as he seeks desperately to carve a living from her earth. The Basketmaker people appear, followed by the Pueblo and Hohokam. As always, death commands, and these prehistoric people leave only their giant cliff houses, irrigation systems, and artifacts for future generations to marvel over.

Here lies a desert where beauty lures men to their death. Glimmering gold entices the novice into traps of shifting sands where water flows only in men's aspirations. This land of contrast seduces the adventurer through desert, bejeweled with cholla and guarded by the forces of the devil — the rattlesnake, the heat, and the lawless; yet he feels amply rewarded by the sight of the giant cactus at sunset, raising its arms like a desert priest in benediction over this land of beauty and death.

A strange procession commences to cast its shadows through this courtly land. Explorers, fur trappers, missionaries, miners, settlers — all seek solace or gain in the untrodden wilderness.

The first European intruder to the regal land is a Negro slave named Estevanico. His disastrous journey originates in Mexico City in 1539. Tales of the Seven Cities of Cibola to the north had trickled into Mexico City for years. The Spanish viceroy, Mendoza, before equipping a major expedition to these cities of solid gold, glowing with treasure, assigns the Franciscan priest, Fray Marcos de Niza, to investigate the report. The priest's guide and companion is Estevanico.

Upon reaching northern Sonora, Mexico, the slave strides in advance to gather information. Lacking in education, he is to indicate the country and send back news of the legendary Cibola in the shape of crosses via Indian courier. "A cross one-hand in length would indicate average country." Estevanico responds warmly to nature's overtures and the brown-robed Franciscan is pleased and surprised when four days later an Indian courier appears carrying a cross taller than a man.

Estevanico, taking advantage of his color, which is strange to the Indians, tells them tales which might have been the cause of his violent death. Legend says the slave, enjoying his newfound freedom, presents himself to the natives as a supernatural being and demands the finest gifts, entertainment, food — and young maidens for his bed. The awed Indians of southern Arizona accommodate him while death hovers nearby.

When Estevanico reaches Zuni, one of the mythical cities of Cibola, he makes the same demands. These fierce warriors resent the thought of a stranger, even a god, despoiling their women. Now, Zuni gods are immortal, so to test this foreigner's claims there is the snap of bowstrings and the whistle of arrows. The slave sprawls in death much to the "surprise" of the Zuni. Thus does Arizona succor her first European visitor.

A friendly Indian brings news of the Negro's fate to Fray Marcos on the 21st of May, 1539. With great difficulty the Franciscan persists and from a hill sights this city of Cibola. The friar erects a cross on a heap of stones and takes formal possession of the regal land in the name of the Viceroy Mendoza and the Spanish king. His duty completed, the friar hastens homeward *"con harto mas temor que comida,"* (with a lot more fear than food.)

Arriving in Mexico City, Fray Marcos confirms the existence of the cities of gold. The regal land plays tricks on the unwary and so the priest and others to come fall unwilling victims of an optical illusion. Though at midday the adobe walls of the Zuni village are lifeless, the flare of the lowering sun plates them a flagrant gold. Today's photographer takes advantage of this color change, but for these early visitors it is the cause of their ultimate disgrace.

In 1540, the conquistador, Coronado, commands a large mounted army in search of the famous Cibola. Across shifting sand dunes, through treacherous mountain passes, jagged escarpments, and fertile valleys, the mail-coated Spaniards ride. Zuni succumbs after a short pitched battle but proves to be a poverty-stricken village. A lieutenant of Coronado discovers the Grand Canyon during this expedition and so gives us one of the Wonders of the Modern World. The frustrated Coronado persists in the search for Cibola, marching his army as far as the present state of Kansas — and disaster.

Other armored Spaniards appear on the Arizona scene and are followed by the sandaled missionaries. Father Kino labors for 24 years in southern Arizona among the Pima and Papago Indians. This beloved missionary and explorer introduces cattle and horses into a state which in centuries to come will be famous for its great ranches. Indian revolts, massacres and bloodshed obscure the Arizona picture for many years. Historical San Xavier del Bac Mission, built in 1700, crumbles under the onslaught of the fierce Apache Indians, only to be rebuilt by the zealous missionaries.

Spanish attention turns from the gold of Cibola to silver and precious stones. Numerous mines are opened throughout Arizona, but the eager miner often finds only intangible minerals — amethyst hues that rest on the ridges and wrap the abrupt gorges of the range in wondrous beauty; the garnet and opal tones on the mountain peaks as the rising sun dispels the pale grey mist that has gathered during the night; and gold in the setting sun. Some of the fortune hunters escape the scalping knives of the Apache and pry riches from the avaricious land. From the Planchos de la Plata Mine the Spanish take one piece of native silver weighing 2,700 pounds, according to local folklore.

Trappers, hunters, and prospectors drift into the territory after 1800. The steel nerves and accurate guns of such men bring a crude but swift form of justice to the untamed country. Over the regal land during three centuries fly the flags of Spain, Mexico, the Confederacy, and the United States.

Early attempts to colonize California come from the desert land. The coastal metropolis of San Francisco owes its founding to a soldier stationed at the Spanish presidio of Tubac in south-central Arizona. Captain Juan Bautista de Anza with a group of poverty-stricken Sonora colonists establishes the great bay city in March of 1776.

Political intrigue appears on the Arizona-Mexico scene and on a March day in 1857, Arizona's filibusterer, Henry A Crabb, and 100 of his followers crumple before a firing squad in Sonora, Mexico. Violence and blood continue to run through the land. On a spring day in 1862, in central Arizona, blue and grey garbed soldiers battle the Civil War conflict.

In this land of contrasts a lighthouse rises from the desert floor and a Temple to the Sun God is envisioned, while diamonds, opals, and rubies are reported along mountain creeks of northern Arizona. A California editor of the day travels through the territory and says, "This is a land of marvels. The painted desert . . . is the beauty of death, and a mimicry of life."

Arizona is isolated by poor transportation and communication but the nation watches it with interest. Attempts are made in Congress as early as 1857 to organize a territorial government for Arizona. The first bill is introduced by a California legislator but fails as a result of railroad jealousies. In 1860, Missouri offers a bill to provide a "temporary government for the Territory of Arizona," which also fails. The final creation of the territory is due partly to the Civil War. The Confederates invade Arizona and here they find gold. So the Confederate government quickly organizes Arizona into a territory separate from New Mexico, with the full approval of the Territory's residents. This recognition by the Confederacy, coupled with the efforts of Ohio, New Mexico, and California, leads to the passage of a bill in Congress creating the Territory of Arizona. The bill is made official with the signature of President Lincoln on the 24th day of February, 1863.

On a frosty December morning in 1863, a small insignificant place near the New Mexico border is the scene of an important event for Arizona and her people. At Navajo Springs the newly appointed federal officials raise the Stars and Stripes, take their oaths of office, and proclaim Arizona a territory.

To this land of beauty and death, men continue to stride in search of gold, fame, adventure and escape. From these pioneers develop ranchers, miners, businessmen, and settlers. We are concerned here with a unique breed of men that develop in this frontier — fighting editors.

A "Fighting Editor" may have been born in Rhode Island or Louisiana, may have been a student at Rutgers or a farmer; but all have two beliefs in common — one in themselves and one in ARIZONA. Freedom of the press often finds itself to the point of license, but any difficulty can be settled by a six-gun in the grey dawn light.

Stories which these editors print will become an important part of our history. However, their own lives and deeds seem more thrilling than any of the stories which find their way into type. This, then, is the story as fought and written by eleven Arizona editors who typify the spirit of America a century ago. In revealing the deeds of these fighting editors there unfolds the history of their towns and life in a bygone era, how they faced numerous problems which they finally conquered, and how these unheralded pioneers turned wildernesses into bustling metropolises.

To these editors is due much of the credit for molding the raw land and adventurous people into organized communities. These writers, battling to obtain statehood for their territory, cannot be called literary geniuses. They use poor grammar, neglect spelling, and ignore the dictionary. But from the early papers on the Atlantic coast, rallying the patriots in the Revolutionary War to those in Arizona, who are crusading for military protection from Indians, the editors lead the fight — and win it. Here is the story of the West, not as it is envisioned by the modern writer, but in the words of the men who lived in and fought for Arizona, America's last frontier.

A young editor writes, "I can die at my post but I can never desert it." On a brisk fall day in 1837, a seething mob shoots him to death as he stands by his printing press — not in the lawless West but in Alton, Illinois; the editor dying because he refuses to relent in his editorial crusade condemning Negro slavery. In the humid towns of Georgia and on the fog-bound California coast, editors often die in defense of the ideas they have put into print. From such as these spring the Fighting Editors.

THE WEEKLY ARIZONIAN.

Vol. 1. TUBAC, ARIZONA, MARCH 24, 1859. No. 4.

THE ARIZONIAN,
A WEEKLY PAPER.
DEVOTED TO THE GENERAL INTERESTS OF ARIZONA.

— TERMS —

Three Dollars per annum, in advance.

RATES OF ADVERTISING

One Square, of 10 lines, or less,	one insertion,	$2 00
" " " "	" three "	4 00
" " " "	" one quarter,	10 00
" " " "	" one year,	30 00

All communications and business letters must be addressed to The Arizonian, Tubac, Arizona.

Sonora and its Resources.

We copy from Wilson's "Mexico its Peas-

the river after a great flood. On arriving at the other side, he found the crest of an immense *lode* laid bare by the force of the water. The greater part of this was pure massive silver, sparkling in the rays of the sun. The whole town of Batopilos went to gaze at the extraordinary sight as soon as the river was fordable. This Indian extracted great wealth from his mine, but, on coming to the depth of three Spanish yards (*varas*), the abundance of water obliged him to abandon it, and no attempts have since been made to resume the working. When the silver is not found in solid masses, which requires to be cut with the chisel, it is generally finely sprinkled through the *lode*, and often serves to nail together the particles of stone through which it is disseminated."* "The ores of the *Pastiano* mine, near the Car-

priating it to the king's use. This put a stop to private enterprize; and, after the Indian war set in, Arazuma became almost a forgotten locality, and in a generation or two afterward, the account of its mineral riches began to be discredited.

We have the following record in evidence of the masses of silver extracted at Arazuma. Don Domingo Asmendi paid duties on a piece of virgin silver that weighed 275 lbs. The king's attorney (*fiscal*) brought suit for several other pieces, which together weighed 4033 lbs. Also for the recovery, as a curiosity, and therefore the property of the king, a certain piece of silver of the weight of 2800 lbs. This is probably the largest piece of pure silver ever found in the world, and yet it was found only a few miles distant from the contemplated track

Public Lands to Actual Settlers.

We have several times heard inquiries in regard to the act of Congress donating public lands within the Territory of New Mexico to actual settlers. The enactment, which was adopted in July, 1854, grants 160 acres of land to every white male citizen of the United States, or every white male above the age of twenty-one years, who has declared his intention to become a citizen, now residing in New Mexico, and who was so residing prior to 1st January, 1853, and to every white male citizen of the United States, and to every white male above the age of twenty-one years who has declared his intention to become a citizen, who should

"We have no law . . ."

Conducting a paper in a frontier
country is always a perilous,
precarious, and thankless task . . .
Edward E. Cross

First Lieutenant Sylvester Mowry, 4th U.S. Artillery, wipes the drops of sweat from his dust-streaked face. He looks with disgust at his battered, frogged-blue Army uniform, tilts his regulation cap farther back on his head and cusses the Army, the new gold rush, the Apaches, and Fort Yuma.

Mowry rereads the letter in front of him — his letter of resignation from the Army. Affixing his signature with a deliberate pen, Mowry frowns. He remembers that day in 1852 at West Point when he first received the bars of a lieutenant. But this is

1858, and Mowry is stationed at Fort Yuma on the southwestern border of Arizona. Arizona, though, is still a part of the New Mexico Territory.

The only future for an Army officer in Arizona is chasing murdering Apaches across the desert into their time-worn mountain strongholds! Mowry regrets that the infamous Johnson Massacre hadn't been more successful.

Johnson, an American trapper, had been killing Apaches for the Mexican government. He received $100 for the scalp of an Apache warrior, $50 for the scalp of a squaw, and $25 for that of a child. Later, when the Mexican government offered a large reward for the killing of Juan José, famed Apache chief, Johnson readily accepted the offer.

The chief and Johnson were old acquaintances, so Johnson had little difficulty in locating the wary Apache. Apache scouts, however, learned of the proposed treachery and reported to the chief. Juan José discredited the report and went to greet Johnson and his band of fur trappers.

When the two met, Juan addressed his old friend, "Don Santiago, we have never lied to each other. Give me your word of honor that the report is false. If it is untrue, bring your men to our camp and spend the night with us."

The trappers accepted the chief's hospitality, and upon arriving in camp prepared to distribute a gift of *pinole*[1] to the women and children. While the unsuspecting Indians gathered around the *pinole,* Johnson took a blunderbuss loaded with balls, chains, and other missiles. Many Apaches sprawled in the agony of death as the clamor of the gunshot faded away. Angry screams of the betrayed Indians rent the air. At the same instant another fur trader shot at Chief Juan. Severely wounded, the chief clinched his opponent and cried:

"Don Santiago, save me!"

As Johnson approached, Juan held a drawn knife against his adversary. The chief addressed Johnson in Spanish.

"For God's sake, help me. I could kill your white friend but I don't want to."

Ignoring the plea, Johnson shot the chief. In turn the surviving Apache warriors attacked Johnson and his men. The treacherous Johnson escaped but many of his men were not so fortunate. The avenging warriors attacked two nearby white

2

encampments, and before dawn 24 innocent white men died, as hundreds more would die in the years to come.

To protect the frontier from these relentless Indians, the government establishes a few military posts throughout the area. The Army protection is flimsy and officer Mowry is disgruntled.

Upon leaving the Army, Mowry joins trapper Johnson and others in a mining venture. Purchasing the Patagonia mine, they erect buildings and furnaces and change the name to the Mowry Mine. The mine yields some $950 per ton in silver, and Mowry's opinions of Arizona brighten with his income.

Desiring greater government assistance to aid in developing the Territory and its resources, Mowry seeks the office of delegate to Congress. He would represent the Territory of New Mexico, which still includes Arizona. Elected to the office of delegate, Rhode Island-born Mowry travels eastward to assume his new duties.

In the same year another New Englander, Edward E. Cross, travels from the nation's capital to Arizona by way of Texas. Cross, a journeyman printer, ex-editor of the *Cincinnati Times,* and special correspondent for the *New York Herald,* does not meet Mowry when he first enters the Territory. Cross becomes editor of Arizona's first paper, the *Weekly Arizonian,* at Tubac. The meeting of the editor and mining engineer must wait; but when they do, it will be in a blaze of bullets.

Using a Washington hand press, Cross offers the first issue of the *Weekly Arizonian* on March 3, 1859. As his readers are comprised of a few miners, a handful of adventurers and hangers-on from the days when Tubac was a Mexican presidio, Cross states very simply the aims of the paper in his first editorial:

THE ARIZONIAN

We commence today the publication of a weekly newspaper under the above title, devoted to the interests of Arizona and the development of its resources.

The territory we have selected for our home is unlike any other portion of the United States. Separated on the one hand by the broad, unsettled wastes of Texas and New Mexico from the Atlantic States, and on the other from the golden sands of California, it resembles neither region in its climate, soil or resources.

Attached as we now are nominally to the Territory of New Mexico, and situated many hundred miles from its seat of government, the western portion of Arizona is a region without the shadow of anything that claims to be law. The highest crimes may be committed and justice can never overtake the fugitive. So far as we know, no judge or justice, either Federal or Territorial, has ever visited this portion of the country. One great object we shall have in view will be to advocate the establishment of law and government in Arizona.

In politics our opinions are fixed, and when the social requirements of our state demand it, we shall speak our sentiments freely and fully. For the present, and until government extends to us the right of suffrage, we shall ignore the subject, till our citizens are vouchsafed the right to take part in the great political questions which agitate the Union.

In general news, we will endeavor to give our readers a summary of the events which are passing in the world. The limits of our paper are necessarily small, but they are thought to be sufficient for our wants at the present time. We shall enlarge them as the necessities of the Territory justify.

In the enterprize (sic) we have now begun, we have little hopes of pecuniary gain. The reading population of Arizona is small, and the expense of publication great. It is not, therefore, with very bright prospects of pecuniary return that we begin our labors. Yet, if we feel that we have the sympathy and good wishes of the people of our country, and that our labors contribute somewhat, however little, to procure for them the boon they are now asking of the General Government, we shall feel amply rewarded for the toils and labors we have undertaken.

(*Weekly Arizonian* of March 3, 1859)

Cross could not have found a better town in which to establish the Territory's first paper. Located on the Santa Cruz River, Tubac boasts of a kaleidoscopic population of some 600 persons. By far the largest of the four settlements in Arizona, Tubac

4

is a center of great mining activity. A resident of this outpost, which was first founded by the Spaniards in 1752, says:

"We have no law but love, and no occupation but labor. No government, no taxes, no public debt, no politics. It is a community in a perfect state of nature."

Tubac hosts many Spanish women, for civil wars in Mexico and the California gold rush have called most of their men.

The Mexican señoritas really have a refining influence on the frontier population. They call the American men '*Los God-dammes*' and the American women '*Las Camisas-Coloradas.*'[2] If there is anything that a Mexican woman despises, it is a red pettycoat. They are exceedingly dainty in their underclothing — wear the finest linen they can afford; and spend half their lives . . . washing.

This accretion of female population adds very much to the charms of frontier society. The Mexican women are not by any means useless appendages in camp. They can keep house, cook some dainty dishes, wash clothes, sew, dance and sing. Moreover, they are expert at cards, and divest many a miner of his week's wages over a game of monte.

An idea that it is lonesome at Tubac would be incorrect. One can never be lonesome who is useful, and it is considered at the time that the opening of mines which yielded nothing before, the cultivation of land which lies fallow, the employment of labor which is idle, and the development of a new country, are meritorious undertakings.

The table at Tubac is generously supplied with the best the market affords, besides venison, antelope, turkeys, bear, quail, wild ducks, and other game, and we obtain through Guaymas a reasonable supply of French wines for Sunday dinners and the celebration of feast days.

It is astonishing how rapidly the development of mines increases commerce. We had scarcely commenced to make silver bars, — 'current with the merchant' — when the plaza of Tubac presented a picturesque scene of primitive commerce. Pack trains arrive from Mexico, loaded with all kinds of provisions. The rule is to purchase everything they bring, whether we want it or not. They are quite willing to take in exchange silver bars or American merchandise. Whether they pay duties in Mexico is none of our business. We are essentially free traders.[3]

5

Miners and other laborers receive their wages once a month in cardboard money. With silver bullion too bulky for everyday buying, the Heintzeman Mining Company has engravings made in New York and paper money printed on pasteboard about two inches by three. Each piece is a *boleta* (voucher for money) and animal pictures show the value of the piece for the numerous illiterates in the valley. The smallest sum is for 12½ cents, and this is represented by a pig; 25 cents is a calf; 50 cents a rooster; one dollar a horse; five dollars a bull; and ten dollars, the largest denomination, a lion.. The *boletas* are accepted by all the merchants who now have an interest in the success of the mine and are dependent upon it for their continued prosperity.

The usual routine at Tubac, in addition to the regular business of distributing supplies to the mining camps, is chocolate or strong coffee the first thing in the morning, breakfast at sunrise, dinner at noon, and supper at sunset.

Sunday is the day of days at Tubac, as the superintendents come in from the mining camps to spend the day, and take dinner, returning in the afternoon. One Sunday we had a fat wild turkey, weighing about twenty-five pounds, and one of the engineers asked permission to assist in the *cocina*.[4] It was done to a charm, and stuffed with pine nuts, which gave it a fine flavor.

In the spring of 1857 a garden containing about two acres was prepared at Tubac, and irrigated by a canal from the Santa Cruz River. By the industry of a German gardener, with two Mexican assistants, we soon produce all the vegetables, melons, etc., that we require, and many a weary traveler remembers, or ought to remember, the hospitality of Tubac. We are never a week without some company and sometimes have more than we require; but nobody is ever charged anything for entertainment, horseshoeing, and fresh supplies for the road. Hospitality is a savage virtue, and disappears with civilization.

. . . Tubac might well be regarded as the headquarters of civilization in the Territory. Men of refinement and education connected with the mines are here occasionally assembled, and even the fair sex are well represented. The gardens afford a pleasant place of retreat in summer, with their shady groves of acacias and peach trees; and deep pools in the river, overhung by willows, are cleared out and made into bathing-places, in which all who please might refresh themselves with a luxurious bath.

Despite the peaceful setting of Tubac, murder is a frequent visitor. The citizens, angered by the incessant violence, organize a people's tribunal. Justice has been too long delayed or not invoked; for the nearest civil court is Santa Fe, New Mexico, a distance of some 500 miles.

The tribunal first tries a Mexican for the unprovoked killing of an American. After passing on the facts of the case, the tribunal chairman, Editor Cross, orders the prisoner sent to nearby Fort Buchanan until he can be taken to Santa Fe for trial.

Before adjourning, the tribunal unanimously adopts this resolution:

> RESOLVED: That in the future, until the establishment of law and courts among us, we will organize temporary courts, and administer justice to murderers, horse thieves, and other criminals, ourselves.

Heartened by the action of the tribunal in electing a temporary justice of the peace and constable, Chairman Cross turns to his newspaper columns. Speaking for his fellow citizens, Editor Cross addresses a new plea to Congress in this editorial:

WHAT OUR GOVERNMENT CAN DO FOR ARIZONA

> . . . The first great boon we have asked is a territorial organization; one which gives us a means of making and enforcing laws to protect life and property, and which will encourage the enterprising to come and settle within our limits. If this boon must be denied for a time, till other questions are settled, the next best thing for us, is the establishment of a separate Judicial District with a United States Judge and officers. This can be done without prejudice to the great question of a Territorial organization, and will give a semblance of a disposition on the part of government to extend to this distant region the first dawn of favor.
>
> With a court of law and Record, and probably a branch

office of the Surveyor General of Territory established at some suitable point, the people of this portion of the Territory could have many advantages. High crimes, such as murder and theft would be punished. Titles to property could be recorded and disputed claims settled. Boundary lines fixed, and many a disputed point now settled with the revolver and bowie knife, adjusted as becomes civilized and intelligent men — the interests of the country developed and emigration invited. We trust that the matter will receive early attention and a favorable consideration.

(*Weekly Arizonian* — March 10, 1859)

Not content with just writing for his own paper, Cross sends articles to the eastern papers which he represents. While believing strongly in Arizona, Cross feels that the East is wrong in thinking that Arizona is a sort of paradise. His articles are widely copied and quoted. His first dispatch finds its way to the columns of a paper in Washington, D.C.

Important From Arizona
THE HUMBUG EXPLODED!
The Gila Gold Mines a Failure, etc.

A correspondent, writing from Tubac, Arizona, under date of January 30, says:

The President in his late message to Congress, says, referring to Arizona: "The population of that Territory, numbering, as is alleged, more than *ten thousand souls,*" etc. Now, whoever alleges this, alleges what is not true. Raking and scraping together every human being within the proposed limits of Arizona — American, Mexicans, and Indians, white, black, yellow, and red — you cannot make a total of eight thousand inhabitants. The Indian population cannot be estimated with much certainty, but every tribe is greatly over-estimated, as is usual in such cases. The Mexican population at this end of the Territory is very small, not over one hundred and forty men, women, and children at Tubac, and perhaps twice that number at San Zavier (*sic*) and Tucson.

An old resident of the Mesilla valley, who knows everybody declares that there are not more than forty American residents in the valley, and not one solitary American woman! There are exactly sixteen American ladies in Arizona. Summing up the entire American population, including the men employed at the overland mail stations, and allowing largely for transient persons, *we barely make two hundred and fifty.* I think this is a very liberal estimate. Some of the 'oldest inhabitants' hereabouts declare that it is impossible to find even two hundred American residents in this territory. The vote for Mr. Mowry is no criterion of the population, for to quote the President's language, "it alleged that *everybody* voted — men, women, children, Indians, and Greasers." I do not pretend to say that such is the case — I only give the common rumor here abouts.

In regards to the Gila gold mines, the *Republican's* correspondent says:

We have bad news from the Gila gold mines. Every few days some "seedy," dead-broke, and half-starved individual strays into town with the usual story — "No gold there — all a d———d humbug!" One fellow told me I might judge of the state of things at a place where fifty cents was a big bet at monte! Provisions and clothing command the most extraordinary prices: Flour $16 per hundred, sugar $1.50 per pound, and coffee $2 per pound. Everybody that can get away is leaving, and fresh fools arrive constantly, *allured by the false reports published in the newspapers.*

There has been an enormous amount of falsehood uttered and published concerning this country and its resources. As an agricultural country it is worthless. Rain seldom falls, and there is very little permanent water. Were it not for the Indians, something might be done at stock raising, but under the existing order of things, there would be far more loss than profit. Silver mining will eventually be very profitable, as no country in the world is more abundant in silver ores and metals. Several silver mining companies are now in operation, with fine prospects.

(We will no doubt eventually get the truth from Arizona. As to the correctness of the above letter, we presume a paper with the reputation of the St. Louis Republican would not publish such an account as is here given, unless it came from a responsible source. — *States*)

(*Washington States* of Feb. 26, 1859)

A stockholder of the St. Louis and Arizona Mining Company, Editor Cross seeks the development of Arizona's resources. On this issue he is in accord with Sylvester Mowry, delegate to Congress from the Territory. Cross also joins Mowry in the fight to gain for Arizona the status of an independent territory. However, Mowry's mining company and the St. Louis and Arizona Company, in which Cross has an interest, have been waging an almost silent warfare for political control of the proposed Arizona Territory.

Still not having met, Cross and Mowry begin to exchange letters, which are printed in the eastern papers. The language becomes bitter and the battle for political control is soon submerged in personal animosity.

After Cross questions the truthfulness of Mowry's statement on Arizona, the delegate then writes to the paper:

Letter from Lieutenant Mowry — Arizona Affairs

EDITOR STATES: In your paper of Saturday, under the announcement, in large capitals, *"The Humbug Exploded,"* you publish an anonymous letter, copied from a St. Louis paper. Believing I know the source from which this letter emanated, I should not notice it here, were it not for the direct attack upon the statement in reference to the population of Arizona, viz: that it contains a population of more than 10,000 souls, exclusive of Indians. For this statement, I am responsible; and I again assert, that, so far from being exaggerated, it is below the actual number.

The person who wrote the letter you publish, has never seen enough of Arizona to write intelligibly about it; and in this item of population, he has stated what is absolutely untrue. Mr. Otero, the delegate from New Mexico, has certified in writing that, of his own knowledge, there were more than eight thousand people in the Rio Grande valley alone two years ago, and that the present population of the territory is at least ten or eleven thousands. If it is necessary I can call witnesses, now in Washington — certainly *ten* — whose respectability and position cannot be questioned, who will testify, at the bar of the Senate or House, to this same fact.

The letter you publish says there are not two hundred

Americans in the Territory. My list of American correspondents in Arizona contain three hundred and twenty-six
names, and I have supplied them, and several hundred
more, with newspapers this session. At one time my correspondent at Fort Yuma informed me there were seven
hundred Americans at the Gila mines. The list referred to
does not include the employees of the Overland Mail Company, who must number from one hundred and fifty to
two hundred more. The reference to my vote is simply an
absurd falsehood.

A number of gentlemen in Arizona wrote to their
friends in Washington among whom I recollect Hon. Jefferson Davis, Hon. John Letcher, and Hon. S. H. Wood-
son — stating emphatically that the vote was as fair and
legal as at any election in any part of the country, and
represented about one-fifth of the population. The whole
vote was 2,852. It is useless for any man to attempt to break
down these facts, except in the cowardly manner of an
anonymous letter. Had he been writing the truth, he would
not have been afraid to give his name.

With reference to the Gila gold mines, what has been
published I am in no degree responsible, for I have told
what I saw . . .

With regard to the agricultural resources of Arizona, I
have the statements of Bartlett, Whipple, Campbell, Gen.
Lane, Jack Hays, Nugent, and Bonneville to stand against
this anonymous "individual," who *says so many falsehoods
have been published about Arizona,"* and who has made
good his own charge by what he has himself written. I
have never claimed more than this, that Arizona had sufficient arable land to support a large population— sufficient
to make a wealthy and flourishing State. I assert it, and
have proved it by more evidence than it would be sufficient
to hang twenty such fellows as the writer of this anonymous letter if he was on trial — a fate, by the way, which
will be apt to overtake him when his letter gets back to Arizona. I shall republish it, with my answer, for general
circulation among my people.

*   *   *   *   *

Congress may adjourn without giving Arizona the
protection she has asked for five years *(sic)*. This will be
accepted by the people of the Territory as a declaration
that they are not entitled to the rights of American citi-

zens, because they have with the vigor and enterprise of American character sought the frontier to plant there the institutions of their country, and to build up in a remote and almost unknown region a State which shall connect the Atlantic with the Pacific.

The case has been presented by me without exaggeration. It remains to be seen if we are still to be left not only to the depredations of the Apache, who is daily enacting in Arizona those scenes which have made Kentucky famous in history as the "dark and bloody ground," but also without the shadow of legal authority to redress a crime or to protect property.

Your obedient servant,
(Signed)
Feb. 27, 1859   SYLVESTER MOWRY.
(*Washington States* of March 1, 1859)

To this, Editor Cross in Tubac replies:

"Arizona Matters — Reply to Lieut. Mowry"

Tubac, Ariz. April 24, 1859

EDITOR STATES: SIR — I have just received Mr. Mowry's latest "manifesto" in reference to Arizona, and in answer to a letter which appeared in the St. Louis *Republican*, dated Tubac, January 30. As the writer of that letter, signed "Gila," I have a few words to say, and I would be obliged if you would give them an insertion in your journal.

I came to Arizona in November, 1858, and my business was partially to correspond with several leading journals in the United States, to give, as far as possible, a true statement of the condition, resources, and prospects of Arizona. I had been a careful reader of Mr. Mowry's voluminous (and, as I now find, *fabulous*) productions regarding this country, and supposed them correct. I found, however, that many of his assertions were not true, and that all were exaggerated. Not only this, but also that his letters and pamphlets were the laughing stock of the western portion of the Territory; that he had never lived in Arizona, and derived most of his information from old Jesuit records and tradition, which are known to be the most unreliable of all authorities. His experience in Arizona had been con-

12

fined to a couple of brief electioneering trips, made in the sparse settlements. Also, that in representing Arizona to be a good agricultural country, he was absolutely injuring the Territory, and deluding people into a long and dangerous journey to a country whose agricultural resources, in all, are not equal to one first-class corn-growing county in Ohio.

I therefore, in writing to the East, endeavored to correct some of the false ideas prevalent concerning Arizona, but never, except once, mentioned Mr. Mowry's name, and then in connection with the vote he claimed to receive. I have the satisfaction of knowing that out of some thirty-five letters of mine which have been published by the Eastern press, *not one of them,* so far as I know, has ever been condemned in this Territory where they have been read; while, on the contrary, Mowry's exaggerations and misstatements are known and denounced everywhere, and even by the few who are now his supporters. I submit this statement to any intelligent man who has lived three months in the Territory.

In my letter to the (St. Louis) *Republican* I made the following points:

1st. That the population of Arizona, especially *Americans,* had been greatly overstated.

2d. That the Gila gold mines near Fort Yuma were a failure, and that false reports published in the newspapers had allured many persons there.

3d. That there had been an enormous amount of falsehood uttered and published concerning this country and its resources.

4th. That Arizona was not an agricultural country; that rain seldom fell, and there was very little permanent water.

Now, sir, I maintain that every point there made is correct, and no one in Arizona will dispute a single item, unless it be some infatuated individual to whom Mowry has promised office.

I shall not trouble you to publish my remarks in confirmation of the above points. They will be sent to the Republican and other journals. Mr. Mowry has culled old Jesuit records, the reports of army officers, and published letters from gentlemen who have traveled hastily through the country on business, to prove his assertions. From the same authorities enough can be selected to show that Arizona is the most desolate region in the world. Why has he not called on such men as Herman Ehrenberg, late chief engineer of the Sonora Exploring and Mining Company, who has lived here five years, and explored and mapped the entire Territory. Or called upon Mr. Fred'k Bronchon, another mining engineer, who has lived three years in Arizona, and who knows more concerning this region of country, scientifically and practically, than ever Mr. Mowry dreamed of? Or called upon Mr. Edwin E. Dunbar, whose truthful letters in the New York Times ought to put Mowry to shame, for the ridiculous humbugs with which he has filled the Eastern press for two years past!

Mr. Mowry has stated that Arizona was a well watered Territory. This is not the case. There is not a *permanent* stream in the Territory, leaving out the Rio Grande and the Colorado, which are the boundaries; and nearly all the water is strongly impregnated with alkali. Also, that the streams abound in fish. The only sort I have ever seen are from one to two inches in length, called, in derision, "Mowry trout." Also, that this is a well timbered country. Another humbug. There is a little pine in the mountain cañons, but it costs enormously to get it out. Very common narrow pine boards are worth $150 to $200 per thousand feet. To procure timber only thirteen feet long and one foot in diameter, to timber their mine, the Sonora Company are compelled to go *fifty miles* away from their works, and for common rafters sixteen feet long, delivered in Tubac, the same company are now paying $4 each, and the contractor will furnish no more at that price. Mr. Mowry has greatly exaggerated the population of the Territory, and his "conventions" and "elections" have been the *merest farces in the world!* You will receive facts enough to confirm the above statements. There are plenty of people here who will cheerfully give their experience and knowledge concerning Arizona . . .

I shall collect from the writings of Mr. Mowry, as soon as possible, a chapter of the misstatements he has made concerning Arizona, and send it East for publication, with certain notes and explanations.

And now one word concerning Mowry's reply. He says he will be very apt to ascertain, to his heartfelt satisfaction, who is the author of the articles in the *States*. The "hanging" question I will cheerfully submit to the citizens of this country, if to expose humbuggery, falsehood, misrepresentation, imposition, and fraud, carried on for two years, entitles a man to Mr. Mowry's hanging operation, I confess I am a fit subject; but from the opinions every day expressed towards the gentleman by the few Americans hereabouts who know his course, I apprehend that he is eminently more deserving and more in danger of lynch-law than myself.

Respectfully, &c.,

EDWARD E. CROSS

(*Washington States* of May 24, 1859)

Not inclined to let lynch law settle the question, Mowry turns from his official duties to defend himself. He, "a bold and swaggering fellow," demands a duel with Cross which will be fought in Tubac. Before leaving for Arizona, Mowry answers his antagonist, Cross, in the Washington paper.

Letter from Lieut. Mowry, in Reply to E. E. Cross,
of Arizona
Tucson, Arizona, July 2, 1859.

EDITOR STATES: The letter signed Edward E. Cross, which appeared in the *States* of May 24th, has just reached me. It purports to be a reply to a letter of mine denouncing an anonymous communication which appeared in the *St. Louis Democrat,* and was copied into the *States.*

Aside from the personalities in which Mr. Cross has indulged, his letter bears on its face its own refutation. I have never written or spoken in regard to Arizona the statements Mr. Cross pretends to quote and denies. As this question has resolved itself into a mere personal affair between Mr. Cross and myself, it is only necessary for me to refer to my lecture before the Geographical Society to show the utter falsity of Mr. Cross' statements. On page 24, last paragraph, I say: "The conclusions to be drawn from the facts I have thus hastily set forth are these: that while Arizona *cannot be called an agricultural State,* she has a sufficiency of arable land to support a large population; that as a grazing and pastural region she has unsurpassed advantages, *but her great wealth is found in her inexhaustible mineral resources.*

In reply to the inquiries of Senator Green, chairman

15

of the Senate Committee on Territories, I said: *"Nine-tenths of the proposed Territory is unavailable for agricultural purposes."* Mr. Green made notes of this conversation, to use in his report or speech upon the bill, and I have no doubt he remembers it. The Hon. Mr. Phelps, of Missouri, remarked in conversation in reference to the relative merits of the Arizona and Albuquerque routes: "Mr. Mowry, you have never claimed that *Arizona was an agricultural States, but a great mineral region."*

Mr. Cross says, I have called Arizona "a good agricultural country." The falsehood is patent on its face. Mr. Cross says, "Mr. Dunbar's truthful letters should have been an example to me." On page 14 of my address will be found a high compliment to the *conscientious regard for truth* is displayed by Mr. Dunbar, and also my statement *confirming his* — that the country of which he treated, and with which he was familiar — that west of the Santa Cruz and south of the Gila — *"is generally an irreclaimable desert."* Mr. Cross says that I should quote from Herman Ehrenberg and Mr. Brunckon. In my memoir of Arizona will be found a letter addressed to me by Mr. Ehrenberg; and during the past year I have had several hundred copies of Mr. Ehrenberg's map of Arizona circulated through Congress and the country at my own expense. I have great respect for Ehrenberg's acquirements, although I have not had the pleasure of meeting him. It will require better evidence than Mr. Cross' insinuation to induce me to believe that Mr. Ehrenberg has changed his opinions of the country, because I was obliged to decline recommending him for the surveyor generalship of the Territory . . .

A few words in reference to Mr. Cross' motive, as this is not the first time he has been hired to do dirty work. Before entering Arizona in November of last year, Mr. Cross and his employer having failed to control me, announced their intention to regulate the affairs of the Territory after their own ideas. They brought with them a press, which has since issued the Arizonian. At the same time Mr. Cross announced that neither Lieut. Mowry nor any other man, except the one named by them, should represent the Territory in Congress. This fact is beyond denial, as there were a number of witnesses to this statement.

In pursuance of this plan, letters have been written to the Eastern States representing the people as opposed to me, imputing language never uttered, and then contradicting their own falsehoods. The Arizonian, to keep up this delusion, in publishing the proceedings of a meeting held at Arizona City, omitted a resolution of confidence and thanks to me as the delegate from the Territory . . .

. . . I have advised friends and capitalists to invest money in the mines of Arizona, and I have shown my own confidence by investing more of my own money than any one of them, except Col. Sam Colt.

Mr. Cross knew when he penned his letter that he had not a friend or sympathizer outside of Tubac and the small party that made up the company with which he came. He has acknowledged as much in conversation with friends of mine, and said he anticipated a personal difficulty with me when I arrived. He never had a truer presentiment in his life. During my absence he addressed a letter to my friend, Judge Hoppin, asking him to become a candidate against me. His letter was treated with the contempt it deserved. His statement that his letters to the eastern press have met with the approval of the people of the Territory is equally false. The only ones they have seen are emphatically condemned by every one outside of Tubac.

Mr. Cross pretends to speak for the people of the western portion of the Territory, with how much truth will be seen by reference to the proceedings of a meeting of the people of Tucson and vicinity, including gentlemen from the Sonoita valley and the vicinity of Tubac. I enclose a copy of those proceedings with this letter. I have already alluded to his suppression in his paper of the expression of the feeling of people in my favor on the Gila and Colorado . . .

The result is at once apparent; finding the country he has abused too hot to hold him, Mr. Cross has announced his intention of leaving at once. If he escapes, by a lucky chance, the punishment which his personalities deserve, he will leave Arizona with the unanimous consent of the people whom he has failed to make subservient to the wishes of his employers. It is a part of the freedom of the press that any man may lampoon another in the papers, and to this fact I am indebted for the blackguardism to

17

which Mr. Cross has resorted. The fact that I have raised
him to the level of a gentleman, by demanding of him
personal satisfaction for the scurrilous language he has
used towards me, prevents my showing him in his true
light . . .

Your obedient servant,
SYLVESTER MOWRY.
(<i>Washington States</i> of July 23, 1859)</div>

The proposed duel holds the attention of the nation. The
newspapers in Washington, D.C., of course, take notice of the
impending fight while readers of California papers learn that
Lieutenant Mowry has reached Tucson and is en route to
Tubac to "seek a hostile meeting with the editor of the *Arizonian!*"

Having traveled over trails of rock and shifting sand, Mowry
arrives in Tubac. He selects as his second T. L. Mercer, while
Cross chooses Jack Donaldson. Preliminaries for the duel begin
with Burnside's carbines being chosen as the weapons to be used
at a distance of 40 yards. With the duel scheduled for the following morning in the plaza, Cross and Mowry spend the afternoon in practice shooting.

Both men prove themselves good shots in the practice session, "Cross plucking the cactus leaves from the top of the Tubac
church (remains of an old Spanish mission) at almost every shot,
and Mowry playing sad havoc with a small cottonwood tree."

On the morning of June 8, 1859, a large crowd gathers to
await the duel. Sporting men from Tucson, farmers from the
Santa Cruz valley, and miners from the nearby hills talk in
small groups in a plaza that is whipped by a heavy wind. The
miners favor Editor Cross; but just in case, everyone carries two
six-shooters and a bowie knife around his waist.

"The duel begins. Three shots are fired by each . . . and nobody is hurt. At the fourth round Mowry's carbine does not go
off and his second demands another shot for his principal. Donaldson, Cross' second, protests most energetically and the onlookers assist him faithfully, declaring the demand to be ludi-
crous, outrageous and everything else. Words wax wroth and
high, and it looks as if a general fight is imminent.

"Cross, however, handing his gun to his second, says, 'Let

18

him have the shot,' and folding his arms with an admirable coolness, awaits the shot.

"Mowry raises his gun as if to fire, but understanding that if he shoots, whether he hits Cross or not, would be the signal for a general fight among men skilled in the use of arms, and to whom fear is a stranger; a fight in which he certainly would be one of the first victims, he (Mowry) lowers his gun, then, again, raising it and discharging it in the air.

"Handing his gun to his second, Mercer, Mowry advances toward Cross, who also advances, and coming together, they shake hands. The pent up feelings of the crowd now find vent in a shout which shakes the Santa Rita mountains.

"A procession is then formed . . . with the principals leading the way to the mining company's store, and then, murder! murder! how the whiskey suffers. A barrel — 42 gallons — of prime Monongahela, purchased a few days previous . . . at a cost of seven dollars per gallon melts like snow before the midday sun. . . ."

Though the California press reports that "Lt. Mowry shot Mr. Cross through the ear, at the fourth round, and the parties became satisfied," the Cross-Mowry duel is a bloodless one.

Both men issue a CARD, or Letter to the Editor, after the duel, which is carried by the *Arizonian* in Tubac and the *Washington States* in the nation's capital:

CARD

EDITOR STATES: Mr. Edw. E. Cross withdraws the offensive language used by him, and disclaims any intention to reflect upon Mr. Mowry's veracity, or upon his character as a gentleman, in any publication he has made in reference to Arizona. Mr. Mowry withdraws any statement that he has made in his letter to the press of July 2nd, which in any degree reflects upon Mr. Cross' character as a man and a gentleman.

Any difference of opinion which may exist between them in reference to Arizona is an honest one, to be decided by weight of authority.

(signed) SYLVESTER MOWRY
EDWARD E. CROSS

Tubac, Arizona, July 8, 1859

Cross even supports Mowry for re-election as delegate in the impending election. However, it is not until 1863 and the Civil War that Arizona wins the status of Territory, independent from New Mexico. Editor Cross leaves the paper in late July, 1859, while Mowry returns to Congress.

The Civil War sweeps the nation, and Arizona becomes involved. Cross receives his commission as a colonel in the New Hampshire Infantry and wins special mention for gallant conduct. Wounded at least eight times in numerous battles, Cross fights for the Union cause for the last time at Gettysburg. A Confederate bullet smashes into him and he lies among the other dead on the battlefield.

The war causes Mowry much embarrassment. Although Mowry's mine is supported by Northern money, Arizona sympathizes with the Southern cause. The Confederacy recognizes Arizona as a separate territory and Southern troops garrison the major Arizona town of Tucson. Mowry decides that he had better back the Southern cause if he wants to do business in Arizona.

The Confederate occupation of Tucson is short-lived, for gallant Union troops, known as the California Volunteers, are marching eastward from the coastal territory. Commanded by General James H. Carleton, and with bayonets flashing in a morning sun, the troops reach Tucson on May 20, 1862. The blue-uniformed Union soldiers meet no opposition, for the Southern Army marches out without offering resistance.

Tucsonians know little of the war and care less. General Carleton, however, proclaims martial law and begins to round up outlaws and those suspected of being Southern sympathizers. General Carleton writes, "I have sent to Fort Yuma, for confinement, starting today, nine of the cutthroats, gamblers, and loafers who have infested this town to the great bodily fear of all good citizens. Nearly every one, I believe, has either killed his man, or been engaged in helping to kill him. I shall send on a detailed account of the causes which justify their arrest and removal from the territory. They shall be held prisoners at Alcatraz until the end of the war. If discharged at Fort Yuma, they will get back here again and give trouble.

"I have sent to arrest Mr. Sylvester Mowry and all the people at his mine. It is possible that I shall be obliged to hold Mr. Mowry as a prisoner. That he has been guilty of overt as well

20

as covert acts of treason, there is hardly a doubt. I consider his presence in this territory as dangerous to its peace and prosperity. Inclosed are copies of certain charges against him and of the instructions for his arrest."[5]

The charges against Mowry are "treasonable complicity with Rebels"; and the order continues, "there is little doubt but what he has rendered assistance and furnished supplies to their forces (the Confederate army). From the moment he falls into your hands, you will interdict all communications by word or sign between him and his people, except such as you shall personally supervise."

After his arrest, Mowry is examined by a military court, found to be "an enemy to the Government of the United States," and ordered to be held over for trial before a military commission. Before being taken to Fort Yuma for imprisonment, Mowry is paraded through the main street of Tucson in chains. A California newspaper reporter of the day writes that Mowry is "taking things quite coolly, puts on a good many airs; has along his mistress, private secretary and servant. I think a dose of military treatment will cure him. He has been guilty of writing secession letters and giving shelter to outlaws."

Although held a prisoner at Fort Yuma for only six months, Mowry is a broken man. General Carleton has assumed the ownership of the Mowry mine, taking all the profits, and leaving the place in ruins. Without the income of the mine and held in suspicion by Arizonians, Mowry decides to leave the Territory. Time shows that Mowry is done an injustice. The first Territorial Legislature of Arizona resolves that Mowry's arrest was unnecessary and asks that General Carleton's order be revoked. The resolution comes too late to benefit Mowry, and he becomes just another victim of the Civil War.

While the war has its effect on Arizona, this Territory is not the scene of any great battle. Only one skirmish is recorded, and this is the battle of El Picacho on April 5, 1862. In the fight Lieutenant James Barrett of the Union Army and two of his men are killed, while one or two Confederate soldiers die and three are taken prisoner. The end of the war finds the Union forces in command of Arizona.

The Territory does not suffer any great loss of life due directly to the war, but many are killed during the endless confusion. The once-populated town of Tubac falls when the regular Army is withdrawn to fight for the Union at the war's onset. "The Apaches beseige Tubac on one side, while the Sonoranians lurk in the bushes on the other. Twenty men hold it for three days, and finally escape under cover of night. There is nothing left. The troops have burned all the stores, provisions, and groceries, public and private, that they could lay hands upon . . ."

When the Americans first entered Arizona they and the Apaches were on friendly terms. Subsequent American treachery turned the Apaches into implacable foes. To understand the death of hundreds of white men at Indian hands, and the years of conflict and desolation, one must know the Apache.

"It is difficult to give a fair description of the personal appearance of the Apache, because there is no uniform type . . . One general rule may be laid down: The Apache . . . is strongly built, straight, sinewy, well-muscled, extremely strong in the legs, provided with a round barrel chest, showing good lung power, keen, intelligent looking eyes, good head, and a mouth showing determination, decision, and cruelty. He can be made a firm friend, but no mercy need be expected from him as an enemy.

"He is a good talker, can argue well from his own standpoint, cannot be hoodwinked by sophistry or plausible stories, keeps his word very faithfully, and is extremely honest in protecting property or anything placed under his care. Around his own camp-fire, the Apache is talkative, witty, fond of telling stories, and indulging in much harmless raillery."

The children learn "at a very early age the names and attributes of all the animals and plants about them; the whole natural kingdom . . . They are inured to great fatigue and suffering, to deprivation of water, and to going without food for long periods.

"The alertness of the Apache in all that relates to tracking either man or beast over the rocky heights, or across the interminable sandy wastes of the region in which he makes his home, has been an occasion of astonishment to all white men who have had the slightest acquaintance with him. He will follow through grass, over sand or rock, or through the chapparal of scrub oak, up and down the flanks of the steepest ridges, traces so faint that to the keenest-eyed American they do not appear at all. On the other hand, he is fiendishly clever in concealing

22

his own line of march when he wishes to throw a pursuing enemy off the track.

"The Apache is a hard foe to subdue, not because he is full of wiles and tricks and experienced in all that pertains to the art of war, but because he has so few artificial wants and can depend upon. . . . nature . . . . On the war-path, he wears scarcely any clothing save a pair of buckskin moccasins reaching to mid-thigh and held to the waist by a string of the same material; a piece of muslin encircling the loins and dangling down behind the calves of the legs, a war-hat of buckskin surmounted by hawk and eagle plumage, a rifle (with the necessary ammunition in belt) or a bow, with the quiver filled with arrows reputed to be poisonous, a blanket thrown over the shoulders, a watertight jug to serve as a canteen, and perhaps a small amount of "jerked" meat, or else of *pinole* or parched cornmeal. He also carries his sacred relics and *medicine* to get all his ghosts and gods on his side.

"To his captive, the Apache is cruel, brutal, merciless; if the captives are of full age, the Apache wastes no time with them, unless on those rare occasions when the Apache wants to extract some information about what his pursuers are doing or contemplating doing, in which case death might be deferred for a few brief hours. Where the captive is of tender years, unable to get along without a mother's care, it is promptly put out of its misery by having its brains dashed against a convenient rock or tree; but where it happens that the Apache raiders secure boys or girls sufficiently old to withstand the hardships of the new life, they are accepted into the band and treated as kindly as if Apaches by birth.

"The endurance of Apache warriors while on raids is something which extorts expression of wonder from all white men who ever have anything to do with their subjugation. Seventy-five miles a day is nothing at all unusual for them to march when pursued, their tactics being to make three or four such marches, in the certainty of being able to wear out or throw off the track the most energetic and the most intelligent opponents."[6]

Cochise, war chief of the Chiricahua Apaches, is probably the most feared of all Apache warriors. Until 1859, Cochise, whose name in Apache is "Chies" or "wood," is friendly with the whites. In the fateful year of 1859, a worthless American rancher asks the military to help recover his adopted son, Mickey Free, and some stock which the Apaches have driven off.

In compliance with the request, 12 soldiers under the command of a recent West Point graduate, Lieutenant Bascom, march to Apache Pass. Bascom has little knowledge of Apache character and is blinded by pride over his first important command. Upon arriving at the Overland Stage station in the Pass, Bascom summons Cochise's band under a white flag. In the ensuing conference Cochise declares that neither he nor any member of his band is responsible, but that they will try to recover the boy and stock if they are given a few days' time. Cochise's denial of the theft is to be proved true later, but young Bascom unwisely calls the Apache chief a thief. He then orders the soldiers to arrest Cochise and the warriors with him.

In a tent surrounded by armed soldiers the Indians stand little chance with their bare fists against rifles and bayonets. Cochise, however, draws a hidden knife and cuts a large slit in the tent wall and flees to the adjoining hills, though wounded in the knee by a bayonet. Lieutenant Bascom still holds six of the Indians, among whom is the half-brother of Cochise.

Cochise, backed by the remaining members of his band, manages to capture three white civilians. Among them is a trader who has been a close friend of Cochise and who speaks the Apache language fluently. The trader begs the rash lieutenant to free his captives, or Cochise would torture his hostages. With an unreasonable stubbornness the lieutenant refuses the request and hangs the Apache warriors before Cochise's eyes. The Apache chief in turn orders that the captive trader be tied behind the horse. Ridden by a warrior, the horse is galloped over the rocky terrain until the trader is an unrecognizable mass of blood and broken bones. The other two captives of the Apaches are tortured to death before the view of horrified soldiers who dare not attack such an overwhelming body of Indians.

Cochise, standing over six feet tall, with straight black hair, snapping eyes, and pierced nose, is a man of honor. He views the soldiers' encampment over which still floats the white flag. Then he makes a vow of vengeance for his six warriors who dangle from ropes, their bodies twisting in the breeze. "Death to the whites!" is the chief's cry.

After the Army withdraws from the West to fight in the
Civil War, Cochise has every opportunity to fulfill his vow. For
the next 12 years, death at the hands of the Apaches will be the
constant companion of all whites in the Territory. Across cactus-
studded deserts and pine-clad mountains, the war cry of Cochise
will be heard, "Death to the whites!"

---

1 Apache corn meal
2 The red petticoats
3 Farish, Thomas E., *History of Arizona,* (State of Arizona, Phoenix, 1915)
4 Spanish word for kitchen
5 Sloan, Richard E., *History of Arizona* (Phoenix Record Publishing Co.,
1930)
6 Burke, John G., *On the Border with Crook.,* (London, Sampson, Law,
Marston, Searle and Rivington, 1892)

THE WEEKLY ARIZONA MINER.

VOLUME VII   PRESCOTT, ARIZONA, SATURDAY MORNING, FEBRUARY 5, 1870.   NUMBER 6.

THE ARIZONA MINER.

PUBLISHED EVERY SATURDAY MORNING,

— AT —

PRESCOTT, YAVAPAI COUNTY, ARIZONA.

SUBSCRIPTION:

One Copy, One Year, $7 00
"   "   Six Months,   4 00
"   "   Three Months,   2 50
Single Copies,   25

Papers will not be sent unless paid for in advance, and will invariably be discontinued at the end of the time paid for

ADVERTISING

The Mormon Question

Just now there seems to be a disposition on the part of those who manufacture public opinion, to raise a breeze about Utah that may eventually light the torch of war in that land of many feminines. The "Saints," them selves are as loggerheads, and therein lies the danger to themselves and their rare old institution. So long as they held to the same opinions, there was little danger of gaps between the hated gentiles. Now, while firmly believing in the sinfulness of polygamy, we do not care to see it and those who practice it blotted out by war, and we hope the necessity ...

[column partially illegible] ... influence. When the waltz was at an end, she would dance no more, and soon retired.

It was midnight when the dancers permit ted me to quit playing, and soon all was silent in the house. The Colonel had and yet returned when I had prepared my night toilet. I walked up and down in my room for about twenty minutes, and was just lying down, when I heard a knock at the entrance door of the hall. Instinctively I opened my door, and saw the mulatto gliding down a stair with a candle in his hand like a ghost; but when he had reached the last step, he commenced to tramp on the floor with a certain vehemence, as if he intended to devour my listener as to whence he came, before he reached the front part of the hall.

The Colonel had arrived. The mulatto showed him to his room, and I, after having formed a great many romantic explanations ...

Complete List of the Theatres Destroyed by Fire in the United States.

The recent destruction of theatres at Milwaukee, at Helena, Montana, at Galveston, Texas, and in this city, induces us to republish what is believed to be an accurate list of the public places of amusement burned in the United States since 1798, with the exception of the ones above mentioned:

Federal Street Theatre, Boston, February 2, 1798.
Daniel Bowen's Museum, Boston, January 15, 1803.
Chestnut Street Theatre, Philadelphia, April 23, 1820.
Park Theatre, New York, July 4, 1821.
Richmond Theatre, Richmond, December 16, 1821.

Conceit—Some Notable Instances Thereof.

Even the philosophers have not shown themselves averse to be sprinkled with the holy water of adulation. Socrates soberly told his judges that they should award him a pension instead of condemning him; and Epicurus assured his correspondent that if he devised glory it was secured to him by the fact that Epicurus had thought him worthy of being written to. Alcibiades let all the world know that the sole purpose of his life, whether he howled a conspiracy, or plundered a city, or cut his dog's tail off, was to make a noise and give the Athenians something to talk about. Aristophanes, more frank even than Cicero, made of the pretenses of his comedies vehicles for the most extravagant self praise, coolly claiming for each success ...

"He wears no mask . . ."

They tried to get my scalp, both the Injuns and the white men, but damn 'em, I'm still here. — John H. Marion

This is Prescott, Arizona, in the tumultuous 1860's. A mining camp without a jail or church — the Territory where every man is judge and jury, and the "Colt" is executioner.

Prescott lies in a picturesque mountain valley of northern Arizona. With paling-fenced yards, houses neatly painted, and windows of glass, this is a New England village transplanted to the heart of the Indian country. By 1870, American wives grace the town and Prescott soon becomes the West's most "Eastern" town. Unlike those in other settlements of the Southwest, the

27

interiors of the Prescott homes are furnished with lamps, rocking chairs, mirrors, tables, and with carpets covering the pine plank floors.

At this time the town has a population of four or five hundred; but, within a few miles, 3,000 gold-crazed men work placer mines. Home of the territorial capital, Prescott is often molested by the warring Apaches. At times guards patrol nightly throughout the town. Men sleep on their guns, expecting Indian attacks at any hour.

Though the pioneers face many hardships they are "free, reckless, and jovial." Mail comes to the West twice monthly by the pioneer Pony Express. The riders, even when accompanied by soldiers, are often killed and the mail captured, plundered, and destroyed. Civilians can send their mail east via the infrequent military express. Such poor communication certainly does not encourage progress.

Though every man packs his own arsenal, gunplay is unpopular. The more adventurous, however, soon find a pastime offering excitement. Two of the town's crack shots, after a number of drinks, are the stars of the drama. Stepping off 10 or 15 paces, they amuse themselves and their friends by shooting pine knots off each other's heads. Dangerous? Not much more so than living in the Territory.

Contrary to the popular idea of a Western town, this settlement hosts no "badmen," neither is it safe to "shoot up the Town," nor "to serve a man for breakfast." Yet, Prescott cannot be termed a moral or puritan settlement for this community boasts 10 drinking halls, but not a bank or banking house, a free school, or a Protestant church. The gambling saloons are never closed, Sunday or weekday, night or day. To the clank of poker chips the "games" go on and the voice of the dealer is uninterrupted.

During its infancy Prescott's needs are served by a few merchants, quartered in the most primitive of shelters. A small wagon sheet stretched between large pines houses the town's first saloon. The bar fixtures consist of one 10-gallon keg containing liquid which faintly resembles whiskey; a half-dozen tin cups, and a canteen of water. The first well-regulated saloon is opened by Tom Hodges on Cortez Street. He sells "drinks and

28

segars (*sic*), and takes 'Burros' in payment, much as was done with Davy Crockett's coon skin."

The first boardinghouse for miners is opened in 1864 and presided over by "Virgin Mary," who builds a log house and christens it "Old Fort Misery." Two goats furnish the milk and the price hangs from the latchstring: "Board $25 in gold, per week in advance." The usual fare includes bread, venison, and coffee with milk. "Virgin Mary" is one of the two women in Prescott during the early part of 1864. Her name is unknown, but grateful miners give her the *nom de plume* because of her charity and benevolence.

The Juniper House, Prescott's first hotel, opens on July 4, 1864. The hotel derives its name from the tree under which the cooking and eating are done. "It is very handy as a man can load up his plate with grub and go to the shady side of the tree to eat." The bill of fare on the opening day reads:

BREAKFAST

Fried Venison and Chili
Bread and Coffee with Milk.

DINNER

Roast Venison with Chili
Chili Baked Beans
Chili on Tortillas
Tea and Coffee
with Milk.

SUPPER

Chili, from 4 o'clock on.

A lot of chili! In a land without ice or refrigeration, meat quickly spoils. Chili acts as a preservative and masks any unpleasantness.

Though the town is called Prescott, this might well be any Western community. Some say the frontier is a region which divides civilization from the unknown. At first the Allegheny Mountains, stretching from New York to Georgia, marked the frontier. As settlements multiplied in the east this dividing area between civilization and Indian dominated country moved constantly westward. With the California gold rush of 1848, a second frontier develops, moving from the west to the east. Lying between these two advancing lines of civilization is Arizona, America's last frontier.

Settlements do not spring from the wilderness overnight. The change is slow and follows a general pattern. The first problem is to remain alive, despite the untiring efforts of the Indians. If the white men are successful in this initial campaign, then part of their efforts are expended in planting crops for food and erecting crude houses. The arrival of families, however, marks the first real beginning of settlement. Next comes the task of erecting schools and churches, establishing law and local government, the opening of stores, and always — the founding of a local newspaper.

Prescott's paper, the *Arizona Miner,* stamps out its first issue on colored mapping paper at nearby Fort Whipple in March of 1864. Its printing press was brought overland from Philadelphia by Richard McCormick, the first secretary of the Territory, and John N. Goodwin, territorial governor. When the civil government moves from the Fort to Prescott, the newspaper comes along to its new primitive, unroofed quarters. A description of its arrival in Prescott, still carrying the motto: "The Gold of that Land is Good," is given by a contemporary paper:

> There was a deep pride in the Arizona hamlet as its entire population gathered around the little hand press to welcome the birth of a journalistic babe of promise that would carry afar the story of its greatness. The only compositor was the pressman: across the iron bed the "devil" energetically distributing ink on a composition roller, but none too skillfully. The paper had been "wet down" the day before and lay in smooth dampness. The forms being inked, the printer thrust a piece of paper upon the tympan points, slowly unhooked the swinging frisket and brought it down to protect the margins of the paper, rolled the bed under the platin, and rolled back the bed. Then there was deep sensation among the bespurred spectators. Possibly a few relieved their feelings and spread the glad tiding of joy by shooting through the roof or the door.

The perils of editing a frontier paper often produce a rapid turnover in editors, and so it is in the early life of the Prescott paper. Richard McCormick, first secretary of the Territory, owns the *Miner*. He selects Tisdale A. Hand as his first editor. Harassing by Apaches, haranguing by fellow citizens, and an attack by an outlaw soon convinces Hand that there are safer and easier jobs than editing. Then, Hand comes to grips with a desperado, Lou Thrift, while at dinner in the Prescott House during the early summer of 1864. The ruffian is a native of Virginia, an ardent sympathizer of the Southern cause, and is likely to insult grossly anyone "wearing the blue." Another newspaper editor gives this account of the Hand-Thrift clash:

The two sit at opposite sides of the table, and in the dispute, Hand is so indiscreet as to call Thrift a liar. At first, Thrift is more astonished than otherwise; soon recovering himself, he proposes to settle the matter there and then with "Colonel Colt" as arbiter. To this, Hand demurs and says he is "unarmed and never carries a pistol".

Thrift replies, "Such cowardly curs as you are ready to shoot off their mouths and then hide behind the law". Thrift carries two six-guns; drawing one, he cocks the gun and places it beside Hand's plate, remarking at the same time, "Now you are armed; cut loose."

Hand is badly frightened and dares not touch the gun; but begs Thrift not to shoot him, and says, "Mr. Thrift, you have the advantage and could kill me before I made a move."

By this time Thrift is simply boiling with rage; jumping up, leaving his pistol on the table, Thrift steps back to the wall some distance away; he hisses through his teeth, "Now you white-livered scoundrel, you have the advantage."

Notwithstanding the cocked gun lying beside his plate, Hand very prudently declines to do any shooting. He lacks the nerve, even with all the advantage Thrift gives him. Even if he had attempted to shoot and had shot, unless the shot is suddenly fatal, Thrift would certainly kill him. Thrift picks up his gun and makes a move to kill Hand; but instead, he slowly returns the gun into the scabbard, remarking as to himself, "No credit to kill a cur like that."

Shortly after this Mr. Hand leaves the country for the East.

A tramp printer who worked with Hand does not lose his newspaper zeal. A. F. Banta remains in the territory and at various times is connected with seven papers. Mystery shrouds much of Banta's life. While boasting that he has held more official positions by election and appointment in the Territory than any other man, he serves as a guide; and, using the name of Charles Franklin, he acts as an Indian scout under General George Crook. In Miss Lutrell's book appears an interesting account of Franklin's (or A. F. Banta's) death:

> When his career was closed and a group of pioneers gathered at the Point of Rocks in Prescott to "shove him off," they stood on the slopes amid the gnarled juniper trees while the venerable Judge Wells breaking the silence — made even more solemn by the sighing of the pines — called the role of the scouts of whom Charlie Franklin had been the last survivor.
>
> "Pauline Weaver," a pause; "Willard Rice," silence; "Ed Peck," still no sound; "Dan O'Leary," an empty echo; and at last "Charlie Franklin," a final pause. "No answer comes from the camp of the scouts," gravely pronounced the Judge . . .

An Iowan, Emmet A. Bentley, occupies the recently vacated editor's chair. His newspaper career is brought to an abrupt end by the efforts of the Indians. Bentley and a friend, Louis St. James, are traveling on horseback through Skull Valley near Prescott when they are ambushed by Indians. Though Bentley is gravely wounded, he resumes his duties at the *Miner* office, but fever quickly sets in and he dies on February 27, 1867, from the wounds received in the Indian battle.

Prescott is less than three years old when John H. Marion tramps down the dust-filled streets of the territorial capital. Tired of a foot-loose, two-year venture in search of gold, the soon-to-be "Father of Arizona journalism" assumes editorship of the *Miner* in 1867. Having worked in the printing business in California, Marion finds in the smell of ink an old friend. He begins his long career, in which he will be cursed by some, blessed by others, but known to all, with:

SALUTATORY

In accordance with a time-honored and necessary custom, we today address the readers of the Miner, for the purpose of informing them what they are entitled to know, that is: What shall be the future course of this paper? To which we answer, in all truth and earnestness, that, while under our control, it will fearlessly, but in a respectful and dignified manner, advocate the ancient and time-honored principles of the grand, liberty-defending Democratic party.

Believing, honestly, that the practices of the party in power have been and are subversive of that freedom which is the birthright of every free white American citizen, we shall labor, with whatever reason our Maker has vouchsafed us, to cripple the monster that has grown fat upon the misfortunes of our country. It gained power and mounted the shoulders of the people by false promises, and has kept its position by fraud, violence, bloodshed and treachery. It has duped good citizens — Democrats and Republicans — into a support of its vile unrepublican measures (for it has no principles) by a terrorism never before attempted to be practiced in a free country, made so by the valor of our ancestors.

Its leaders, in conjunction with a few madcaps of the South, created, nursed and fanned into a hellish flame an unnatural civil war, in which millions of Americans fell victims and drenched their native soil with precious blood, leaving behind them wives, mothers, fathers, sisters and brothers to lament their violent and unnecessary death; besides which, it has saddled upon the country a load of debt that fairly makes the bones of the tax-payers crack under the pressure of the greenback, bondholding, black anaconda which has coiled itself around the Nation . . .

But, thank God, day is breaking, Reason has resumed her sway, and those who have strayed after false gods are returning to worship at the shrine of the deity before which the great and good Washington bent his knee — the Constitution and the laws made in accordance therewith. Democracy will soon again be enshrined in the hearts of the people, and under its just, economical, constitutional

33

sway all wrongs will be redressed, wounds healed, sectional hate will be nurtured no more, and the Republic will live forever.

Aside from politics, we will endeavor to make the Miner more useful than it has ever before been, in making known the resources, mineral, agricultural and pastoral, of the whole Territory; and to further this end, we invite to our columns contributions containing anything and everything interesting or useful to our own citizens of the outside world, as, in the matter of building up the Territory to the position God and Nature intended her to occupy, we mean to know no party, no poltics, and will as cheerfully insert an article or item pertaining to the good of the Territory and her people, coming from a Republican as one from a Democrat. In fact, politics will not at present be the main question treated of by the Miner . . .

We shall never allow the columns of this paper to be used for the purpose of attacking private character, and in the discussion of public men and measures, we mean to be temperate, candid and just, giving credit to all who deserve it, and condemnation to the man, party or measure that merits it . . .

With these few explanations and promises, we lay aside our pick, pan, shovel and horn spoon, put on the editorial harness, and try what we can do with pen, paste and scissors.

(Signed) J. H. Marion
(*Arizona Miner* of Sept. 21, 1867)

Marion soon undertakes a crusade for an honest and effective territorial government. One of the first to come under attack is the governor, "who through ignorance or baseness of purpose has, for the last two years, usurped and used power vested solely in the Legislature, and 'squabbling' the records of the various counties, thereby aiming to create endless trouble, confusion and disorder all over the Territory. . . . his littleness, Richard C. McCormick, who by soft soap and flunkeyism, has wormed his way into the gubernatorial chair of a Territory he has helped to impoverish."

The editor of the *Arizona Miner* then issues a tirade against the McCormick-owned *Arizonian* and its editor. This is the first in a long series of verbal duels with fellow journalists. In his pugnacious and witty style, Marion honors DeLong, editor of the paper in the boom town of Tucson, to the south:

> We are in possession of a brand new thing on parchment. It is no more nor no less than a picture of the brilliant luminary of Tucson, Judge Sydney R. DeLong, the ostensible editor of the *Arizonian*. For it we are indebted to Mr. Gentile, who "took" it by the consent of the learned Judge. Mr. DeLong looks well in a picture; his head and face indicate that he belongs to the Caucasian type of man; his forehead is well suited for flattening out tortillas; his nose projects some distance from his face, and is, we think, large enough to "smell a mice." His mouth appears to have been well cut with some dull instrument, either a crevice spoon or a shovel, and the eyes — those glorious "yorbs" look like empty egg shells.
>
> . . . .we mean to preserve this picture, by having it framed with "brass," and mounted on a braying ass, so as to represent the pious Judge in the act of blowing his trumpet for the patriot (Governor) McCormick.
>
> (*Arizona Miner* of Nov. 21, 1868)

The Tucson editor takes Marion's words in stride. There are enough things to concern DeLong without his taking heed of the upstart in Prescott.

Tucson, at this time, appears to the newcomer as a city of chaos. Rollicking soldiers, rustling gamblers, emigrants on their way to California, cursing teamsters, sleepy-eyed Mexicans and stoic Indians jostle each other on her garbage-littered streets. A few mercantile stores, the fly-ridden, tobacco-filled "Shoo Fly" and Palace restaurants, numerous saloons, and a handful of adobe shacks with cowhide doors compose the town and provide the local paper with news.

Marion does not wait to hear from his colleague before lashing out again. The disapproval of the Tucson paper towards Dr. John T. Alsap, first treasurer of the Territory and one-time Prescott businessman, who is running for public office in Tucson, motivates Marion's second editorial:

35

It must afford our fellow-citizen, J. T. Alsap, un-bounded satisfaction to have the best and ablest citizens of Tucson elect him to preside over the Council, after the foul charges made against his character by the Governor's organ (The *Arizonian*). What contempt these men must hold the whangdoodle editors of the vile organ in? But a short time ago, it denounced Mr. Alsap as a liar, and a man who kept the worst sort of company in its town, yet its purest and best citizens show their confidence in his honor, knowledge and integrity by electing him to preside over them. Go hence, to the pump, unclean scribblers of the Arizonian, and scrub the foul pollution from your vindic-tive carcasses. Avaunt, ye yelping curs, whom it would be base flattery to designate men. Cease your abuse of Yava-pai and her people, quit scheming to injure your fellow-citizens of other counties of the Territory, and if you can-not then make an honest living go and crucify yourself upon a cactus.

(Arizona Miner of Nov. 28, 1868)

Tough language for tough men in a still tougher Territory! The population of Arizona, excepting for a few widely separated families, is a hodgepodge of men. Some are old frontiersmen, or refugees from the war-ravaged Southern states; but many more are Mexican outlaws or fugitives from the law in Texas, New Mexico, and California. San Francisco in particular contributes ruffians, thieves, and murderers to Arizona when the Vigilance Committee offers these hoodlums of the Bay City the choice of a noose or a trip to Arizona.

Marion's attack on DeLong causes little concern in the Ter-ritory. Just another fight — and it will be just another shooting! However, DeLong leaves the *Arizonian* to enter the mercantile business and the one-sided feud is over. Warm days and long evenings come to Prescott before another editor is favored by Marion's ire:

Got the Bighead. — Taggart & Bushyeard, editors and publishers of the *San Diego Union*, are badly afflicted with the "bighead," given to lying and other improper practices. Exaltation to editorial tripods has inflated them muchly, and they will burst, or turn to night-owls before long. Recently, they copied, approvingly, from the MINER, an item relating to mail service, in which we laid our complaints before the authorities in a vigorous but respectful manner. They also seized upon another item upon the same subject, in the same issue of our paper, pinched out one or two lines, twisted their meaning to suit themselves, and, in hopes of getting even with us for past stabs, crowed lustily, about how it had brought the Department and its contractors to time. To believe it, ever since it opened and shut its alligator jaws upon the contractors, and greased them with slime, they have carried the mails regularly, and the people of its county have been blessed with rare mail facilities. Unfortunately for this tipsy organ of a few crazy speculators, its own columns furnish as assertions to refute its empty boast, as may be seen by the following correspondence from a citizen of its county, in the same issue containing the boast.

(Here is published a complaint about mail service from a citizen of San Diego, California.)

Now, Mr. *Union,* be more careful in the future, how you lie, bloviate, and try to injure a contemporary, simply because it is located in a white man's country. Reduce yourself to decent proportions, and we will let you have a *branch* from our main trunk railroad.

(*Arizona Miner* of June 12, 1869)

There is no rebuttal from San Diego. Marion's attention turns to local news — a dance given by the officers of Fort Whipple, the theft of a horse from in front of a saloon, new arrivals in the town. The newcomers have heard, and now believe, that "in Arizona the hoofs of your horse throw up silver with the dust."

The interest in local affairs is interrupted by a "fore'n" source. Marion, as keenly interested in Eastern attitudes towards Arizona as the East is in the exploitation of the Territory, finds a New York editor predicting a dire future for the new Territory. He trains his verbal guns on Charles Dana, America's leading newspaperman and editor of the *New York Sun.*

THE NEW YORK SUN AND ARIZONA

While the military and citizens of this Territory are

37

struggling, with all their might, to gain ascendancy over its savage tribes of Indians, and "conquer" it for the United States, "peace snakes" are erecting barriers to prevent them from so doing. But, they might as well undertake to crush civilization as to stop its steady, onward pace. The bitterest and most shortsighted of those who advise Government to abandon the Territory to "its wild men and wild beasts" is Charles A. Dana, editor of the New York *Sun*, ex-secretary of War, etc.

He actually does this very thing, from motives of economy (?). Bah, Mr. Dana, you are behind the age, and should be ashamed of yourself for advocating so nonsensical a proposition. Confine yourself to your velocipede and to firing squibs at the President for not giving you a fat office, and you will not make yourself entirely ridiculous, as you must eventually do should you keep on writing in the interest of the Indian. Were your advice followed by Government and people, almost every Territory of the Union would in a short time be turned over to the savages. Fortunately, however, there is no danger of your advice being heeded. The cause of your splenetic attacks is too well understood. You are sore headed, Charles, and your intelligent countrymen from Maine to Mexico know it.

You start out upon the hobby that this Territory has no earthly value to the country. Well, admitting that it has not, the fault is not with the Territory. You say that it originally cost the Republic the sum of ten millions of dollars. Yes, Charles, you need not fear, the Apaches won't hurt you, unless your advice should be followed, and the whites be forced to fall back upon New York City.

It is not true, as you assert, that the Territory has been of no benefit to the country, since its acquisition, for there is one gold mine in this country, which has yielded several millions of dollars, and is now yielding one half million per year. We mean the Vulture, near Wickenburg — the largest and richest gold mine yet discovered on the face of the earth. This, too, when by the neglect of the Government, its owners have to work it at a great disadvantage. Has this yield of bullion done the country no good? It has, and you cannot gainsay it. Then there are hundreds of the rich mines here ready to "remit" a hundred fold the cost of the Territory to that Government, whenever Government subdues the Indians that prevent its citizens from working them, and but for you and your kind, Charles, they would to-day be contributing to the wealth of the nation.

You advocated the internecine strife, and through taking good care to keep your precious (?) carcass away from the front, made lots of money out of it. Then you were for putting down resistance to the Government at the cost of the last man (except yourself), and the last dollar.

Oh, fie, Charles! Cease your croaking, and wield your able pen in the cause of civilization, humanity and justice. If you are really anxious to stop Government expenses in Arizona, use your influence to have about three full regiments of cavalry sent to this Territory as soon as possible, and our word for it, the Apaches will soon be subdued, the drain upon the Government at an end, and the Territory placed in a position to be of great service to the whole country.

(Arizona Miner of Sept. 18, 1869)

Marion should plead for more troops! Without a railroad or telegraph, and depending on a handful of soldiers to patrol and protect hundreds of miles, disorder and bloodshed prevail throughout the area. "Mines without miners and forts without soldiers are common, politicians without policy, traders without trade, storekeepers without stores, teamsters without teams, and all without means, form the mass of the white population."

In this setting it is not surprising to find the Prescott editor again upbraiding Dana as follows:

WE RISE TO EXPLAIN

The classical donkey (editor Charles Dana) of the *New York Sun* gets off the following:

"There is a man named Crook,[1] who is employed by the military authorities on the frontier lines to hunt down refractory Indians. The great excellence claimed by Mr. Crook is, that he can travel for three days on the trail of an Indian without anything to eat, drink, or smoke. This is a very nice accomplishment for Mr. Crook; but how it works in regard to the poor savage Indian is not chronicled."

Well, it was certainly an oversight on the part of your informant, Charles, that has left you in ignorance regarding the disposition Gen. Crook makes of the savage when he catches him but we will enlighten you upon the point: There are such things in Arizona as the army breech-loaders. To describe one of these would be somewhat difficult, but they dispense a preparation, lead, seldom used in the pharmacopoeia, which, when administered through their agency, exercises a most beneficial influence upon the nature of the "poor" savage. One dose generally suffices to remove him beyond earthly troubles, and the worst subject becomes as harmless as a child. Now, when the "Mr. Crook" of whom you speak, comes upon a rancheria, he sets his breech-loaders to work, and soon the hostile savages of a moment before, are just as harmless as the bowlers among which they lie stretched. He then leaves them in their innocence and goes in search of another rancheria.

But do you know, Charles, how the "poor Indian" would welcome you, his friend, were you to test the powers of your gentle blandishments upon him? No, you have not the slightest idea. Charles, there is a plant in Arizona known as the cactus. It is frequently three feet in circumference and fifty feet high, and its whole surface is studded with sharp thorns varying in length from a quarter of an inch to an inch and a half.

Well, the poor Indian, after divesting you of your fashionably-cut clothing and reducing you to a state of nudity, would bind you fast to one of the plants which we have described. Your tongue would be cut out so as to prevent you from indulging in any profane language, and you would have the satisfaction of seeing your "poor" friends examine its anatomy, while the action of a slow fire gradually imparted a beautiful rich brown color to the surface of your body. A peculiar, twitching sensation about your hoofs might at length cause you to look downward and you would doubtless feel somewhat startled to observe that your lower extremities were on fire and blazing brightly. Your surprise, Charles, would soon give way to alarm as you observe that more fuel is being placed upon the fire and the flames are rapidly ascending. In this condition we will leave you at present, believing that we have fully explained everything that might seem dark or uncertain.

(*Arizona Miner* of Sept. 16, 1871)

Marion's editorial is not based on just personal feelings in defense of his Army friend and idol. General George Crook and his handful of soldiers are the only organized force standing between the marauding Apaches and the settlers' scalps. When it is necessary within a military fort for officers to cross from one building to another with a cocked six-gun in readiness for fear of Apaches, then even the efforts of a few troops are a godsend.

In personal appearance Crook stands over six feet in height, straight as a lance, broad and square-shouldered, full-chested, and with keen blue eyes. His voice is always low, his conversation easy, and his general bearing one of great dignity. When not confined by military matters, his great passion is a lonely sojourn into the back country for a few days of hunting and fishing.

Crook as a military man is exceptional in that he commands the respect of his officers, troops, civilians, and even the Apaches he pursues. Disliking the formal army uniform, he personally leads his expeditions, dressed in duck suit and white canvas helmet, riding his stout army mule, "Apache." Despite his unorthodox dress, this general relentlessly stalks the Apache into his vast ancestral strongholds and brings temporary peace to the Territory.

Indians say Crook is more Indian than they themselves, and one of his officers calls him the "Daniel Boone of the West." Skilled in the language of "signs" and trails, cool and resourceful, Crook meets and finally conquers the wily Apache. This high-ranking officer understands the ideas, views, and opinions of these Indians that he is ordered to capture. In council with the belligerents, Crook tells the hostiles that if they continue on the warpath, he will fight until every Apache is dead; but if the Indian surrenders, "(I will) treat the Apache just the same as (I) treat any other man — as a man." And Crook is not speaking with a "forked tongue," for he never makes a promise that he cannot keep.

In an infrequent speech, Marion, after the final subjugation of the Apaches, voices his feeling for Crook in this way (*sic*): "We have had many generals here to fight the Injuns, but Crook is the only one who ever succeeded. We had Stoneman; Stoneman was a good fighter, he built a good many roads, and did a good deal of work, but he couldn't fight Injuns. Wilcox had a big reputation as a Civil War soldier, but he couldn't fight Injuns; he had the piles; and so it was with the balance both before and after Crook came. When Crook came he made the Injuns hunt their holes, and we've had peace in northern Arizona ever since."[2]

The commending of Crook for his service by the Sixth Territorial Legislature expresses the appreciation of an indebted Territory. Still, peace is slow to come; it will be some time before the "Injuns hunt their holes."

To the uncertainty of living in the midst of Indians on the warpath, political unrest appears on the Arizona stage. When party lines are drawn in 1870, Marion joins the ranks of the Democrats and becomes their chief exponent. As a public-spirited man, the Prescott editor is an ardent advocate and energetic co-worker in behalf of everything which is in the interest of the Territory. Even at this early time Marion can be rightly called "Prescott's one-man Chamber of Commerce." His enthusiasm for his home town, however, does not blind him to the needs of the Territory.

Interest focuses on the territorial election of 1870. McCormick left the office of governor in 1868 to enter Congress as a delegate from the Territory of Arizona. He now seeks re-election, but finds himself in an embarrassing situation. The governor's old paper, the *Arizonian*, is supporting his opponent, Peter R. Brady, in the race for territorial delegate. McCormick tries economic pressure to bring the *Arizonian* in line; but failing there, he establishes the *Arizona Citizen* in Tucson, and installs John Wasson as editor. Wasson barely has time to draw his first pay-check before P. W. Dooner, irate editor of the *Arizonian,* sends a challenge. Wasson defends his patron in the reply:

FRAUD

The Arizonian is crazily bawling over frauds which it asserts the friends of McCormick intend to perpetrate at the coming election. The editor knew he was penning calummes (*sic*) when he made these charges, for if fraud is intended, the small, unpopular clique he trains with contemplate committing them.

The supporters of McCormick want nothing but a just legal vote, and they mean to see that none other is cast, so the Arizonian Pecksniff may well quiet his nerves and be as comfortable as possible under the defeat awaiting the whole Brady outfit.

(*Arizona Citizen* of Oct. 22, 1870)

While feeling runs high, Marion leaps into the fracas, defending the Democratic candidate, Brady. Each candidate's qualifications are soon lost in a series of editorial exchanges between Marion and editor Wasson of the *Citizen*:

"A GREAT LIAR AND BLOWHARD."

To show who has written himself down as above, and to vindicate our correct course, we give place to the subjoined from the Arizona *Miner* of Nov. 5:

"The editor of the Tucson (Arizona) *Citizen* is fast writing himself down 'a great liar and blowhard,' which fact pains us considerably, as we have heretofore considered him incapable of getting down on his knees and filling the position of affidavit man to a set of thieving politicians. His paper of the 22 Oct. is one tissue of falsehoods. To believe these falsehoods, a stranger would imagine that everybody in Arizona was wrapped up in McCormick, and that his election is a foregone conclusion. We know better, and to show that we have confidence in our knowledge, we will stake the *Miner* office against its value in money or property that Brady will be our next Delegate to Congress."

It would be well for the substantial citizens of Arizona, if somebody accepted the stake offered by Marion of the *Miner*.

Now, Marion, who is proven 'a great liar and blowhard,' you or we? The People have decided that "thou art the man."

(*Arizona Citizen* of Nov. 12, 1870)

Brady is defeated. Even Marion's unfailing faith in the Democratic candidate cannot change the result — 832 votes for Brady and more than twice that number for McCormick.

Wasson, gloating over McCormick's triumph, seizes this opportunity to reprimand the renegade *Arizonian* and her editor, Dooner:

43

PEOPLE'S MASS MEETING

Dooner excels in one thing — that of long faced hypocrisy. He declared after election, that he was too honest to live in Tucson! Satan is beckoning him on to a warm welcome with congenial spirits.

(Arizona Citizen of Nov. 12, 1870)

A former country schoolteacher, Wasson continues in the same issue to spank verbally McCormick's other recent antagonists:

PERSONAL

Toll the bell,
A crowd of damned souls (politically)
Float down the Stygian River.

P. R. Brady (defeated candidate for Congress) heads the floating mass. He knows what is right, and has generally done right, but in the canvass just closed he proved himself too weak to always do right. By listening to and acting upon the advice of pretended instead of real friends, he has brought political if not financial ruin upon himself, and has few sympathizers.

That prince of dead beats, and slanderers, and carpet baggers, Sylvester Mowry (former soldier, delegate to Congress, and owner of the *Arizonian),* is more likely to bring up in the club rooms of the Pacific Street, San Francisco, than the Pacific Club of that city. Miserable and despised Sylvester.

If Granville H. Oury (former delegate from the Arizona Territory to the Confederate Congress) has not yet discovered the place the people of Pima county desire him to occupy, he has, at least, ascertained the one they will not permit him to occupy.

P. W. Dooner (editor of the *Arizonian)* has probably a glimpse of that "future" which he said awaited him if he played the treacherous part he has, instead of continuing as a worthless if not a damaging simpleton. It may assuage his grief some to be assured that we cared nothing for his idiotically vicious abuse, and are now enjoying healthy

laughs at his calamity. Viewed merely as a rare compound
of fool and knave, he is admirable.

The notorious M. B. Duffield (first Marshal of the Territory) will probably emigrate, or remain here within legal
bounds and *bonds* (under bond to keep the peace) . . .

We have sympathy for those who for some weeks have
been apologizing for the company they were in, and trust
the lesson they have just been taught will be of value to
them hereafter, and that they may live to realize its
fruits an hundred fold.

(*Arizona Citizen* of Nov. 12, 1870)

Because news reaches Prescott only by horseback or stage-coach over several hundred miles of unsettled, Indian-infested
desert, the election results are slow to reach the northern city.
Great is the excitement when the returns are finally learned.
Marion listens unbelievingly at first, and then vents his disgust
and anger through his paper's editorial column:

RESULT OF THE ELECTION

Another terrible calamity has befallen our unfortunate
Territory, the will of whose citizens has just been defeated
at the ballot-box . . . Mr. McCormick the vile, and his
backers — the contractors, Federal office-holders, monopolists, and their retainers, have again stuffed the ballot-boxes with fraudulent votes . . .

(*Arizona Miner* of Nov. 26, 1870)

Many join Marion in his bitterness. Added to the defeat of
their Democratic candidate at the hands of the Republican Mc-Cormick, Prescott has recently lost the territorial capital to Tucson. In the election of 1868, there was a widespread belief that
McCormick was trading the capital for the large vote of Pima
County, of which Tucson is the county seat. Credence was given
to their suspicions by the removal of the capital.

In a period when men sleep on six-guns and work with rifles
strapped to their backs, all misfortunes are blamed on Mc-Cormick's "inefficiency" in Congress. The Territory needs sol-

45

diers for protection, a railroad, and a telegraph. For these they look to McCormick. When there is no gratification of these needs, tempers rise and curses fly at the mention of McCormick or the new capital, Tucson.

"The Ancient and Honorable Pueblo," as some of the residents of Tucson are apt to call their town, was founded in 1776, although first visited by Europeans in 1694. From an Indian village, Spanish mission outpost and presidio, to territorial capital, the town lives in constant turmoil. As early as 1825, the town has been encircled with a fortified adobe wall, complete with corner salients. A single gate in the south wall, barred from sunset till dawn, offers relative security from the blood-stained Apaches.

Even after the recapturing of the settlement from Confederate forces during the Civil War, men shoot innocent and unoffending citizens or bowie knife them just for the pleasure of watching their agonies. Men walk the streets and public squares with double-barreled shotguns and hunt each other as sportsmen hunt for game. The town's graveyard fills quickly with murdered men.

Sprawling on the banks of the Santa Cruz River, amid fields of green barley and shaded by cottonwood trees, Tucson creates a vivid impression on the traveler: "the head-quarters of vice, dissipation, and crime. There is neither government, law, nor military protection. The garrison at Tucson confines itself to its legitimate practice of getting drunk or doing nothing."

Another visitor describes Tucson as: "a city of mud-boxes, dingy and dilapidated, cracked and baked into a composite of dust and filth; littered about with broken corrals, sheds, bake-ovens, carcasses of dead animals, and broken pottery; barren of verdure, parched, naked, and grimly desolate in the glare of a southern sun. Adobe walls without whitewash inside or out, hard earth-floors, baked and dried Mexicans, sore-backed burros, coyote dogs, and terra-cotta children; soldiers, teamsters and honest miners lounging about the mescal-shops soaked with the fiery poison. . . ."

In the space of a few years Tucson manages to become dirtier, more crowded and unruly. Along the streets, devoid of sidewalks, wagon trains hauled by placid oxen or quick moving mules and cumbersome prairie schooners still wend their way

46

to unload goods at the stores of local merchants. The dusty, be-whiskered teamsters soon ease their thirst at the "Quartz Rock," "Hanging Wall," or "Golden West" bars. Water, when not bought from the old Mexican who hauls it in barrels in a dilapidated cart from a spring, is obtained from wells. Paved streets, as yet, are unheard of and street lamps unthinkable.

The buildings in Tucson, like the inhabitants, are in direct contrast to those in Prescott. ". . .there are whole blocks of houses in Tucson which do not have a single nail in them, but have been constructed entirely of adobes, with all parts of the wooden framework held together by strips of rawhide. Tucson has no hotels. She does not need any. . . .as her floating population finds all the ease and comfort it desires in the flare and glare of the gambling halls, which are bright with the lustre of smoking oil lamps and gay with the vari-colored raiment of moving crowds."

In this setting walks John Wasson, known to his friends as Joe, editor of the *Arizona Citizen*. Wasson the zealot! Wasson the crusader! Almost the very first columns of his paper demand the "sweeping away of garbage-piles, the lighting of the streets by night, the establishment of schools, and the imposition of a tax upon the gin-mills and the gambling-saloons."

"Devout Mexicans cross themselves as they pass this fanatic, whom nothing seems to satisfy but the subversion of every ancient institution. Even the more progressive among the Americans realize that Joe is going a trifle too far, and feel that it is time to put brakes upon a visionary theorist whose war-cry is 'Reform!' But no remonstrance avails, and editorial succeeds editorial, each more pungent and aggressive than its predecessors. What was that dead burro doing on main street? Why did not the town authorities remove it?"

The readers of the *Citizen* receive the editor's words in typical Southwestern fashion (*sic*): "Valgame! What is the matter with the man? And why does he make such a fuss over Pablo Martinez's dead burro, which has been there for more than two months and nobody bothering about it? Why, it was only last week that Ramon Romualdo and I were talking about it, and we both agreed that it ought to be removed some time very soon. Bah! I will light another cigarette. These Americans make me sick — always in a hurry, as if the devil were after them."

A well-traveled, well-informed man, Wasson soon realizes

that his conscientiousness and energetic pleas for local reform are falling on deaf ears. So when Marion of the *Miner* offers a new topic for debate, Wasson readily replies:

PAH UTE COUNTY

Marion, the truthful, says, "that the land formerly known as Pah Ute Co., Arizona, we all know to be a part and parcel of Lincoln county, Nevada, and that it remains to be seen whether Governor Safford and Secretary Gashford are sufficiently base and lost to all shame as to count this vote."

We know it will make the dear sanctified soul writhe with indignation, but the truth must be told, dear Marion. The vote was counted and being true to truth, we are compelled to say further, that admitting the territory ceded to Nevada to have been legally accepted by that State, (which we deny) still St. Thomas and the citizens that you would have disfranchised because they did not vote your ticket, are in Arizona.

In proof of this statement, we publish an extract from a letter from B. H. Paddock, of St. Thomas, under date of Nov. 12:

"I am satisfied that these settlements are east of the Nevada line. From the point the surveyors are now at, a due south line will go west of this place."

The surveyors have been at work for some time under contract from the government, establishing the line between Nevada, Utah, and Arizona, and it is now ascertained that in any event St. Thomas belongs to Arizona. Truthful Marion, we are sorry for you. We are sorry that you are repudiated by more than two-thirds of the people of the Territory. We are sorry that you cannot indulge in the little pasttime of talking about frauds and corruption, without being compelled to know that you and your own friends are the only corruptionists, and in your madness and disappointment you desire to cast off a part of our Territory and population, because they voted against your wishes; but as tho' the heavens and earth had combined against you, the compass and chain say "no", these people belong to Arizona, even if they did vote for McCormick . . .

(Arizona Citizen of Dec. 10, 1870)

Wasson's attack is unjust when viewed in the light of later developments. Pah Ute County, carved from northwestern Mohave County, was established by the Second Territorial Legislature of Arizona in December, 1865. Congress voted to give a majority of the Pah Ute area to Nevada in 1866. The protests of the residents of the county and a petition from the Arizona Territorial Legislature fail to change the vote in the nation's capital. The Legislature of Nevada accepts in 1867 the cession which is a condition to its annexation, while the citizens of Arizona are still crying three years later over the "stolen land." It is not until 1871 that the Arizona Legislature reluctantly recognizes the area as part of Nevada. Arizona loses millions of acres and Marion is vindicated.

In the monumental task of carving a home from the wilderness, Marion has just begun. Confined to Prescott by editorial duties, he can look back on his first weeks in the Territory and write: ". . . .we have prospected, mined, risked our lives among Indians, suffered hardships innumerable, sewed on many a button, flopped many a flapjack, and upon several occasions, gone to bed, on Mother Earth, tired, hungry and a little alarmed about the permanency of our scalp."

John H. Marion becomes the target of many. This editor remains in a land where the strongest often become weak and the weak soon perish. Armed with an accurate, quick-moving, and effective pen, Marion succeeds in a town and territory where even strong men's guns falter and then tumble through the hands of their owners into the Arizona dust.

Burned fields, unmarked graves, silent military posts, and deserted ranches dot the Arizona landscape. From abandoned mines and ruined towns the surviving pioneers flee to the protection of the walled city of Tucson or militia-guarded Prescott. Screams of the stragglers mingle with the war cries of the Apaches. The Army has long since marched east to fight in the Civil War.

Rampaging Apaches dance with glee. "Have we not defeated the soldiers? The *dogs* with their noisy bugle have run away to the east. Now, we, the Apache, will drive away all whites. Those

49

that try to stay will be killed. The land of our fathers will once again belong to us!"

More settlers die under the scalping knives of savage warriors. Men shovel parched earth on the graves, as their women watch tearfully, unbelievingly, and hopelessly. Occasionally the frontiersmen do best the Indians — an Apache dangles at the end of a rope on the limb of a sprawling desert tree; another lies nailed to a cross on a rocky ridge.

These become signposts of the frontier!

With the end of the Civil War the nation struggles to regain its feet. The battered and bloodied Union Army can afford to return only a token force to the Arizona Territory. A few hundred soldiers are assigned to guard thousands of miles where death lurks behind every boulder and bush.

The fearless Prescott editor chooses the pen as a weapon in this territory where the arrow, rifle, bowie knife, and six-gun wage the battle of the frontier — crime vs. law; plunder vs. settlement; wilderness vs. civilization; and life vs. death. He is one of the few men in the "despised, maligned and neglected" Territory to do battle in the unceasing verbal war which will bring to Arizona the renown, fortune, protection, and standards that are Marion's dream and the settlers' prayer.

American outlaws, Mexican bandits, and other outcasts of society increase the hellish confusion created by the Apaches. Even more despised on the frontier than the Indians are the renegade traders. These unscrupulous white men in return for "much gold" furnish the natives with guns and ammunition to supplement their native lances, bows, and arrows in the war against the whites. Whiskey is in constant demand, for liquor and a war dance prepare young warriors for tomorrow's raids. All this the renegade trader will furnish for a price!

Marion expresses the pioneer's contempt for these scoundrels when one of them very nearly becomes a victim of his "customeers":

CAPTURE OF A PACK-TRAIN BY THE COYOTERO APACHES —

From Messrs Young and Bryant, who recently came through from New Mexico, we learn that while they were in camp at Zuni, Sol Barth and George Clinton, formerly of this county, with some Mexicans, arrived at the villages from the White Mountains, almost naked and in a starving condition. They had left Zuni but a short time previous, with a pack-train of some twenty head of animals, loaded with goods and trinkets specially suited for trade with the Indians. With them was an Indian guide. After crossing the Mogollon range and descending into the valley of the Rio de los Milpas, and while going through a deep and narrow box canyon, the members of the party were seized, one by one, by Indians, deprived of their arms, stripped of their clothing and threatened with death, and would have been murdered but for the interference of an Indian who knew Sol.

After being released by the Indians, they took the trail for Zuni, distant 80 or 90 miles, without food or water of any description, arms, and but very little clothing — some of them having been stripped of their boots. When the pangs of hunger became unbearable, they killed a dog which accompanied them and lived upon the meat for five days.

If what we have heard of Sol Barth be correct, we do not pity him for his misfortune. It is believed here and in New Mexico that he has been in the habit of trading these Indians powder, lead and arms, and if such be the case, we regret that they did not take him down to the village and let their squaws torture him to death.

(Arizona Miner of Nov. 14, 1868)

The frontiersmen are fortunate in that not all Indians are Apaches. Many tribes, each a sovereign nation, lie within the Territory's limits. Some tribes join the Apaches in their war against the whites, yet others maintain a historic friendship with the settlers. Three of these tribes, the Pimas, Papagos, and Maricopas, in central and southern Arizona, are lifelong enemies of the Apaches and now become strong allies of the whites. The Walapais,[3] living on the edge of the Grand Canyon in northern Arizona, are only annoying to the settlers of Prescott. These Indians steal an occasional horse, not to ride into war, but to fill their empty cooking pots.

Suddenly the Walapais take the warpath in 1868. This once peaceable tribe is stirred to action by the causeless killing of

Waba Yuma, their head chief, by a white man named Mitchell. Though the Walapais had been looked upon with the contempt that frontiersmen commonly feel for peaceable Indians, they prove vicious enemies. General McDowell reports, "the officers from Prescott say they would prefer fighting five Apaches to one Walapai."

With the subjugation of the Walapais comes punishment for their leaders. "Walapai Charley" is taken prisoner and sent to Alcatraz prison. To his tribesmen's protests Marion writes:

> Wallapai Charley — This notable Indian scoundrel, was, shortly after arriving at San Francisco, set to work by the military authorities there, who did not understand that General Price sent him in to have a good time and see enough of the whites to awe his proud, murderous spirit. It is said that the Wallapais are anxious to see Charley again, and threaten to kill all the whites between Prescott and the river, if Charley is not soon returned to them, right side up with care. Bah! the red dogs would like to murder *whites* whether or not Charley is ever returned to them.
>
> (*Arizona Miner* of Aug. 14, 1869)

After months of peace the Walapais again take to the warpath. Before leaving for their old strongholds in the Canyon of the Colorado, they fire into the Agency buildings. There appears to be no explanation for this sudden turn of events and the press is filled with dire predictions on account of "the well-known treachery of the Indian character."

Captain Thomas Byrne, 12th Infantry, is supervisor of the Walapai reservation. Realizing full well the cost to the government in blood and dollars if the outbreak is not stopped at its inception, he rides bareback after the fugitives. When the Walapais see the cloud of dust on their trail, they fire into it; but the officer is unscathed and rides up to the knot of chiefs who stand on the brow of a lava mesa. The sullen Walapais are soon telling of their grievances, especially those against the captain. The new agent on the reservation has been robbing them blind in the most barefaced manner. In their ignorance of military affairs, the chiefs imagine that it is Byrne's duty to regulate all affairs at his camp. They do not want to hurt their friend, the captain, and will let him return safely; but they have been cheated and must take the warpath and plenty of it! Tommy says patiently, "Come back with me, and I'll see that you are righted." The chiefs follow the solitary, unarmed officer. Going directly to the beef scales, the officer discovers tampering. A two-year old Texas steer, which, horns and all, would not weigh over 800 pounds, marks 1,700 on the crooked scales. In the treaties with the Walapai the government grants them a food ration to be distributed by the agent. This agent not only cheats on the beef ration but even sells most of their salt and flour to nearby miners, the Indians being swindled out of everything but their breath.

Thoroughly enraged, Tommy seizes the agency and assumes command, to the complete satisfaction of the Walapais. The agent leaves that night for California, never to return.

Crooked agents, unscrupulous traders, and white killers hide their tracks well. Only with the passage of time will the injustices done to the Indian unfold and the frontiersmen learn why "the pesty redskins have gone on the war-path." The only reports seeping into the *Miner* office are the names of the most recent victims and the fact that their Indian murderers had fled before any pursuit could be organized.

Disorganization prevails throughout the Territory. Without the telegraph, news travels only as fast as a man on horseback. The *Miner's* editor is one of the first to realize that warring Indians are just one of the problems facing the settlers. Believing that an aroused public in the East can bring pressure to bear for the relief of the Territory, Marion addresses this editorial to them:

ROLL OF MURDERED ARIZONIANS

With Some Account of What the People
of this Territory Have Done
and Suffered in the Past Six Years.

We have demonstrated our ability to live in this new country, when we had to import every pound of provisions eaten by us, at a cost of from 25 to 100 cents per pound, every article of clothing, every implement and article used by us, at prices fully as high in proportion. Since then, we have ceased to import many articles, having produced them at home, and consequently enjoyed them for much less money. This, too, in time of war and general stagnation. Our foe — the Indian — has frequently come down on us like the wolf on the fold, killed many good and true men, and robbed us of our property, but, we have always recuperated, and to use a homely but expressive phrase, "come up to the scratch," like men . . .

To hold their own, or get ahead, the people of new as well as of old countries must not be tormented or harassed with war. They and their property must be protected by government, else they cannot accumulate and develop. These are acknowledged facts, and no one will have the hardihood to gainsay them.

Now let us see if the people of this Territory have had sufficient protection from a government that is pledged to protect all its citizens, and which was organized and is continued for that special purpose: The Territory is said to contain nearly 130,000 square miles, over which are scattered in tribes and bands, about 30,000 Indians, 5,000 of whom are deadly enemies of the white race. To conquer these Indians, and protect life and property, there is, it is said, about 2,000 troops in the Territory, fully one-half of whom are employed in doing camp and garrison duty, with perhaps from 200 to 300 always on the sick list. Now, most of these troops are scattered in small bodies throughout the southern and middle portion of the Territory, convenient to large towns and settlements, while a few companies — perhaps four or five — are posted far away from any settlement of importance, and where, in our humble opinion, they ought not to be, so long as the entire force is so small.

Then, again, the cavalry are poorly provided with horses, and the infantry with pack trains, so that when they do move after Indians, their movements are most generally, altogether too slow to catch the fleet-footed miscreants that prey on us. Again, so soon as officers and troops get to know the country, and the ways and haunts of the Apaches, they are sent out of the Territory, and new, green men, put into their places. Again, commanding officers here are 1,000 miles from the headquarters of the General commanding the Department, and, of course, have to act in

54

accordance with his instructions and orders, and beg him for troops and material.

Again, the settlements are scattered far and wide so much so that it would take at least four times the number of troops in the Territory to render them proper protection, and chase the Apaches.

Knowing these facts, people at a distance will not wonder at the slow pace this Territory has advanced, or the great length of the almost fruitless war that has been waged against the Indians. The wonder ought to be, that we have held our position in the Territory, despite every drawback, and it is a wonder. At times, our people have been almost ready to abandon the contest and throw up the thankless, unprofitable job of holding the Territory for a country that left them to shift for themselves. But, at these junctures, braver counsels would prevail and new determination be formed to stick to it at all hazards. They have stuck to it, retaliated on the savages, and by dint of hard work, have succeeded in making homes for themselves, cultivating the soil, opening and working mines, until we are now almost "out of the wilderness," and the labyrinth of difficulties with which we were formerly surrounded.

In a few years, should government not abandon us entirely, we will be able to shift for ourselves. Even now, we raise nearly enough grain to feed ourselves, the troops, the Apaches, and the animals belonging to all three of the aforesaid parties. We also raise vegetables of every kind, and mine out, annually, over $1,000,000 in gold, silver and copper — of which we have an inexhaustible supply.

To give our fellow citizens of the States an idea of the murderous war that has been waged against us, while accomplishing these things, we, below, give a partial list of the persons murdered by the savage aborigines of the Territory, from March 4, 1864, up to the present time. The list is, of course, incomplete, many persons having been murdered, of whose death no record has been kept. We will commence with Yavapai county; where, on March 4, 1864, the savages whom we had partially clothed and fed, dug up the hatchet, and without cause or provocation, commenced a career of murder and robbery unparalleled in the history of the West, by murdering five Mexicans and two Americans, whose names are to us unknown.

(Marion lists here the names of 153 white men killed by the Indians, together with the dates and places of their murder) . . .

We have no means of getting at the value of property stolen and destroyed during this time, but people can form an opinion upon that subject when they are told that nearly every white citizen now in the Territory, or who has ever resided in or passed through it, has lost a horse, a mule or a donkey, while from many persons whole bands of horses, mules, cattle and sheep have been stolen. Then the savages have descended upon ranches, and robbed many men of their crops. The only consolation we have for our great losses in life and property, is the fact that hundreds of the murderous race of savages that infest this Territory have been sent to their long homes and will trouble us no more. But, thousands yet remain, who are more determined than ever upon driving us from the Territory, a feat which they feel certain of accomplishing, having, in long ago, murdered and driven out a greater number of semi-civilized Indians. Will they succeed in expelling us? We think not. Yet, should government do no more for us in the future than it has in the past, the result is doubtful. ,

Reader, does not the above lengthy record of crimes sufficiently prove the folly of trying to conquer the Apaches with a few companies of troops? If you think so, raise your voice for vigorous war, until the last hostile Indian in Arizona is reconstructed.

(*Arizona Miner* of Jan. 22, 1870)

Less adventurous pioneers lose faith in the Territory in the face of what appear to be insurmountable hardships. Though mountains are rich with gold; though cattle wax fat on luxuriant native grasses, and homes overlook majestic valleys, there is little reward for staying in the Territory. The Indians butcher the miners as they work their claims, steal cattle from under the guns of guards, and burn homes over the owners' heads . . .

An "iron horse" could save the Territory! Where the Indians now attack mail riders, ambush stagecoaches, and plunder freighters, the railroad could get through. From numerous trips to new mining districts, Marion knows that the extensive gold and silver deposits in the Territory are of little value. The cost of bringing in heavy mining machinery by mule teams is almost prohibitive. A railroad would take gold and silver bullion safely to eastern cities. New settlers would travel over the rails to bolster the white forces in their battle of life vs. Indian. Supplies moved by rail would be cheaper and no longer would it "take a lady's stocking full of gold dust to buy a sack of flour."

Numerous schemes are presented for the construction of the railroad; but it is not until September, 1877, that the first engine snorts across the Arizona boundary. The Prescott editor contributes money to the project and enthusiastically supports it through the columns of his paper. Great is the celebration as the first train wheezes its way into Prescott.

Crime adds to the problems of transportation, communication and protection when Prescott grows too large for its village government. The county sheriff can't hang every offender on "some pine limb around the hill in west Prescott." Sentencing a person to jail, however, presents a problem. Marion doesn't want to see fellow citizens serving their terms chained to a huge ironwood tree under the Arizona sun, as is done in the neighboring town of Wickenburg. The Territory must have a large "escape-proof" jail:

WANTED — A PENITENTIARY

We again call the attention of the proper Territorial officials to this great want of the Territory — a want upon which we have heretofore dilated. Get that revenue money and start the building.

(*Arizona Miner* of Sept. 14, 1872)

Violence is the leading obstruction to justice. Judge Howard, outstanding lawyer of Prescott, defends most of the persons charged with crimes. His latest client is Fagan, a heavy drinker, who is convicted of assault with a deadly weapon. The well-liquored Fagan had rambled into a favorite saloon with his dog at his heels. As Fagan gulped the saloon's fiery liquor a well-placed boot crashed into the dog. With a startled curse Fagan pulled a knife. Fists smashed into flesh and chairs flew through the air in the general fight that ensued.

57

As Fagan's name is called at the sentencing he sidles up to his counsel, Judge Howard, and, in a stage whisper, tells the Judge, he's proud of the defense he made. He certainly did all that a man could do for another man, and asks him to do one more favor, and that is, stand up there and take the sentence for him.

The trial judge joins in the spectators' laughter and asks if Judge Howard would receive the sentence or if it should be given to the prisoner. Fagan receives the sentence; but a very light one, thanks to his Irish humor.

Humor is rare and much sought after on the raw frontier. Settlers are usually too occupied in the grim battle for survival. Holidays, however, are a cause for celebration even in Prescott. Tables are laden with the meat of the deer, its cousin the antelope, and wild turkey.

In the pine-clad hills surrounding Prescott intermittent snow falls, ushering in the Christmas season. To be ignored are high prices, the murder of friends, and hard work. Here is a time of joy, laughter, music, food and wine.

On the great day all join in a celebration around the community Christmas tree. Halves of tallow candles, tied to the branches with twine, shed their flickering light over the tree. Bright ribbons, gathered from trunk bottoms by ladies recently arrived from the East, give added lustre to the scene. Crude toys, fashioned by bewhiskered men, lie under the tree. Melody flows from the only musical instrument in Prescott — a violin, out of tune and minus a string. The fiddler cares little that the only air he can play is the "Arkansaw Traveller."

Standing shoulder to shoulder are sun-bronzed miners, bespurred ranchers, and wives of local merchants. Joyous carols, eager faces, and candy-smeared children fill the room. Christmas has come to Arizona!

Vincent Colyer, the "red-handed assassin" and "cold-blooded scoundrel," acts as peace commissioner to the Indians. When the troops fail to conquer their wily adversaries in the field, Congress sends Colyer to negotiate a treaty of peace with the Apaches.

Marion sees little value for the words of a peace agent where the guns of soldiers are unsuccessful. The Territory has a future; but that future can be bought only with all-out war, not trinkets and fancy words.

58

THE DARK SIDE

We, like most newspaper scribblers, are too prone to delineate the bright side of everything, and perhaps, it is better to do so than to frighten and discourage people with angry looking charcoal sketches of men, matters and things; yet, truth should never be forgotten, and it compels us to tell our readers that in trying to cast the horoscope and take a peep into the future of the Territory, we can discern some black stains — some devilish-looking clouds hovering in and about our unfortunate Territory.

Congress — that most unfeeling, hypocritical assemblage of stallfed cormorants — still sticks to its motto of "millions for the protection of Negroes, but not one cent more than the inadequate amount now paid out, from year to year, for the protection of white citizens of Territories," or to aid in the development of these Territories. We, of Arizona, have asked for better mail facilities, for a regiment or two of troops, and for a small sum of money to be expended in building a wagon road from New Mexico to connect with other roads in the Territory, but instead of giving us better protection from Indians, troops have been withdrawn, and none have yet arrived to fill their places.

Indeed, we fear that Vincent Colyer, and a horde of cowardly thievish Quakers and peace men will be sent out among the peaceable Indians, rekindle hell's passion in their bosoms, back them up in committing crime, and then screen the wretches from punishment. There is not the least danger of their making the hostile savages any worse than they are, for the Old Scratch is so big in them that it is utterly impossible for the Indian department and its Quaker policemen to make them any worse. Should the squawking Quakers succeed in the game now being played by them — that of having Sheriden[4] and his Lieutenant, Baker, reprimanded, for killing a lot of red devils in Montana, we may bid good-bye to every hope of peace in this Indian accursed Territory. No military officer will then dare kill an Indian, even though his buckskins were dripping with white blood.

Still, Government sends its agents among us to collect taxes, and by so doing belittles itself in the eyes of the people of all other civilized nations. No wonder that foreigners who have visited our Territory have stared at us widely when told that we were forced to pay taxes to a government that fails to give us protection. But for its failure to do so, native and foreign capital would flow to the Territory and be invested in mines, ranches, etc. Roads would be built, the country would be settled and the Indians conquered or driven out of it. The Territory is really worth fighting for, and it is the earnest prayer of its suffering people that Government will not much longer act the fool with the murderous savages who now bar the door to prosperity in Arizona.

(Arizona Miner of April 16, 1870)

The Prescott editor, taking advantage of a news item, verbalizes his feelings for the reasoning ability of some government officials:

Among the most recent discoveries made by General Belknap, Secretary of War, is that there are not less than fifteen thousand mules in the supposed service of the Quartermaster's Department, most of which are engaged wholly in the business of "eating their heads off." — Examiner.

We'll bet a trifle that there are twice fifteen thousand two legged asses in the employ of the other departments, most of whom are engaged wholly in the business of destroying the substance of the people.

(Arizona Miner of July 16, 1870)

To Marion, one of the biggest "asses" is Peace Commissioner Colyer. A member of the Church of Friends and Board of Indian Commissioners, Colyer is directly responsible to the president. As he has authority even greater than the military, Colyer attempts to place the Apaches upon reservations where the government can give them food and clothing. Preaching this gospel of peace, he believes that the Arizona press represents an ungodly and unregenerated people, rather inferior even to the Indian.

In line with the Colyer policy, Indian chiefs will go to Washington to confer with the "Great White Father." The trip, perhaps, will bribe the chiefs into bringing their clansmen unto the reservations. Who knows? This trip may even impress these war lords with the benefits of "civilization."

60

Marion's contempt for such a policy is not to be kept in silence.

APACHE INDIANS TO VISIT WASHINGTON

WASHINGTON, January 19. — The Annual report of the Board of Indian Commissioners called the attention of the President and Congress to the present condition of the Apaches of Arizona, asking for a special appropriation of $30,000 to prevent a threatened war with those Indians, and inviting their Chief and a dozen of his braves to visit Washington. The President endorsed this proposal, and the House voted the appropriation.

The foregoing shows that the fools, or knaves, — don't know which to call them — are not all dead yet. "To prevent a threatened war." Good gracious! Just as if the Apaches had ever been at peace with any one. Out upon such twaddle.

(*Arizona Miner* of Feb. 18, 1871)

When Cochise, chief of the Chiricahua Apaches, receives a written invitation from C. Delano, secretary of the Interior, to visit Washington, Marion's rage knows no bounds.

Cochise go to Washington? Unthinkable! Has not that "fiendish killer" tied whites to burning wagons, left them pegged naked over ant hills, and dragged them to death behind his galloping horse? Has not this Apache led his tribe for 12 years on raids through the Territory that left theft, murder, and rape in their wake? Cochise, war lord of the Apache and scourge of the whites, is the sworn foe of the frontiersmen and should be treated as such.

Exasperated further by Colyer's statement that the *Arizona Miner* reflects "the opinions of traders, army contractors, barroom and gambling saloon proprietors — who prosper during a war; that the frontiersman, miner, and poor laboring man of the border, pray for peace," Marion writes:

"GOD HELPS THOSE WHO HELP THEMSELVES."

If the Colyer policy of treating hostile Indians prevails much longer, the best thing our people can do is cease

61

business for awhile and go to hunting up and slaying Apaches. We have stood enough fooling, in this line, and might stand it awhile longer, if Government had not made the Apaches worse than they have commonly been, by feeding and arming them at its reservations; then threatening them with punishment, after a certain date, provided they did not change from natural-born hyenas to innocent lambs, or tractable rams; then, when they for the tenth time, at least, had defied the Government, left their reservations and commenced anew the work of plunder, Government goes back on its words, crawfishes, and tells the commander of its forces here to be sure and not let the Indians and his troops come together, we think it is about time for our people — poor and demoralized as they are — to act upon the saying at the head of this article.

The writer of this will follow the lead of any brave white man against any number of Government pets — whether Red or White — or, he will mortgage what little property he has to help defray the expenses of a campaign against the foes of the Territory.

(*Arizona Miner* of March 23, 1872)

When Marion learns that Colyer is at Fort Whipple near Prescott, he rides out for a talk with his adversary. Colyer gives this account of the meeting:

"Mr. Merriam, (Marion) the editor of the 'Arizona Miner,' and several other gentlemen, called to invite me to address in public meeting the citizens of Prescott on the Indian question. I read to Mr. Merriam his editorials, published before my arrival, wherein he said, 'Colyer will soon be here. . . .We ought, in justice to our murdered dead, to dump the old devil into the shaft of some mine, and pile rocks upon him until he is dead. A rascal who comes here to thwart the efforts of military and citizens to conquer a peace from our savage foe, deserves to be stoned to death, like the treacherous, black-hearted dog that he is. . . .' I told him that I had no hankering after that kind of 'mining.' "

"The gentlemen assured me that they would protect me with their rifles and revolvers; but as my official duties were wholly with the Indians, and the officers of the Government having them in their charge, and I was unable to see sufficient reasons

62

for addressing a public meeting in which I should have to be protected with rifles and revolvers, I respectfully declined."[5]

Marion flings a last verbal barrage when Colyer's resignation as peace commissioner and member of the Board of Indian Commissioners is accepted:

FAREWELL, FRAUDS

Whitman is under arrest for various shortcomings and Colyer, the cat's-paw of the Indian Ring thieves, is in disgrace.

"It is a long lane that has no turning," Mr. Colyer. You, no doubt, feel sorry that the necessity for removing you should have arisen. We hail it as good evidence that the Secretary of the Interior and President Grant have Fowlerized your bumps and found you to be a very foul fraud. It is hard on you to be shelved in such a manner, although you have been let down easy. Don't you wish you hadn't told so many falsehoods about matters and things in this unfortunate Territory, and, above all, don't you wish your name here wasn't "Greene?"

Ah, you natty little criminal, what, now, will become of the squaw you made love to at Camp Apache, and what about the promises you made the Apaches, to feed, clothe and, by the aid of soldiers, to protect them from the settlers; and your lying affidavitmen — can't you come out and console such of them as have not already silently stole themselves out of the Territory?

"Vengeance is mine" saith the Lord. You and your kind have scourged Arizona, and now the Lord is taking vengeance upon you.

You clung to position longer than the Secretary of the Interior wished you, and you had to be kicked out at last!

How changed your circumstances must now be from what they were while you were here, traveling through the Territory, dispensing presents to murderous savages and bribes to affidavit-men, with lavish hands. Ah, supercillious upstart, you are no longer clothed with power to take white men's farms from them and declare said farms parts and parcels of Indian Reservations. The clank of protecting sabres will never again be heard by you in Arizona, unless, indeed, you may conclude to come back at your own ex-

63

pense and take up a residence in that shaft, of which we reminded you while here.

Thanks, a thousand thanks to President Grant for shelving you, and may God have mercy on your soul for the wrongs you have inflicted on Arizona and her people.

(Arizona Miner of March 30, 1872)

Sharing Colyer's disgrace is Royal E. Whitman, a lieutenant of the 3rd Cavalry, U. S. Army, who was in charge of the Apache reservation near Fort Grant. In line with a government peace policy of 1870, Apaches who surrendered were placed on reservations and protected by Army guns from possible revenge by the settlers. Whitman was accused of having Indian mistresses, establishing a settlers' store, blacksmith shop, and butcher shop on the reservation to line his own pockets.

Citizens of Tucson believed that the Apaches from Fort Grant were responsible for numerous killings and thefts. Enlisting the support of friendly Papago Indians, a handful of whites and Mexicans took up the trail of a war party which had recently attacked the settlers and peaceable Indians near Tucson. The pursuing party claimed the trail led to the Camp Grant reservation.

In the dewy freshness of dawn the avenging citizens struck. The Apache sentinels, a buck and a squaw, were playing cards before a small fire. Stout hands clubbed them to death before they could give the alarm. This attack on April 30, 1871, entered the annals of Arizona history as the Camp Grant Massacre.

An angry and sickened Lt. Whitman looked in horror at the remains of his wards. The Tucsonians had done their work only too well. An army officer gives a description of the terror-filled Apache encampment:

CAMP GRANT MASSACRE

The camp had been fired, and the dead bodies of some twenty-one women and children were lying scattered over the ground; those who had been wounded in the first instance had their brains beaten out with stones. Two of the best-looking of the squaws . . . were first ravished and then shot dead. Nearly all of the dead were mutilated. One in-

64

fant of some ten months was shot twice, and one leg hacked nearly off. While going over the ground, we came upon a squaw who was unhurt, but were unable to get her to come in and talk, she not feeling very sure of our good intentions.

So sudden and unexpected was it, that no one was awake to give the alarm, and I found quite a number of women shot while asleep . . . The wounded who were unable to get away had their brains beaten out with clubs or stones, while some were shot full of arrows after having been mortally wounded by gunshot. The bodies were all stripped. Of the whole number buried, one was an old man and one was a well-grown boy — all the rest women and children. Of the whole number killed and missing about one hundred and twenty-five — only eight were men. It has been said the men were not there — they were all there.

(The raiders captured the older children and took them back to Tucson to be sold into slavery.) About the captives, the Indian men say, "Get them back for us; our little boys will grow up slaves, and our girls, as soon as they are large enough, will be diseased prostitutes, to get money for whoever owns them. Our women work hard and are good women, and they and our children have no diseases. Our dead you cannot bring to life, but they that are living we gave to you, and we look to you (Lt. Whitman), who can write and talk and have soldiers, to get them back."

A furor sweeps the Territory and the nation. Claims and counterclaims fill the air. Some maintain the Camp Grant Apaches had nothing to do with the frequent raids and the murder of settlers. Others, including the Arizona press, believe that Colyer's policy of protecting Apaches with soldiers encouraged Indian warfare.

"Murder," cries the nation.
"Self-defense," echoes the Territory.

President Ulysses S. Grant threatened to place the Territory under martial law if all who took part in this massacre were not arrested and brought to trial. Finally, one hundred Americans, Mexicans, and Papagos were indicted and tried in December

65

before the U. S. District Court. With a virtual instruction from the presiding judge for acquittal, the Tucson jury deliberated only 20 minutes to return a verdict of "Not Guilty."

Whitman was arrested for failing to protect the Apaches, but was later acquitted. Not knowing the true events of the massacre, the Prescott paper takes great delight in the forced resignation of Colyer as a result of the massacre.

Though possibly guilty of an unjustified attack on Colyer, Marion does not retract any of his editorials. After all, that fool Colyer makes peace treaties with fiendish Indians and then uses American soldiers to make the whites live up to the treaties. Everyone knows that there is gold and silver all over the reservations granted to the Indians. The prospector and miner want that gold — they have a right to it. To hell with the treaties!

To the surprise of his friends and the delight of the back fence gossips, Marion suddenly forsakes the life of a bachelor. Nearly as homely a man as ever walked on two legs, he proudly proclaims: "Being a firm believer in the axiom that, 'It is never too late to do good,' we boldly announce, to all old and new patrons and readers of the Miner, that we, the editor, have mustered sufficient courage to 'pop the question' to one of Arizona's fairest and best daughters, who has, for some unaccountable reason, said 'yes' to our proposal, and agreed to become Mrs. Marion. With her, and with but little else, we propose to take a new departure; to commence anew the battle of life; to earn an honest livelihood out of the Miner, to which we must, hereafter, if possible, devote more excruciating toil and thought; to labor for the advancement and prosperity of Arizona. . .

"Wedding to take place at the residence of Mr. and Mrs. Edward W. Wells, in Prescott on the 16th (Sept., 1873). Reception at the residence of the parties of the first and second part, in the evening of the same day, to which latter trying ceremony friends from here, there, everywhere, are cordially invited to come and not stay too long."

Marion, the old renegade, getting married! Leading the rejoicing citizens of Prescott is the staff of the *Arizona Miner*. A flag near the newspaper's office flies at half-mast. "Marion has departed" reads the banner over the office door. Foot races are run in the street and the winner, a *Miner* employee, freely distributes his prize — a keg of beer.

Taking his new role seriously, Marion seeks to improve his paper. A major problem is finances — and hence:

> More Subscribers Wanted. — Our anxiety to "benefit" the public, and raise a stake to be expended in celebrating the coming National Anniversary, prompts us to offer great inducements to persons, who don't take the MINER, to have their names enrolled among our honored paying subscribers, and thus become happy in this world, and glorious in the next.
>
> These inducements are as follows: From and after date, every new subscriber who pays seven dollars down, for one year's subscription, will receive a copy of the paper for one year, and be entitled to our support, should he see fit to run for Delegate. As there may be some old fogies who prefer a farm, or feet in a ledge of "pay-stone," we have about made arrangements with Judge Berry, Register of the Land Office, to give each man a farm in Tonto Basin, or the valleys of the White Mountain streams, where they can have the pleasure of living near neighbors to thousands of "amiable, tractable" Apaches. Miners, or those whose hopes of making piles are imbedded in the primary rocks, will receive "feet" in ledges that have never paid a cent, so that they may be rest assured of one thing i.e. that if they ever contained "pay," it is there yet . . .
>
> *(Arizona Miner of March 26, 1870)*

After years of pleading, demanding, and even threatening for an improved territorial government, Marion takes a more active role by being elected a member of the Ninth Territorial Legislature.

Little happens in Prescott or the Territory that is not recorded by Marion's faithful pen. From the birth of a baby and the arrival of new goods at a local store, to Indian raids and the progress of mining — all are chronicled by this tireless editor. Marion, promoter of the Territory; Marion, watchdog of the people's interests; Marion, crusader for an honest, efficient, and progressive government; Marion, who misses only one big story! To others must fall the job of reporting that tragic day in Prescott history — July 27, 1891.

Flags at half-mast curl lazily in the warm breeze of a summer day. The District Court lies empty, its members adjourning quickly in stunned silence. Prescott is hushed with inactivity, its citizens refusing to recognize reality.

The news spreads quickly, "yes . . . drawing a bucket of water from the well behind the house. He just collasped." And several hundred miles to the south of Prescott, another editor painfully writes of Prescott's tragedy.

"What, Marion dead! was the grief-laden exclamation of surprise which fell from every lip, as the sad news became known, and even then some refused to believe it until they went to the late home and with their own tearful eyes saw the earthly remains of the best and bravest friend that Prescott and Arizona ever had — one who battled ever for the right, for his adopted home and for his friends, who never quailed before mortal man and who was only vanquished by death."

Order somehow emerges from chaos. Companies of the fire department are alerted to meet in full dress uniform for the funeral. Led by the 9th Infantry Band, the long funeral cortege slowly wends through the Prescott streets to the nearby hills. "The Prescott Fire Department — Mechanic's Hook and Ladder Co. No. 1, Toughs Hose Co. No. 1, Dudes Hose Co. No. 2, O K Hose Co. No. 3; printers, all of whom had been in the employ of deceased at different times; Aztlan Lodge No. 1, F. & A.M.; hearse with remains of deceased; mourners; Arizona pioneers on foot; members and visiting members of Prescott bar, and citizens on foot, in carriages and on horseback," form a kaleidoscopic procession.

These mourners pay glowing tributes to Marion, friend and champion of Arizona. They realize that it is Marion who played an important role in bringing closer to the Territory a railroad, telegraph, law, nation-wide recognition, and an end to Indian warfare.

Sons and daughters of these mourners will only too soon forget. Tomorrow the Territory which Marion helped to build will let him rest in an unmarked grave. In her grief Prescott does not realize that Marion's fame will be so short-lived. A fellow journalist of the day eulogizes the renowned Prescott editor:

When the names of the territory's early heroes shall

be enrolled; when those who have been most instrumental in shaping her destiny shall be written on history's pages, the name of John H. Marion will lead all the rest.

One might sometimes differ from him in political matters, might get vexed and annoyed at some of his blunt sayings or brusque way; but always, in season and out of season, we loved and admired him for his devotion to and untiring labor in behalf of this community. As a friend he was firm and unchangeable, ready to share every sorrow and trouble and to divide with him the last dollar. As an enemy he was unrelenting and defiant.

He wore no mask, he knew his friends, his enemies knew him.

---

[1] Brig. Gen. George Crook, commander of the Military Department of Arizona.

[2] Farish, Thomas E., op. cit.

[3] Also known as Hualapai.

[4] Major General Philip H. Sheridan, commander of the Military Department of Missouri.

[5] Farish, Thomas E., op. cit.

The Arizona Sentinel.

Vol. 1.　　ARIZONA CITY, YUMA COUNTY, A. T., SATURDAY, JULY 27, 1872,　　No. 20.

Who is to blame?

Wanted Immediately . . . a Fighting Editor for the Sentinel. — C. L. Minor

"Arizona City!" roars the stagecoach driver as he sights the sandy streets of the river settlement.

The traveler, wracked from the jostling ride, peers intently at the town.

"A great wide stretch of avenue is lined for a quarter of a mile by straggling adobes . . . a few of which have lost their usual grey, ashen hue under a coating of whitewash. Looking eastward he sees the green line of willow trees and bushes that bend over and fringe the green Colorado river. Across its waters

71

his eye rests upon the uncouth group of buildings perched upon the sand-dune that has for so many years borne aloft 'Old Glory' and told the weary traveller of 'mine Uncle's' care and guardianship. The setting makes the gem, for sure it is that Fort Yuma is no jewel.

"The wide horizon's stretch, the strange peaks that almost quiver in the morning haze, the far-off 'Purple Hills,' the wavy line of odd-shaped mesa and bluff; these for a western perspective unite to make a rare picture of strange tones, colors, and atmospheric effects."

The stagecoach rolls to a stop and the driver dismounts. A postmaster hastens forward to receive the mail. Contemplating the coach and its passengers are "the lazy Indian, in his breechclout or ragged pants; the more picturesque Mexican; and the cynical, careless stalwart American." The travel-bruised passengers climb from the coach.

Travel by stagecoach does not draw the sightseer. It takes urgent and important business to induce a frontiersman into these "carriages of the devil." As no reservations are required, you pay the fare in gold or silver and climb aboard with no questions asked.

A veteran traveler tries to ride next to the driver on the top of the stage. Some good tobacco, a stray cigar, and perhaps a little pull out of a convenient flask will make the drivers, each of whom is called "Jehu," both pleasant and talkative. Generally men of nerve, sobriety, and intelligence, the overland drivers form a class by themselves. "Their histories are peculiar; their language also; their ways are usually quiet, and from their ranks have come men of mark."

The old hand at coach riding gives this advice to the newcomer: "If the top of the coach is not heavily loaded, and is guarded by a rail, the traveler will do well to put a pre-emption thereon as a sleeping place. Of course, he has provided himself with a large canteen, holding a gallon at least, and with his blankets, a good driver, and a fair day, it will go hard if he does not make himself as comfortable as the circumstances will allow. If an inside seat is secured, let it be one at the back and next to the side. A good precaution is to carry a stout strap, which can be passed round the coach door, and the body, so that when

72

sleeping, the jolting of the vehicle will be thus prevented from throwing the passenger out of his seat.

"In no place is the spirit of courtesy and mutual accommodation more needed than in a crowded stagecoach starting out on a long journey. Rolling day and night over gravelly mesa, sandy river road, and stony mountain pass, there will be ample room for the exercise of all the finer courtesies and social amenities.

"The roads are almost as nature had made them, rough and rocky, abounding in ruts, pitfalls, and heavy sands, and every mile of the way from the Rio Grande is beset with dangers. Fierce and barbarous Indians lurk behind the rocks and in the deep arroyos, ever on the alert to plunder and murder. . . ."

Strangers arriving in Arizona City by stagecoach are a common sight; hence, our traveler arouses little curiosity when he decides to remain in the town. He is not asked for his name, as men are sometimes killed for asking such a question. Rather, he is asked, "What are you called?"

"C. L. Minor," he replies. As is customary on the frontier, no further questions are asked. A man's name, where he came from, and where he is going is his own business, unless he volunteers the information. Minor chooses to keep his past a secret, as do so many on the frontier.

A printer by trade, Minor casts about the town for a suitable job. Finding that Arizona City has never had a newspaper, he establishes the *Arizona Sentinel* and issues the first edition on March 10, 1872. Though knowing the mechanics of printing, Minor finds a problem in the writing of news. He has no reporters to write the news, nor are there radios, or a telegraph, or railroad which could carry the news.

But on the frontier one thing is always news — the Indian. And in the Arizona Territory, editors are continually writing about the Apache, most warlike of all Indians. It is not too strange to find Minor denouncing them in one of his first editorials:

THE APACHES

These fiends in human form are on the war-path in all directions. Every week brings us intelligence of horrid butcheries perpetrated by these devils, and yet notwith-

73

standing all this, the Government would have us to meekly submit to our fate. If the Government and the Indian Ring cannot keep the Apaches on reservations, why not let General Crook and his small body of efficient men, who, knowing the nature of the beast as well as we do, send them to that peaceful reservation "from whence no traveler returns."

(Arizona Sentinel of March 23, 1872)

Conflicts usually arise wherever two different and distinct types of civilization meet; but the white man's war with the Apache Indians probably exceeds all others in its intense hatred, and the unbelievable atrocities committed by both sides. The Apaches show little mercy to any white unfortunate enough to fall into the enemies' hands.

The Apache ravishing of an entire white family of nine is only one of numerous incidents. Royce Oatman, his wife, and seven children are en route to Arizona City from Illinois. The family journeys westward, in the mode of the day, by wagon caravan. At Santa Fe Pass dissension arises as to future plans and leadership of the caravan. The immigrants divide into two groups, with the Oatman family and their friends moving south toward Tucson and then Arizona City. Just short of Tucson the party loses a number of horses and mules to thieving Indians. Upon reaching Tucson the travelers are warned that the Apaches are raiding along the Gila River Valley, through which they must pass. All of the party but the Oatman family elect to remain within the security of Tucson.

Although most of their possessions have been stolen, traded, or sold, this family keeps two wagons, two yoke of work-worn cows, and one team of oxen to pull the cumbersome wagons over the rough desert floor. Progress is slow. On the ninth morning out of Tucson the family sights "several Indians slowly and leisurely approaching in the road."

Olive Oatman, the oldest daughter and a survivor of the massacre, gives this account. "After the Indians approached. . . . they asked for tobacco and a pipe, that they might smoke in token of their sincerity and of their friendly feelings toward us. This my father immediately prepared, took a whiff himself, then passed it around, even to the last.

74

"Suddenly, as a clap of thunder from a clear sky, a deafening yell broke upon us, the Indians jumping into the air, and uttering the most frightful shrieks, and at the same time springing toward us flourishing their war-clubs, which had hitherto been concealed under their wolf-skins. I was struck upon the top and back of my head, when with another blow, I was struck blind and senseless.

"As soon," continues Olive, "as they had taken me to one side, and while one of the Indians was leading me off, I saw them strike Lorenzo, and almost at the same instant my father also. I was so bewildered and taken by surprise by the suddenness of their movements, and their deafening yells, that it was some little time before I could realize the horrors of my situation. When I turned around, opened my eyes and collected my thoughts, I saw my father, my own dear father, struggling, bleeding, and moaning in the most pitiful manner. Lorenzo was lying with his face in the dust, the top of his head covered with blood, and his ears and mouth bleeding profusely. I looked around and saw my poor mother, with her youngest child clasped in her arms, and both of them still, as if the work of death had already been completed; a little distance on the opposite side of the wagon, stood little Mary Ann, with her face covered with her hands, sobbing aloud, and a huge-looking Indian standing over her; the rest (of the Oatmans) were motionless. . . .all upon the ground dead or dying."

Olive and a younger sister Mary Ann are dragged by the Indians into captivity. Lorenzo, though badly wounded and left for dead, recovers and begins a search for his sisters that is to last five years. Mary Ann, unable to endure the rather primitive life of the Indians, dies while still a prisoner. Through the efforts of Lorenzo, a sympathetic carpenter at Fort Yuma, and the assistance of friendly Yuma Indians, Olive is released from her five years of captivity. Thus closes the saga of the Oatman Massacre.

Betrayal, treachery, and insincerity have sown distrust among both whites and Indians. Many opportunities for Indian capitulation are thwarted by a white man's rash violation of Indian surrender under a white flag. To the white, an Indian is a murderer. To the Indian, a white is a trespasser. The harsh treatment of Mangas Coloradas, a war lord of the Apaches,

75

though perhaps justified, only prolongs the war for several years and costs numerous lives.

"The name of Mangus Coloradas is the tocsin of terror and dismay throughout a vast region of the country. . . .He combines many attributes of real greatness with ferocity and brutality of the bloodiest savage, the names of his victims, by actual slaughter or captivity, would amount to thousands, and the relation of his deeds throughout a long and merciless life would put to shame the records of any other villain."

Caught while plotting treachery against the miners of the Santa Rita Mines, Mangus receives a whipping at their hands. This is too much for his proud spirit, and thereafter Mangus is the sworn foe of the whites. Mangus had privately visited some of the more prominent miners with offers to show them the location of gold, which was of no value to him. He made this kind of an offer:

"You good man. You stay here long time and never hurt Apache. You want the "yellow iron" (gold): I know where plenty is. Suppose you go with me, I show you; but tell no one else. You like "yellow iron" — good! Me no want "yellow iron." Him no good for me — can no eat, can no drink, can no keepee out cold. Come, I show you!

"For a while each person so approached kept this offer to himself, but after a time they began to compare notes, and found that Mangus had made a like promise to each, under the ban of secrecy and the pretense of exclusive personal friendship. Those who at first believed the old rascal, at once comprehended that it was a trap set to separate and sacrifice the bolder and leading men by gaining their confidence and killing them. . . .When next Mangus visited that camp, he was tied to a tree and administered a dose of 'strap oil,' well applied by lusty arms."

As treacherous as are Mangus' actions, the whites in later years seem to act still more treacherously. A mining party aids troopers of the California Column in inducing Mangus to believe that further resistance is in vain. Now an old man, Mangus surrenders and tells his bodyguard of Apache warriors in broken Spanish: "Tell my people to look for me when they see me." Mangus Coloradas is murdered by the Army on the night of his surrender with at least two different versions of his death being given.

76

General West, commander of the California Column, claims that seven soldiers under the command of a noncommissioned officer were guarding Mangus. When the chief attempted to escape about midnight by rushing the guards, he was shot.

A trooper in General West's command gives another version. He reports that on the evening of the arrest the General addressed the soldiers guarding the Apache chief in this fashion: "Men, that old murderer has gotten away from every soldier command and has left a trail of blood for five hundred miles on the old stage line. I want him dead or alive tomorrow morning; do you understand? I want him dead!"

A civilian witness maintains that the soldiers heated their bayonets in a fire and then burned the legs and feet of the captive Apache chief. When the chief protested the soldiers shot him.

Where men fight treachery with treachery and avenge murder with murder, a quick peace is impossible. For the murder of Mangus the Apaches swear 100 whites will die. The war rages on for years while this and other vows of vengeance are fulfilled.

Some frontiersmen do not live to see the conquest of the Apaches; others do not wait for it. Minor turns to other topics for comment. Having settled down to the life of Arizona City and the drama of everyday living, Minor uncovers a challenge in local government.

The newspaper editor finds no corrupt political ring, but rather gross mismanagement. Alleging the inefficiency of officials, Minor soon has a fight on his hands. And a gunfight is the usual reward for questioning another's business on the frontier. Minor believes, however, that it is the paper's duty to tell Arizona City how its government is run.

Minor wisely decides that gathering advertisements, editing the news, and then printing it consumes all his time. In anticipation of the coming battle Minor runs this advertisement.

WANTED IMMEDIATELY

A large, broad-shouldered, bulldog head, short-haired man, is wanted immediately at this office, to serve as fighting Editor for the Sentinel. We have tried to do our own work, besides "playing the devil," but when it comes that we have to fight besides, then we are not equal to the emergency. After mature deliberation, we conclude that engaging a fighting Editor is the cheapest. Applicants will please send weight — whether light or heavy — also the number of men he has "chawed up." Terms — half the profits. Blood pudding furnished everyday. None but the principals need apply.

(Arizona Sentinel of Oct. 5, 1872)

While waiting for a fighting editor to assist him, Minor looks into the official activities of the county's district attorney. Minor first questions why taxes owed to the county by the recently deceased sheriff are not collected. The sheriff might be dead, but the taxes are still due. Finding that the district attorney has apparently made no effort to collect from the sheriff's estate, Minor asks:

WHO IS TO BLAME?

Last week we took occasion to call attention to the matter of the delinquency of our late Sheriff — Mr. Dana — and by so doing have incurred the wrathful displeasure of our District Attorney. As a journalist, we claim the right — nay, we consider it our duty — to correct whatever of wrong in public affairs that may come to our knowledge, and which lies within the scope of our powers of correction.

Our columns are not devoted to personal abuse. This has been our purpose from the beginning — and they are not to be so prostituted now. The most despicable feature of a venal press is the execrable practice of making a moral blacking-brush of it to tarnish (or attempt to) the private character of persons who have, by accident or otherwise, incurred the ill will of its editor. This kind of business we put behind us, as did the Savior of the world, the Mephistopheles of the Bible. What we said of the individual in question was upon the best authority, and with no intention to wound the feelings of anybody.

That no misapprehension may abstain in the premises, we give to our readers, in explanation of the item referred to, the following correspondence, which will give the gist of the whole matter:

78

SENTINEL OFFICE
Arizona City, Oct. 1st, 1872

Jose M. Redondo, Chairman
Board of Supervisors:

My Dear Sir: — As there seems to be some misunderstanding, or apparent misunderstanding, concerning the matter of collection of the amount of the delinquency of the late Sheriff — Mr. Dana — will you do me the favor of giving me the facts in the premises, that the responsibility touching the non-payments of the same may be placed exactly where it belongs and that our fellow-citizens may know who is to blame (if anybody) in the matter? An early reply is desired.

With much respect, I am very truly your obd't serv't,

C. L. Minor
Ed. SENTINEL.

C. L. MINOR, ESQ:

In reply to your communication of the 1st inst., I have to say that sometime in January last, the Board of Supervisors of the county REFERRED the matter of the deficiency of James T. Dana, late Sheriff, to Clarence Gray, Esq., District Attorney, with instructions to take such action in the premises as would secure the county.

Sometime after this, Mr. Stewart, one of Dana's bondsmen, tendered to me through Mr. Barney, the amount of his portion of such deficiency. I told Mr. Barney to see Mr. Gray, as the matter was in his hands. I AM NOT AWARE THAT ANY STEPS HAVE BEEN TAKEN TO COLLECT THE SUM DUE THE COUNTY BY MR. GRAY. Soon after Mr. Dana's death, the sureties on his bond offered, in County Warrants, the full amount of Dana's deficit, and deposited the warrants with Col. Jas. M. Barney, subject to the order of the Board of Supervisors. The Board refused to accept the warrants on settlement, demanding the cash. The tender of Mr. Stewart was after the Board refused to receive the warrants.

Jose M. Redondo,
Chairman, Board of Supervisors

79

Error has never been right, nor can falsehood ever become true. We have given the facts as they have come to us, without bias or prejudice, and for what they are worth, we give them to you.

The statement of Chairman Redondo has peculiar significance, which will not fail to attract the attention of those most interested. No blame in our point of view, can be attached to the Board of Supervisors in not accepting county warrants in liquidation of the debt of the delinquent Sheriff, because the law requires the payment of all taxes to be in legal tender. Not being a lawyer ourself, we must, as a citizen, confess, however, that we are at a loss to know why contracting parties may not pay off mutual claims, by mutual promises to pay. It seems to us that any other view of the matter would savor largely of repudiation.

Whether the District Attorney is derelict in duty in the collection of the amount of Mr. Dana's defalcation, is a matter for the public to judge of . . .

(*Arizona Sentinel* of Oct. 5, 1872)

Meanwhile, the word has spread throughout the Territory that Editor Minor is seeking a fighting editor to join him in his attack on local politicians. A Tucson editor, John Wasson, good-naturedly ribs his fellow journalist.

The District Attorney of Yuma county seems to have had an unpleasantness with the editor of the Sentinel. According to the dim light we have on the subject, no harm seems to have been done, unless it may be in anticipation, as the editor seems to be anxious to secure a fighting associate. — *Arizona Citizen.*

Yes, brother Wasson (editor of the Citizen), we did advertise for a fighting editor, and have received several applications for the place, none of whom, however, fill the bill; and, besides, some of our friends have recommended a gentlemen at Tucson by the name of M. B. Duffield. Will our friend of the *Citizen* be kind enough to tell us what *he* knows of Duffield's qualifications for fighting?

(*Arizona Sentinel* of Oct. 19, 1872)

80

Tucson editor Wasson should recognize that Duffield is a fighting man. It is this same Duffield whom Wasson threatened to kill. In a rage of passion Wasson had taken his gun to hunt for Duffield; but when the two met on the streets of Tucson, Wasson lost his courage and fled back to the newspaper's office where he penned vile but empty threats against Duffield.

Editor Minor would indeed find that M. B. Duffield had all qualifications to become a fighting editor. Duffield came to the frontier from New York. Appointed by President Abraham Lincoln, Duffield was the first marshal of the Arizona Territory. He, as does Minor, covers his past with a blanket of silence.

Duffied stands "not less than six feet three in his stockings, is extremely broad-shouldered, powerful, muscular, and finely knit; dark complexion, black hair, eyes keen as briars and black as jet, fists as big as any two fists to be seen in the course of a day; desputatious, somewhat quarrelsome, but not without amiable qualities. It is said he is the only man in the Territory who dares to wear a plug hat without fear of having it shot off by ruffians."

Once Duffield obtains a reputation as a crack shot, numerous ruffians and gun-slingers attempt to outdraw him, thereby building their own reputation. One such gun-slinger is "Waco Bill," who comes with a wagon train from Texas. Having consumed "half or three quarters of the worst liquor — coffin varnish — in town, he is anxious to meet and subdue this Duffield, of whom such exaggerated praise is sounding in his ears."

" 'Whar's Duffer?' he cries, or hiccups, as he approaches the little group of which Duffield is the central figure. 'I want Duffer; he's my meat. Whoop!'

"The words had hardly left his mouth, before something shoots out from Duffield's right shoulder. It is that awful fist, which could, upon emergency, have felled an ox, and down goes our Texas gun-man sprawling upon the ground. No sooner has he touched Mother Earth than, true to his Texan instincts, his hand seeks his revolver, and partly draws it out of the holster. Duffield retains his preternatural calmness, and does not raise his voice above a whisper the whole time that his drunken opponent is hurling all kinds of anathemas at him; but now Duffeld sees that something must be done. In Arizona it is not customary to pull a pistol upon a man; that is regarded as an act both unchristianlike and wasteful of time — Arizonians nearly

81

always shoot out of the pocket without drawing their weapons at all, and into Mr. 'Waco Bill's' groin goes the sure bullet of the man who, local wits say, wears crape upon his hat in memory of his departed virtues.

"The bullet strikes, and Duffield bends over with a most Chesterfieldian bow and wave of the hand: 'My name's Duffield, sir,' he says, 'and then 'ere's mee visiting card.' "

Duffield could be an effective fighting editor; but perhaps not realizing the necessity for "freedom of the press," he confines his fights to barroom brawls.

The same issue in which Editor Wasson laughs at Minor's need for a fighting editor also carries an editorial on a near tragedy. Minor's apprehension of a coming battle with his political antagonist has become a reality. Minor has expected a showdown gunfight, but the attack comes as a surprise.

ASSASSINATION ATTEMPTED

In the days of Macchiavelli, one of the distinguishing features of Italian society was the work of the midnight assassin . . .

That the race of murderers of this class has not died out yet, was made alarmingly evident from our experience of last Saturday night. At about the hour of 12 o'clock, that night while we were sitting at our desk, reading, we were suddenly startled by the report of a pistol and the hiss of a flying bullet uncomfortably close . . .

(*Arizona Sentinel* Oct. 19, 1872)

Minor upholds Yuma tradition by refusing to run from impending disaster. This community on the Colorado River had had a peaceful enough beginning as a Spanish mission outpost in the early 1700's. Within a few years, Spanish soldiers were stationed at the mission to protect the increasing number of Spanish settlers in the area from the Yuma Indians. Relations were cordial until the horses of the soldiers destroyed the crops of the Yumas. The Spanish were slow in making good the loss, with the result that the aroused Indians planned a revolt. They struck on a Sunday, July 17, 1781, while the soldiers and some 150 settlers were attending mass at the mission. All of the

82

Spanish men were killed, their women and children made slaves of the Indians. This revolt ended Spanish interest and activity in that area.

With the gold rush to California in 1848, many of the fortune hunters in their eagerness to reach the gold fields chose to cross the Arizona-California desert rather than make the long voyage by boat around South America. The road blazed by these gold-seekers passed near the future site of Arizona City. The road, known as the *"Camino del Diablo"* or the "Devil's Highway" was whitened with the bones of some 3,000 to 4,000 wayfarers; killed, not by the war arrows of the Yuma Indians, but by hunger, thirst, and fatigue.

In 1854, a surveying party on the way to California reached the spot on which Arizona City was to be founded. The surveying party wished to cross the Colorado River by ferryboat. The operator of the boat, a German, demanded $25 to transport the party. Lacking money for the fare, Charles D. Poston, leader of the group, relied on his wit to solve the problem. "Setting the engineer of the party, and under him the whole force, at work with the instruments, amid a great display of signal-staffs, they soon had a city laid out in squares and streets, and represented in due form on an elaborate map, not forgetting lots on the river's edge, and a steam ferry. Attracted by the unusual proceedings, the owner of the ferry crossed the river and began to question the busy surveyors, who referred him to Poston. When the riverman learned from Poston that a city was being founded so near to his own land, the German became interested. As the great future of the place was unfolded in glowing terms, and the necessity of a steam ferry for the increasing trade, he became enthusiastic and began negotiations for several lots. The result was the sale of a small part of the embryo city, and the transportation of the survey party across the river in part payment for one lot." Poston did file the survey of the town in San Diego, California, in 1854.

The new settlement was known at first as Colorado City, being named after the river on whose banks it was located. Discoveries of gold in nearby areas brought sudden prosperity to sand-blown Colorado City. Unfortunately an unprecedented flood in 1862 destroyed the town. With the rebuilding came a new name for the settlement — Arizona City.

83

With a population of some 1,200 in 1871, Arizona City consists of four stores, a customhouse, two saloons, a post office, two blacksmith shops, a hotel, some houses, and a stagecoach station. With the arrival of the stage comes long-awaited mail and news of the other communities in the Territory.

In a mail pouch delivered to the *Sentinel* office is a letter from Editor John H. Marion in Prescott. Word of the attempted assassination of the *Sentinel's* editor has spread throughout the Territory. The Prescott editor is the first of many to offer congratulations and encouragement to Minor, editor of the *Sentinel*.

The attempt on Minor's life seems to give him greater incentive in seeing that District Attorney Gray is removed from office. While pressing the attack, Editor Minor gives this warning to Gray — and anyone else who desires to declare "open season" on editors:

A WORD TO THE WISE, Etc.

We have been threatened with violence if we undertook the exposure of a certain official in this county. That little game has been tried before, with what result everybody knows. We hold that the official character and conduct of every man is public property, and that it is the duty of journalists to expose the short-comings of an unfaithful public servant, no matter who it is.

We are personally responsible for everything in these columns, except notice be given to the contrary, and will try to take care of ourself if attacked. The truth is the truth, and will prevail, no matter if the universal army of affidavit men swear against it.

(Arizona Sentinel of Nov. 2, 1872)

Though a fighting editor for the *Sentinel* does not come forward, Minor is successful in his campaign against District Attorney Gray. This official is defeated by the voters in the next election. Editor Minor congratulates the voters for removing Gray from office, while summing up the citizens' grievances against Gray in this editorial:

84

THE DISTRICT COURT AGAIN

The legal mill is grinding, but like those of the Gods, rather slowly. The Grand Jury has been exceedingly industrious. They rain imitation indictments into Court, about as fast as that institution can rain them out on account of insufficiency. The people of Yuma (county of Yuma) never did a wiser or better thing than when they dismissed from office the man who holds the office of District Attorney just now. The Grand Jury did their whole duty, but every one of the first batch of indictments by them presented to the Court (and they were numerous) was summarily *quashed*. This District Attorney has been in office nearly a year, but we do not know of a single case, in the whole of that time where he has convicted anyone, unless he happened to be defending him, and then he did it to perfection in nearly every instance . . .

(Arizona Sentinel of Nov. 23, 1872)*

After fighting successfully to give Arizona City a progressive and honest local government, and even running for public office, Minor decides to sell his paper and leave the territory.

THE WEEKLY ARIZONA MINER.

VOLUME VII — PRESCOTT, ARIZONA, SATURDAY MORNING, FEBRUARY 5, 1870. — NUMBER 6.

THE ARIZONA MINER.

PUBLISHED EVERY SATURDAY MORNING,

AT

PRESCOTT, YAVAPAI COUNTY, ARIZONA.

SUBSCRIPTION:

One Copy,	One Year,	$7 00
" "	Six Months,	4 00
" "	Three Months,	2 50
Single Copies,		25

Papers will not be sent unless paid for in advance, and will *invariably* be discontinued at the end of the time paid for

ADVERTISING.

The Mormon Question.

Just now there seems to be a disposition on the part of those who manufacture public opinion, to raise a breeze about Utah that may eventually light the torch of war in that land of many feminines. The "Saints," themselves are at loggerheads, and therein lies the danger to themselves and their rare old institution. So long as they held to the same opinions, there was little danger of gaps being opened in their ranks to the ingress of the hated gentiles. Now, while firmly believing in the sinfulness of polygamy, we do not care to see it and those who practice it blotted out by war, and we hope the necessity

influence. When the waltz was at an end, she would dance no more, and soon retired

It was midnight when the dancers permitted me to quit playing, and soon all was silent in the house. The Colonel had not yet returned when I had prepared my night toilet. I walked up and down in my room for about twenty minutes, and was just lying down, when I heard a knock at the entrance door of the hall. Instinctively I opened my door, and saw the mulatto gliding down stairs with a candle in his hand like a ghost; but when he had reached the last step, he commenced to tramp on the floor with a certain vehemence, as if he intended to deceive any listener as to whence he came, before he reached the front part of the hall.

The Colonel had arrived. The mulatto showed him to his room, and I, after having

Complete List of the Theatres Destroyed by Fire in the United States.

The recent destruction of theatres at Milwaukee, at Helena, Montana, at Galveston, Texas, and in this city, induces us to republish what is believed to be an acurate list of the public places of amusement burned in the United States since 1798, with the exception of the ones above mentioned:

Federal Street Theatre, Boston, February 2, 1798.

Daniel Bowen's Museum, Boston, January 15, 1803.

Chestnut Street Theatre, Philadelphia, April 29, 1820.

Park Theatre, New York, July 4, 1821.

Richmond Theatre, Richmond, December 16, 1821.

Conceit–Some Notable Instances Thereof.

Even the philosophers have not shown themselves averse to be sprinkled with the holy water of laudation. Socrates soberly told his judges that they should award him a pension instead of condemning him; and Epicurus assured his correspondent that if he desired glory it was secured to him by the fact that Epicurus had thought him worthy of being written to! Alcibiades let all the world know that the sole purpose of his life, whether he headed a conspiracy, or plundered a city, or cut his dog's tail off, was to make a noise and give the Athenians something to talk about. Aristophanes, more frank even than Cicero, made of the *parabases* of his comedies vehicles for the most extravagant self praise,

" . . . A judge of whiskey"

There is no greater or more beneficient work than that of education . . .

William J. Berry

WANTED:

A nice, plump, healthy, good-natured, good-looking, domestic and affectionate lady to correspond with, Object – Matrimony.

She must be between 22 and 35 years of age.

She must be a believer in God and immortality, but no sectarian.

She must not be a gad-about or given to scandal, but must be one who will be a help-mate and companion, and who will endeavor to make home happy.

Such a lady can find a correspondent by addressing

the editor of this paper, Post Office box 9, Yuma, A.T.
Photographs exchanged!
If anybody don't like our way of going about this interesting business, we don't care. It's none of their funeral.

(*Arizona Sentinel* of July 10, 1875)

Many ask why editor William J. Berry seeks a wife when he is already married. Married to the *Arizona Sentinel!* A newspaper, especially one on the frontier, can be as demanding as any wife.

"Judge" Berry, as he is commonly called, receives the honorary title as he is a practicing lawyer. Coming to the Territory in 1862, Judge Berry arrives in Yuma, formerly called Arizona City, from Prescott. Berry, a man of large stature, buys the *Sentinel* from C. L. Minor just before the latter leaves the Territory.

The gray hairs on Berry's head explain a varied and interesting lifetime. Before assuming the editorship of the *Sentinel,* he has been a miner, lawyer, candidate for Territorial delegate to Congress, a gunsmith, and member of the Board of School Trustees.

A grade school was opened in Yuma in 1871, but it is far from a success. Children see little value in a classroom when they can watch the river boats move slowly against the current of the Colorado River. It's a lot more fun to feel the cool river mud ooze through their toes than to study from a dull old book.

Berry and the others ignore the whims of the youngsters and plan for the Territory's future. By boasting of Yuma's fine school system Berry hopes to enlist the support of parents whose children insist on playing "hookey":

EDUCATION

Last week we visited the public school, in charge of G. W. Nash, esq., and found everything in excellent order.

The school room itself is far better than we expected to see in these ends of the earth, being large and well lighted and ventilated.

The girls and boys in attendance seemed happy, healthy and contented, and an air of neatness and cleanliness pervaded the room . . .

It must gladden the hearts of all true friends of education to witness the rapid strides that our young Territory is making in this most important work. Now, thanks to the wisdom and energy of our excellant Governor, we have already as perfect a system of free schools as exist in any of the States, or in the world. All our schools yet organized have excellent teachers, and as fast as other districts are organized teachers are provided, and there is no child in the Territory of Arizona who may not obtain an education free of cost.

Can this be said of any other Territory of the United States? We think not. And let it not be forgotten that we are indebted to Gov. Safford for this great boon. He came here deeply impressed with the importance of engrafting the free school system on our young Territory, with all the improvements that experience and genius would suggest, and set himself about the work with an energy and devotion that overcame all obstacles. He visited repeatedly, all the towns and settlements in our wide-spread Territory, where his voice was heard earnestly and eloquently advocating the claims of every child to an education. He drafted the school laws, and urged them upon the consideration of our legislators, until they were passed; and he makes pilgrimages to all the schools and encourages both teachers and pupils by his presence and by his voice, until the children of Arizona have learned to know Gov. Safford as their friend. This is glory enough for one man . . .

Light, more light! is the cry that goes up from the masses of humanity, and the cry is being nobly responded to. The hope of the perpetuity of free institutions rests upon the free schools of the country. That bigotry that still exists in some quarters, that is an enemy to free schools, is fast passing away with its votaries, and will soon be known no more; while light and truth will still go marching on in infinite progression.

(*Arizona Sentinel* of Dec. 13, 1873)

Although this picture of education in the town and Territory is somewhat exaggerated, it is the work of such men as Editor Berry which prepares the Territory for the establishment in 1885 of a university.

Among the most famous of all frontier teachers is Miss Mary

E. Post, of Yuma. Miss Post, a former teacher in Iowa, was teaching at Ehrenberg, Arizona, when she was offered the Yuma school position. Moving to the lower river settlement, she quickly finds many friends among the wives of Army officers at Fort Yuma. Miss Post is joined by her brother in 1874, who conducts classes for the boys. It is less than a year later when a financial crisis threatens to close the school and Editor Berry pleads for the townspeople's support.

OUR PUBLIC SCHOOL

We understand from our school trustees that the funds will not suffice to pay the teachers for the full term that they were employed to teach, and that they are about to ask subscriptions to complete the necessary amount. We hope they may meet with success. Any one who has visited our school and noticed the progress made by the pupils, would be sorry to see the school closed now, just when the scholars have commenced to take and feel such a lively interest in their studies. The hardest work that teachers have in all their labors is to make the scholars feel an interest in their studies. When this is accomplished, half their work is done. Our school is just now in working order, and more real progress will be made in the next two months than in all past time . . .

(*Arizona Sentinel* of March 13, 1875)

The school problem dissolves, but Miss Post unwillingly contributes to the romance of the Territory's first legal hanging.

"Rawhide" McCartney, a prominent Yuma merchant, is murdered and his store looted. Manuel Fernandez is arrested for the crime, but not before he and his confederates spend two nights filling wagons with the stolen goods. After a trial, Fernandez is found guilty and sentenced to be hanged.

The court acts very deliberately, as this is supposedly the first legal hanging in the Territory; though more than one outlaw has dangled at the end of a lynch rope. Noting the interest in the coming hanging, the sheriff busies himself issuing invitations for the spectacle. In the excitement, the unthinking sheriff orders the erection of the scaffold in front of the jail which faces the school. A shocked Miss Post realizes that all her students will

90

have an excellent view of the event. To prevent tender young minds from witnessing such an affair, classes are dismissed. The hanging goes off without incident — watched by all the youngsters in Yuma!

Outlaws and violence are an old story to Yuma. As far back as 1867, a Vigilance Committee has been operating. In their fight against lawlessness, the citizens of Yuma receive the wholehearted support of Editor Berry.

Doors can be barred against a robber, and a six-gun may conquer the desperado, but Editor Berry believes there is still a greater danger to the frontiersmen — the ignorant Eastern writer. Life in the West depends on capital, supplies, and further emigration from the East. When biased and inaccurate reports appear in Eastern newspapers and magazines concerning life on the frontier and threaten to destroy the West's future, the pioneers can no longer hide behind locked doors or drawn guns. To the defense of the West must come the editors living in that frontier.

Unfortunately, a few Westerners aid those who abuse the West in the hopes of bettering the future of their own area at the expense of neighboring territories. Such a Westerner is taken to task by Editor Berry.

A JACKASS

It remained for San Francisco, the great metropolis of the Pacific Coast, to send to the United States Senate the biggest fool of them all. Senator Hager, in his speech in the Senate, on the Indian Appropriation Bill, asserted that Arizona was a "nearly worthless country." What does he know about Arizona? Nothing. He is totally ignorant of the Territory and its resources and to make such a barefaced, gratuitous lying assertion, is disgraceful to the country and to his constituency . . .

(Arizona Sentinel of March 20, 1875)

Little beauty can be seen in the Territory by a newcomer unless there is beauty in the sharp harshness of a radiant sun on crumbling adobe houses, or in the green of the cottonwood tree shading an almost lifeless river. Arizonians will curse their own Territory, but woe to the visitor who criticizes this country. As

91

is true throughout the Territory, Yuma's Editor Berry is the most ardent supporter of his own town. With a population of 1,500, Yuma is no bustling metropolis, but it manages to be the center of great activity. In addition to being the county seat it is also the location of the Army's Quartermaster Depot.

Heavy freight wagons crowd the windswept streets, for Yuma is considered a seaport. Goods are sent by ship from California to the mouth of the Colorado River where they are transferred to river boats for the trip to Yuma. With submerged boulders, sandbars, snags, occasional floods, and tidal waves at the mouth, this river is always playful; and becomes dangerous when it races, twists, struggles, and writhes in its channel like some monster in its death agony.

After discharging their cargoes in Yuma, the shallow draught boats return to the Gulf of California, carrying troops, passengers, wood, hides, pelts, ores, and bullion.

When not working together for the advancement of the Territory, frontier editors seldom agree, even hunting up debatable questions to provoke an argument.

Such is the case with Judge Berry and John Marion. Berry and Marion are old friends, for the judge lived in Prescott for nine years prior to coming to Yuma. In Prescott he hung out his shingle, "William J. Berry, Attorney at Law and Gunsmith." While there he also served as district attorney of the county and first registrar of the United States Land Office.

The crusading Judge Berry, finding little excitement at the moment, expends his energies in good-natured bantering with Editor Marion. Though the editorial intercourse begins in fun, it soon takes on an angry tone.

EDITORIAL MEANESS

We were never more puzzled in our life than we are now to account for the conduct of that cuss of the *Arizona Miner*. We have been badly, yes, most shamefully treated by him. "To prove this, let facts be submitted to a candid world."

On the completion of the line of Telegraph, connecting Yuma with Prescott, we, by the kind permission of Col. Rockwell, A. Q. M. and Commodore Haines, Superintendent, sent a congratulatory dispatch to the editor of the

Miner announcing the joyful event. Everybody knows that this is a military telegraph, but as above stated we were permitted to send that, the first citizen telegram that ever passed over the wires. We esteemed this a high privilege, and expected and had a right to expect that it would be gladly received and courteously responded to. Was this done? No, no response ever came.

We waited several days and Commodore Haines repeatedly telegraphed to John H. Marion, the said cuss who presides over the *Miner,* asking him to send some response to our greeting. On the day of our going to press, last week, we particularly desired some recognition of our aforesaid telegram, that we might publish it, and Commodore Haines again telegraphed to the editor of the *Miner* asking him to send response immediately. But none came! nor has any come yet.

Now we ask all our editorial brothers and all right thinking men. "What do you think of such conduct as this?" Can anything be more uncivil or discourteous? We cannot account for it, particularly as the relations between the editor of the *Miner* and ourself have always been of the most cordial and friendly character. We fear that our worst apprehensions are realized, and that Marion's glory has departed. It may be that he is sick. If so, we take this all back. If not we mean it all, and more too. We had our fears. Take a rusty old bachelor editor and raise him to the summit of connubial felicity, and in nine cases out of ten it is more than he can stand. His brain reels, reason totters and he is a goner.

Alas, poor Marion! we ne'er shall look upon his like again! We write this more in sorrow than in anger. Adios amigo. "Sic transit gloria mundi."

(*Arizona Sentinel* of Nov 22, 1873)

The completion of the telegraph line is the beginning of a new era in Arizona. This quick system of communication hastens the development of the Territory and brings greater prosperity. After years of anticipation, great ceremony marks the setting of the first telegraph pole at Prescott. To the music of the 23rd Infantry Band the wife of General Dana breaks a bottle of champagne on the first pole. At the same time the line from Yuma is built toward the north. On November 11, 1873, the two

93

lines are joined and the first message carries congratulations to General George Crook on his being promoted to a Brigadier General on that same day.

Prescott Editor Marion, although the speaker at the dedication of the line, continues to ignore Judge Berry's greeting. The judge, though, is finally noticed and he returns the remarks in like manner.

"The editor of the *Yuma Sentinel,* Judge Wm. J. Berry, weighs a little over two hundred pounds, and is a dead shot with rifle, pistol or bowie knife; his foreman, Mr. J. C. Bacon, expresses himself in several languages, and the "devil" of the institution is named "Jesus;" so that editors who may feel like pitching into the institution had better defer doing so, and thank us for the information." — *Arizona Miner.*

Why didn't you qualify that a little, John?

While you noticed our proficiency in the use of arms, why didn't you tell the people of our pacific disposition, which you know so well? — how that we are mild as a sucking dove etc., etc. In the description of us that you have given to the world, a stranger would infer that we are a dangerous character, which is far from the mark, as our bosom overflows with the milk of human kindness. Look out old fellow; or we'll give a description of you one of of these days.

(*Arizona Sentinel* of Dec. 6, 1873)

Where Berry is recognized as a good editor, gunsmith, and lawyer, an unhappy domestic affair and an over-indulgence in liquor dull his brilliant career. Neither, however, seems to hamper his ability in the use of firearms, but a dead editor is of little good to his paper or town. When another territorial election is imminent, Berry wisely decides to hire an assistant.

OUR FIGHTING EDITOR

. . . We have selected a gentleman who possesses fine accomplishments in that line and can whip anything that walks on two legs. He is not quarrelsome and by no means a rough, but if any person should feel agrieved and get at any little innocent that we make in the SENTINEL during the canvas, he has but to call upon the said fighting editor, who will give him ample satisfaction. By this arrangement we will have time to attend to our legitimate duties without having to nurse black eyes.

(*Arizona Sentinel* of Aug. 22, 1874)

Having found a fighting editor to defend the *Sentinel* and its editor, Judge Berry returns to his long-standing feud with Marion of the *Arizona Miner*. Marion has questioned Berry's right to the title of judge, while conceding that he is a judge of whiskey. To this, Berry retorts.

THE ARIZONA "MINER"

In the daily issue of this most scurrilous sheet of October 27th, we find an article in reference to ourself, which is altogether characteristic of the dirty nincompoop who edits that journal.

We shall not attempt to reply seriatim to the charges brought against us in said article, but will simply say that it is a batch of infernal falsehoods from beinning to end. The infernal wretch who edits the *Miner* and who wrote that article, well knows, as every man in Arizona knows, who ever saw him, that he is nothing if not a black-guard. He accuses us of being a gunsmith. We are proud of that, as many a man in Arizona knows that we are a good one. At the same time we are a better editor and a better and more respectable man than he is which fact is also well known. He charges us with demanding high prices for our gunsmith work. To that we have now to say, that we never got as much as our work was worth, and lost fifteen hundred dollars by trusting certain infernal scoundrels in Prescott and vicinity.

The miserable liar also says that he let us write a communication for the *Miner*, years ago. Why the miserable cuss used to beg us to write for his dirty abortion, and since we quit writing for it, many Arizonans say that the *Miner* is not worth a d — n, and that is our opinion too, though we never expressed it publicly before. Marion says we used to reside "up in *Osegon!*" Where is Osegon? (*sic*) We would like to know . . .

In regard to our being a "judge of whiskey," we will simply say that no man ever saw Wm. J. Berry laid out under its influence; while we had the extreme mortification of seeing the editor of the *Miner,* in a party given by Col. Baker in Prescott, laid out in the refreshment room, dead drunk, with candles placed at his head and his feet, and a regular "wake" held over him.

It was then for the first time that we discovered Darwin's connecting link. As he lay, with his drunken slobber issuing from his immense mouth which extends from ear to ear, and his ears reaching up so high, everyone present was forcibly impressed with the fact that there was a connecting link between the catfish and the jackass. What we have here faintly described is the truth, to attest which there are plenty of living witnesses. Now dry up, or we will come out with some more reminiscences.

(*Arizona Sentinel* of Nov. 7, 1874)

When two editors have such vivid personalities, each wants the last word. Since there is no pressing business at the time, a good fight adds sparkle to an infrequent moment of calm in the Territory. Marion then replies to Berry's latest editorial with:

ELEPHANT BERRY

We had intended to let the mammoth ape whose name appears as editor of the Yuma *Sentinel* severely alone, until a day or two ago when a citizen of Prescott requested us to inform our readers that Berry uttered a gratuitous falsehood when he stated . . . that "he lost $1,500 by trusting certain infernal scoundrels in Prescott and vicinity."

This being a reasonable and legitimate request, we now assert that Berry lied when he said so, and that it would take more than $1,500 to pay for the whiskey which Berry "bumed" during his long sojourn in Prescott, not to speak of that which he guzzled in our sister county of Mohave, previous to the day upon which he found himself debarred from the privilege of swallowing whiskey in Cerbat.

Again, we have been asked our reasons for not giving the lie to certain assertions of his, regarding ourself. Well, one reason is: Berry is a natural and artificial liar, whom nobody was ever known to believe. Then, he did tell one truth about us, i.e., that drink once got the better of us . . . We were drunk that night, and have never yet attempted to deny it. But, Berry drank ten times to our once, and the only reason he did not fall down and crawl on all fours like the beast that he is, was that there was not sufficient liquor in the house to fill his hogshead. Berry says no one ever saw him get drunk. When he lived in Prescott his first great care was to fill himself with whiskey, after which it was his custom to walk like the swine that he is, on all fours, to his den.

He cannot have forgotten his visit to Lynx Creek, in 1864, when he rolled over a pine log dead drunk, and served a useful purpose for a jacose man. Yes, Judge, we own up to that little drunk of ours; but, unlike you, we were not pointed out and derided as a regular whiskey bloat; nor did any person ever attempt to use us for a water-closet, as you were used that day on Lynx Creek.

As to your being a better editor than the writer of this, it is for the public to judge; not for you to assert, although you asserted it.

You have called us a blackguard, regardless of the old story about the kettle.

Then you have accused us of toadying to Gen. Crook; you, who have toadied and bent your knees to every placeholder, capitalist and bar-keeper in this section of Arizona; you, who made an ass of yourself by firing an anvil salute in honor of Gen. Stoneman, who, you will recollect, never acknowledged the "honor done him." And you take up the cudgels for thieving Indian agents and, by so doing, go back on your record, made when you used to write and speak against the "Indian Ring Robbers and Murderers."

Ah, Judge, you have had many masters; have been everything (except an independent man), by turns and nothing long. Had you changed your shirts as often as you have changed masters, there would be one sand-bar less in the Colorado river, and we would not know that you are in Yuma when, according to your published statement, you should be in San Francisco.

Hoping that these few lines will find you drunk and obedient to your masters, as usual, we say, in your own "classic" language, "uncork and be d — d."

(*Arizona Miner* of Jan. 5, 1875)

The once-friendly Berry-Marion editorial interchange closes with a last epithet flung by Judge Berry.

JACKASS MARION

We had not intended to make any reply to, or have any controversy with that miserable "what is it?" whose name appears as editor of the Prescott *Miner*. Such dirty, low creatures are beneath the notice of respectable journals . . . We are sorry to have to dirty our columns by any reference to this abandoned creature, and would not have done it, had not a professional chemist sent us an analysis of the constituent part of the interesting subject. Here is the analysis:

Constitutional liar	200
Jackass ability	200
Lunar Caustic	200
Iodide of Potassa	200
Sweet Spirits Nitre	200
	1,000

But we dismiss the disgusting subject. We would remark, however, by way of explanation to our readers, that the publication of the above analysis has caused the peculiar color of our paper this week.

(Arizona Sentinel of Jan. 30, 1875)

Editor Berry might print this issue of the *Sentinel* on yellow paper rather than the usual white, but it is not connected with the mention of a fellow editor Marion. With Arizona still lacking a railroad, printing paper for the *Sentinel* must be shipped in by wagon or riverboat. These methods of transportation are not too dependable and Berry, like others, sometimes finds that, on the day of printing, the newspaper's paper stock is nonexistent. Then begins a frantic search throughout the town for paper, from the butcher or any other available source. So it is with this particular issue of the paper, although Berry claims the color is used to depict his rival.

In poor health, Berry's own editorial career soon comes to a close. "Always good natured and kind to everybody in Arizona," except to Marion, Berry will be forgotten in Yuma for his editorial career, his ability as a lawyer and gunsmith, and even for his sharp words. The continued growth of Yuma and the increase of schools here and throughout the Territory, however, serve as a lasting memorial to his foresightedness and leadership.

As is customary in the pioneer press, one of the departing editor's last duties is a salutatory addressed to his friends and readers of the paper. Accordingly, Judge Berry pens this farewell:

> In taking leave of those with whom I have long held intercourse through these columns, it seems to me proper to drop the plural pronoun, the editorial *we,* and use the simple pronoun. In fact, I have never properly been *we,* since I have been running this journal, as I have had no companion to share the sanctum with me, not even a dog, or cat, or pig or chicken, except sometimes when a neighbor's hen would come in and lay an egg in a box behind the press . . .
>
> Well, kind friends, I have tried to publish a good paper, and it is with pride and satisfaction that when I review the files of the *Sentinel* I can find nothing that I ever wrote that I would wish to blot. I have always been the firm friend of the right and the uncompromising enemy of the wrong. I have always advocated the principles of justice, mercy and truth, and I have never sacrificed truth to policy or expediency. Since the *Sentinel* has been under my control no word has ever been admitted to its columns that could injure any person in reputation or property. I have advocated the best interests of the Territory and its people without sectionalism or partiality.
>
> (*Arizona Sentinel* of Dec. 30, 1876)

"A grand old man . . ."

... we shall rise from the ashes.

Judge A. H. Hackney

Men are not satisfied just to conquer the wilderness; they must civilize it, often without plan. The story repeats itself on any frontier, whether it be in the settling of New York, Kentucky, Texas, or Arizona. The fight for life against Indians and nature is the first battle, then comes the building of homes and planting of crops. These are the battles of men.

Though the men have been the conquerers, women are the civilizers. Many of the first women in a territory are dance hall girls and entertainers, women who ply their trade at night and

101

offer solace and kindness during the daylight hours. Still another class of women, wives of soldiers and officers, travel to the outlying military posts, bringing with them their children and establishing a link to the life of a southern town or a northern hamlet. Women travel ever westward, clutching children, and, when need be, a gun to fight at the side of their men. Regardless of their past, these women join together on a frontier to carve homes in a land that men have spilled blood to conquer.

Hidden in the history of every frontier town is the story of women. So it is with Globe City in the Arizona Territory. Founded by the Anderson brothers in 1873, Globe City becomes the center of great silver mining. In fact, according to local legend, the town was named when one of its founders proclaimed that his silver discovery was as "big as the whole globe."

Located in the Pinal mountains, Globe begins as a tent city on boulder-strewn, brush-covered Pinal Creek. The mining camp sprawls in the bottom of a mountain ravine which is denuded of pines. Any new building and houses are constructed of adobe, as the little available lumber sells for $100 or more per 1,000 board feet.

The town gains its first newspaper when Judge Aaron H. Hackney issues the *Arizona Silver Belt* on May 2, 1878. Judge Hackney is not new to the editorial business, for he owned a small weekly in Silver City, New Mexico, before coming to Arizona.

Born in Pennsylvania, Judge Hackney journeyed to St. Louis while still a youth. Here he lived for 25 years, working as a reporter on the *Missouri Republican*. The title of Judge seems to be bestowed on Hackney through no connection with the courts but because of the respect of his fellow citizens. To them the names of Hackney and Globe City become synonymous.

The women of Globe, struggling to bring a refining touch to the community, find a supporter in Judge Hackney. A church and religious services become one of the first desired additions to the town. Without churches, schools, dances, music, and laughter, pioneers and their children probably will live only to fight and to die like the Indians they are trying to conquer.

Though the Arizona Territory was first visited and later settled by Catholic missionaries in the 16th and 17th centuries, Protestant churches are still to be established. Church buildings

102

do not rise overnight, so the venerable judge offers his newspaper office for Sunday services. The meetings are well attended, and Judge Hackney writes:

> We challenge any old community in the United States to produce a more intelligent looking audience than that which meets every Sunday evening . . .
>
> (*Arizona Silver Belt* of June 4, 1881)

Services continue to be held amidst the printing press and type of the *Silver Belt* for more than a year. The minister, Rev. J. J. Wingar, rides horseback to Globe from a town some 30 miles away. After preaching on Sunday, the minister returns over a mountain trail to his own church. A steady church attendant, Judge Hackney joins the minister in a campaign to erect a church building in Globe, for already the worshippers overfill the small newspaper office.

Within months, the new church building nears completion. No longer will the popular services be held in the courthouse or in a still larger building at a nearby mine.

> DIVINE services will be held in the new church next Sabbath evening. After next Sabbath, religious services will be held there temporarily, until the interior of the church is completed, and the edifice is formally opened by dedication . . .
>
> J. J. WINGAR, Pastor
> (*Arizona Silver Belt* of June 12, 1880)

While the adults are singing hymns and listening to sermons, the religious training of their children is not neglected. Youngsters, with faces freshly washed, attend Sunday school in the Methodist Episcopal Church.

Churches in the West generally lack both organs and choirs; and this is true of Globe. However, the town is entertained by a brass band, an almost necessary institution on the frontier. A community band enjoys great popularity for it was the Army bands that brought the first music to a territory.

The band gives almost nightly performances during the long

103

summer evenings. Wives and children cannot be entertained in the local saloon, and this is before the day of motion pictures. Citizens of Globe, proud of their musical group, began to build a bandstand. The completed stand is eight-sided with carved pillars supporting the ribbed roof, which is covered with canvas.

In the Southwest still another musical group, Mexican serenaders, enjoys popularity. Composed of young men, the serenaders play their guitars and sing songs of love under their favorite girl's window. These men may be hired by any untalented lover to play for his lady fair. Songs of the serenaders float in the air on many a night in Globe. Although Judge Hackney enjoys listening to these men from afar, he believes that these groups are a nuisance when they continue to sing until dawn.

> GLOBE has three musical institutions; a band that discourses sweet sounds, a musical pair of gentlemen — Webster and Schofield, — who play on the guitar and harmonica respectively, and produce exquisitely beautiful music, and a crowd of serenaders whose voices harmonize perfectly. We challenge any frontier town to produce anything more charming in their respective lines than these three. We have only one fault to find, and that is with the serenaders — we think they ought to get to the doxology before midnight.
>
> (*Arizona Silver Belt* of July 9, 1881)

Though Globe can support a band it cannot maintain a theater or a company of players. The mountain town, however, is visited by traveling vaudeville shows occasionally and enthusiasm runs high whenever a performance is scheduled. Good actors are a welcome amusement change from watching the weekly horse races which are run on the main street of Globe.

Residents of Globe seize any opportunity for a celebration. In addition to the usual festivities on Christmas and the Fourth of July, the holidays of the different nationalities composing the population justify nights of merrymaking. Among its citizens, Globe can count a number of Chinese and Mexican nationals. Most of the Mexicans and some of the Chinese work in the mines; while a number of the Chinese are servants in the homes

104

of wealthy mine owners. A few of the Orientals even open places of business, generally restaurants.

The Irish contribute their share of hilarity to Globe. With the arrival of Saint Patrick's Day the Irish promise to make the day a gala one, according to Editor Hackney's report.

> In view of the fact that Saint Patrick, Ireland's patron saint, "was a gentleman who came of decent people" and from the further fact that "he gave the snakes and toads a twist" which "bothered them for ever," *(sic)* the Irish lads of Globe have concluded to commemorate his birth, at the rink, on the 17th instant, in a manner "gay and frisky."
>
> (*Arizona Silver Belt* of March 13, 1886)

The rink is the scene of many a dance, as is Stallo's Hall and the Bucket of Blood dance hall. Though the miners are entertained by the local dance hall girls, the more permanent residents of Globe choose to hold regular dances. Beginning with an evening supper, the dance hosts the entire family from toddler to grandmother. Editor Hackney is not to be outdone and whenever a "social" is in progress the judge is on hand as neighbor and reporter.

THE SOCIAL

> We have dancing parties so frequently in Globe now that it seems unnecessary to state more than the fact that one occured last week: but when we remember how "Bright the lamps shone o'er fair women and brave men" we can scarcely help going into rhapsodies about it, although we played the unenviable part of wall flower ourself. It was a Godsend when the supper was announced, because then we could distinguish ourself. That was always our strong hold. We staid *(sic)* with that supper till the peanuts had disappeared, and then "Folded our tent like the Arab, and as silently stole away." All the beauty and bravery of Globe was there. The floor of the dancing room was kissed by as dainty feet as ever touched No. 2 slippers, and the rafters rung with laughter more musical than the boys can get out of the brass band. We could not say more if we took out all the advertisements and filled the columns up with Jenkmism.
>
> (*Arizona Silver Belt* of Oct. 16, 1880)

Sounds other than music soon claim the attention of Globe's women. Pain because of sickness, accidents, or battle wounds is a frequent visitor and this is before the age of miracle drugs. Frontier medicine, to say the least, is crude and too often ineffective. Here there are no gleaming operating rooms, sterile instruments or white-coated doctors.

It takes a newly arrived bride from Colorado to respond first to the cries of pain that are heard frequently in the mountain town. Mrs. Garrett S. Van Wagenen leads the crusade to give Globe its first hospital. In the past a doctor who came to the community to build a mining smelter had treated the injured in the back room of a store building. The women of the community aided him by keeping the place clean and nursing the numerous patients. The temporary dispensary might have continued indefinitely had it not been for a case of smallpox.

Jane Van Wagenen had fed a new patient and then spent the rest of the afternoon with the sick man because his condition seemed so serious. To the horror of the doctor and Jane's husband, it is discovered that the patient has smallpox. Husbands begin demanding that their wives stop the nursing, for smallpox is one of the most dreaded diseases on the frontier. Undaunted, Jane discusses with her friends the need for a regular hospital. From these discussions is born the Globe Hospital Association.

The hospital drive is nearly stopped at its inception due to lack of funds. However, the persistent Mrs. Van Wagenen begins seeking donations first from saloons. Owners willingly contribute, one even taking poker winnings off his gambling tables for her. The players, before any can become offended, are informed that they should be glad to contribute for they will probably need the use of a hospital after some night's brawl.

Carrying the contributed money in a borrowed hat, Mrs. Van Wagenen joins her feminine co-workers. After great deliberation, the ladies buy a four-room adobe house on a quarter block of ground at the corner of Cedar and Pine Streets.

Since the new hospital needs curtains and sheets for the beds, the community is invited to an ice cream social for the benefit of the hospital. In the midst of the planning, Judge Hackney is consulted and he assures the ladies of his support.

106

Editor Hackney gives not only his personal support but implores the help of his readers in the following editorial.

THE HOSPITAL

The ladies of Globe realizing that all mankind's concern is charity and having waited until "hope withering fled" for men to take the initiatory step for properly caring for the afflicted who happen to be with us, have taken upon themselves the arduous task of erecting and supporting a home for those who will need their ministering care, and to more properly give effect to the undertaking they have resolved to build a hospital and have progressed so far in the good work as to have elected officers, namely: Mrs. E. F. Kellner, President; Mrs. G. S. Van Wagenen, vice President; Mrs. A. G. Pendleton, Secretary; Mrs. Jas Wiley, corresponding Secretary and Mrs. John H. Hise, Treasurer. A good selection of earnest and intelligent women who will not falter in the work until their charitable ends are fully accomplished. Their next step will be to avail themselves of the law authorizing an incorporation and have concluded to designate the association as the Globe Hospital Association, which will render it perpetual. Thus permanently established, the directory, from time to time, can so add to the building as to meet the necessities of our growing community. The ladies who, in the largeness of their benevolence, have undertaken this great work will require assistance and we know of no one in the circle of our acquaintance who will not only bid them god speed, but give material aid in furtherance of the desired object, and while individuals are expected to extend a helping hand the county through its Board of Supervisors which is already charged with the care of the indigent sick is also expected, as a matter of economy, to further the undertaking. And in order to render the intended hospital worthy of our county and people, legislative aid should be invoked in order that an annual poll tax may be collected of adult males for its support.

(*Arizona Silver Belt* of Nov. 18, 1882)

Into the newly erected hospital flows a continual procession of wounded men, most of their injuries caused by saloon brawls.

107

As a mining camp, Globe is not infested with many of the quarrelsome cowboys that manhandle most frontier towns. Whiskey, however, bolsters many a man to swing a blow or draw the gun at his side so that fights over dance hall girls, personal grievances, or just for the hell of it are a common scene. Too common, in fact, to suit Judge Hackney.

> It is quite time that order should prevail in Globe. There are but few lawless characters here who have taxed the forbearance of law abiding citizens and greatly offended the ears of families by boisterous and vulgar talk, such as has the true ring of a Five Points brothel, and not in a few instances such utterances have led to scenes of violence and bloodshed . . .
>
> (*Arizona Silver Belt* of Aug. 19, 1882)

This editorial also mentions a house having been stoned. It is unfortunate that Editor Hackney is not more explicit, for there are nearly as many bawdy houses in Globe as saloons. "Big Bertha, Jew Rose, The Hobo Queen, Texas Jenny" and other colorful names grace the halls of such houses. The girls often work around the saloons in the lower end of town and gain a reputation as singers and dancers. "At the upper end of town the saloons are more genteel and quiet and never employ entertainers."

Though practicing a somewhat dubious occupation, these bawdy house girls make a definite contribution to the frontier. Some of them come from well-known and respected Eastern families. Then comes some tragic incident which causes the young lady to move West; and because she is unable to live without money, she assumes a *nom de guerre* and enters the services of some madam. So it is that these women come first to a community where "nice" ladies wouldn't be found. To these women with a past, the frontier owes the founding of many a present day town, innumerable acts of kindness, and the establishment of many schools and churches. Some of these "questionable" women forsake their past life to marry and raise families whose names will go down in history.

It should not be thought that business houses in Globe cater only to vice. In 1880 the town supports: "one Church, sixteen stores, one Drug Store, twelve Saloons, five Hotels, one Bank, one Lodging House, two Meat Markets, two Restaurants, one Brewery, one Wholesale Liquor store, four Blacksmith shops, one Photograph Gallery, two Jewelers, four Feed Yards, two Shoemaker shops, one Tin shop, two Paint shops, three Barber shops, one Brick Yard, a Masonic Hall, and three Wash houses."

Newspapers seldom print the good everyday events of the community, for it is the dramatic, the spectacular and the bad which make news. So it is in the *Silver Belt*. Horse thieves, robberies and shootings overshadow the details of Mrs. Brown's garden or Jack Barton's new horse. But a horse and garden are nothing new, though in Globe shootings now seem to be regular incidents.

While Judge Hackney faithfully chronicles each new act of lawlessness, he doesn't regard the frequent explosions with favor. Little does the editor realize the violence that is soon to visit Globe when in this editorial he blames the citizens of the community for the present bloodshed.

A LAX ADMINISTRATION OF THE LAW

The frequency with which murders are committed in this country is due to carelessness on the part of the people who live in the immediate vicinity of the crime, and the almost total immunity from the punishment that ought to follow . . .

(*Arizona Silver Belt* of July 30, 1881)

Editor Hackney's admonishment to his readers seems to fall on deaf ears. It takes murder to arouse the citizens of Globe to action; but once aroused, they soon start enforcing the law.

The story begins when a packer on the mail route charges on a foaming horse through the main street of Globe, shouting that the Apaches have attacked the stagecoach carrying the mail and that the express messenger, Andy Hall, is dead.

A sheriff and posse ride to the scene of the crime. The mail lies untouched but the express box containing $10,000 in gold for a local mining payroll is missing. Two sets of tracks at the scene show the posse that the crime was committed by white

109

men and not by Indians, as first believed. At dusk, after a long search, the body of messenger Hall is found where he had made his last stand against the robbers. Still clutched in his hand is a revolver with one shot unfired. The weapon had been presented to the express messenger for faithful service by the Wells-Fargo Company.

The posse also discovers Dr. Vail of Globe near the scene of the crime. The dentist is dying, but in his last few feeble words he tells how he accidentally came across the robbers after the attack and that they shot him when their suspicions were aroused. He identifies the men as "one a tall, dark complected man, and the other a small, light complected man, and that they both belong to Globe."

The posse returns to town, bringing with them the bodies of the murdered men. The next day, three arrests are made. One is a wood contractor for the town, John Hawley; the second, Lafayette Grime, a cowboy-miner, and the third his brother, Cicero Grime, the town's photographer. The events of the next few hours are carefully recorded by Editor Hackney and from the news columns of the paper comes the following story, beginning with the return to Globe of the murdered men's bodies.

The bodies were brought to Globe, and presented a ghastly appearance — especial — (sic) that of Andy Hall — whose breast was exposed, his clothing saturated with blood and so many wounds in sight that a hasty glance was all that was necessary to show that more than one man had done the work — and not amateurs at that, but by men who evidently had served an apprenticeship in the trade of crime. Kindly hands were not wanting to speedily wash and dress the murdered men, and as they lay in their coffins in the church on Monday last, they looked almost as natural as when in life. Mrs. Miller and Mrs. Wiley obtained flowers from Dr. Stallo and wove them into garlands and crosses, and placed a handsome floral tribute on the coffins.

The only clue to the perpetrators of the robbery and murder was the imprint of their boots in the soft ground at the place where the attack was made. One track was that of a number four boot, and as children do not attack the United States mail the track was necessarily made by a very small man. A measure of the track was taken on a gun barrel and Lafayette (Grime) was hunted up, and his boot corresponded to the measurement. It was well known to several persons in Globe that in order to get a shoe to fit him he had to get a woman's shoe, and suspicion fell on the guilty party at once.

The accused Lafayette Grime quickly confesses to his part in the affair and implicates his brother, Cicero, and wood contractor Hawley. Lafayette makes two statements to the arresting officers in which he tells of the plot to rob the coach and of the actual attack.

L. V. GRIME'S FIRST STATEMENT

"When my brother and I went to Hawley's house, we talked about putting up a bridge at the lower end of town. Hawley said something about an Indian racket; that we might rob the stage and lay it to Indians. Brother (Cicero Grime) spoke up and said, 'I think that would be easy to do, no one would be suspicioned,' and we three, my brother, Hawley and myself, agreed to it. He was first to come ahead of the mail, but I understood it to be settled that he was to come behind or with the mail. He (Cicero) came down Sunday ahead of the mail and said they were coming and the box was heavy, and the messenger along with it. He (Cicero) then went along into Globe.

"Hawley and I were to divide the money as soon as we could get away from the trail, and I was to take my part and my brother's, and Hawley was to take his one-third.

"In case they were well armed my brother was to give us a sign, but when he came along he said they were not armed; that they (packer and express messenger) had a gun, but no cartridges; that it seemed that the gun would not work."

(signed) LAFAYETTE V. GRIME

L. V. GRIME'S SECOND STATEMENT

"On Sunday morning Hawley and I started from Globe about four o'clock, following the road to the milk ranch, then we took up a right hand canyon to water, turned and went to the Pioneer trail; followed the trail to where we stopped, about three or four hundred yards; took up

111

our positions on the hill. I was nearest the road. When the mail got down to the foot of the hill where he told me to shoot, and where he said he would shoot at the same time, we commenced to shoot at the mules.

"Hall rode back up the hill and appeared to be trying to see who it was. Hall stood up on top of the hill looking for a chance to pass through. When I fired at the mule below with the pack on, he hollered to Porter (packer on the route), 'Frank, I'll stay with you, old boy, Don't run.' When he saw us both shoot, he says, 'there is more than one, and we better get out of this.' He dismounted and went back over the hill.

"Hawley had emptied about sixteen shots from an old style Henry gun. When they (Porter and Hall) got out of sight I shot at random down the canon, then I went down to where the mule with the box on had stopped; found it standing there. I cut the ropes with a hatchet, (I had taken the hatchet, and a prospect pick up and hid them there the day before for the purpose.) I broke the box open with the hatchet, took out some papers and threw them away; I then took out the money and a watch and put them into a pair of canteenes (*sic*), and struck out across the canon with them, and told him to come on. He (Hawley) hollered and wanted me to come back and take in the mail; I told him we had enough and to come on. He came to where I was and we both struck over the hill; he was mad because I did not take in the mail; said he was there to protect me, and we might get several thousand dollars out of the registered mail.

"We travelled about a mile and Vail overtook us, and stated that he was shot at and he thought by white men, and said he thought it was Lindsey Lewis, and I told him he better rush on into town, and he said he did not want to go in, alone, for it might be Indians. He dismounted soon and walked with us across a small ridge. Going down the canyon they (Hawley and Vail) went so fast I could not keep up with them; he (Vail) mounted and started on; as I struck the bottom of the hill he started up a little knoll; I over took Hawley by that time, and Hawley threw a cartridge into his gun and says, 'We will have to kill him.'

"Traveling up the canyon we stopped to rest, when Hall came up and we recognized him as the messenger;

he said he had been shot by Indians; when he first saw us he dropped behind a bunch of bear grass; then said, 'you are white men, I thought you were Indians, we better get into Globe.' We said we were going to soon, and we all got up and started together; I don't think Hall was ever behind both of us at any one time; he carried his pistol in his hand nearly all the time; he said he was wounded in the thigh, but not bad; had a small bullet in his hand which he said was from the wound; can't tell whether he suspicioned we were the men or not. We travelled on together; I was ahead most of the time; about one and three-quarter miles we stopped to look over a ridge and decide which way we would go; I stood a little in advance of him and at this place Hawley shot Hall in the back; I think the first shot was a dead shot. Hall ran about ten steps and turned towards me and fell on his knees; I thought he was shooting at me, he fired four or five shots; I then walked away and shot at him; Hawley kept shooting; I don't know how many shots he did fire.

"We started to go off and I saw two boys in the canyon; I recognized Eugene Middleton but did not recognize the other; about 300 yards from there we sat down to divide the money. We poured it out on the ground and I counted something over $1,600; he (Hawley) was taking it up and putting it into the canteenes (sic) again; the rest of the money was there on the ground, and I went to see if Middleton and the other one were coming up; I saw them coming toward us, and I told him to get the money and come on, as we hadn't time to finish counting it; he said we better divide it and part as soon as possible.

"He says, 'here's your money, I don't want to know what you do with it,' and I said I wouldn't go back and count that money while men are coming up on horseback; he says, 'all right, we will part and make this all right some other time.' We parted there; don't know whether he took my part or not, but think he did; I kept my eye on him till he was out of sight; was afraid he would shoot me.

"I got to town about half-past three or four o'clock; don't think Hawley got in till 9 o'clock, I saw a man pass my brother's house about that time; I thought he came to see me, whether I had got in all right; that's the last time I saw him (Hawley) . . ."

(signed) L. V. GRIME

With the confession of L. V. Grime after his arrest at the Mack Morris mine, Sheriff Lowther of Globe and U. S. Marshal Gabriel act quickly. Cicero Grime is arrested at his home in Globe and Hawley also is taken into custody.

Cicero Grime and Hawley agree that the details of the crime as given by Lafayette are correct. Hawley makes a separate statement which ends with: "If I must be executed, I want to be shot instead of being hung, as the crime was shooting; if there were eight shots in Hall put eight in me, and make sure work."

Through some confusion, the officers finally end up at Bloody Tanks, a spring some nine miles from Globe, with their three prisoners under the surveillance of a posse. Then, according to Editor Hackney, "the prisoners are placed on horseback, and are speedily brought to Globe. When the party reaches the lower end of town their horses are spurred and whipped to their utmost speed through the main street till the jail is reached — for it is a race for life! The big sycamore (Globe's hanging tree) stands in the middle of the road and the ropes are already prepared. The street is lined with people who, no doubt, would mete out speedy justice to the murderers could they get their hands on them then.

"When the citizens are satisfied that the prisoners are secure in the jail, a committee gets together, decides on a plan of action, and just at nightfall organize, procure arms and proceed to the jail, where a demand is made for the prisoners. Sheriff Lowther refuses to give them up, but finally consents to take them before Justice George A. Allen, justice of the peace, for an examination."

Stallo's Hall is the scene of the trial and the defendants are given legal council. The evidence is such, however, that Justice Allen can do nothing less than bind the prisoners over, without bail, until they can be tried by the next grand jury. This is as good as a death sentence.

Hoping to escape hanging at the hands of "Judge Lynch," Lafayette Grime and Hawley agree to take the posse to the place where they buried the loot. Guarded by horsemen, the two men ride through the darkness of night for some 12 miles. There the money is recovered by lantern light from its hiding place under two trees.

It is shortly before two in the morning when the party returns

114

to Globe. Upon their arrival, the men are given time to make their wills. Hawley deeds his property to his wife, while Lafayette gives his cattle to the girl he had planned to marry. Cicero Grime's life is spared because he acted only as a lookout in the robbery and did not fire any shots at the murdered men. Judge Hackney reports, "Cicero Grime would certainly be sent to his long account were it not for the earnest and eloquent pleadings of Frank Fitch, E. O. Kennedy, Rev. D. W. Calfee, Charles M. Clark, and the moving petition of Mrs. W. F. Vail, the widow of one of the murdered men, to spare his life. Their pleadings are not prompted for the erring husband and father, but in response to the wildly beating heart of the anguished wife and four helpless children, who are present, mutely imploring the life of him who had succored them as best he could in pinching want."

Any chance that the condemned men may have is lost when the express agent reads a telegram from his superintendent who had been informed of the robbery. J. J. Vosburg, the agent, reads the message to the assembled crowd, "Damn the money. Hang the murderers. (signed) Valentine."[1]

Someone begins to toll a funeral knell on the bells of the Methodist Church around the corner. Led by express agent Vosburg, the crowd moves deliberately and silently from Stallo's Hall. Before them walk the prisoners who make no complaint and show no signs of fear. The crowd slows as it approaches the sycamore tree and then two quick arms fling twin ropes over a sturdy limb of the tree. Nooses are dropped over the men's heads while 100 men grasp the ropes to pull the condemned murderers to their death upon the command of the agent.

Rev. Calfee is present but makes no attempt to stop the impending execution. He does step forward with an offer to pray with the men. Hawley roughly refuses, "No, what the devil is the future to me; it's the present that's bothering me. I want to get away from this mob." Grime answers more gently, "Mr. Calfee, I don't believe that anything you can say would aid me where I am going. I deserve to die."

As the handcuffs are removed from the prisoners so that their hands may be securely tied behind their backs, Grime grunts, "Damned if I'll die with my boots on!" With that he proceeds to plop in the mud-covered street and yank off his high-heeled cowboy boots. Then he rises to stand at the side of the unflinching Hawley.

Hands are tied, nooses readjusted. Townsmen tighten their grip on the rope. "Now!" shouts the express agent. The ropes grow taut. Hawley and Grime are jerked into the air where they swing in their death struggles. Steady hands wind the ends of the ropes around the tree and the ever-silent crowd slowly disperses.

The editor of the *Silver Belt* scarcely has time to recover from the violence that has torn through Globe when he hears of another stage robbery. Though the penalty for stage robbing is severe, the road agent can find many victims. Mining payrolls and refined bullion must travel by stage and these offer an opportunity for quick riches.

Editor Hackney again complains that the job of enforcing the law and eliminating bandits is left solely to the peace officers. The aging editor tugs angrily at his white beard as he writes:

DARING STAGE ROBBERY

On Saturday night about 11 o'clock, when Stewart's Black Canyon stage coming down from Prescott had reached a point on the plain about two miles above Gillette, the driver and Capt. G. C. Gordon, of the Sixth Cavalry, Camp Bowie, who was seated on the box, discovered two horses secured to a tree a short distance ahead and a few yards from the road. The driver remarked "robbers" and almost immediately two men sprung from behind a mesquite bush, and with shotguns leveled ordered the driver to halt. The passengers were ordered to stand in a line with hands up, when one of the robbers "went through" them, taking money, checks, watches, etc., while his pal covered them with his gun. The checks were returned, when the robber turned his attention to Wells, Fargo & Co.'s express box, which he broke open and rifled of its contents, as well as tearing open the letters. He went about it as coolly as though engaged in some legitimate occupation, laughing and joking with the passengers meanwhile.

While engaged in this, to him, lucrative occupation, the up stage from Phenix (*sic*) was heard approaching. He paid no attention to its coming til his "pard" informed him it was time to "take it in," when he quietly left his work and the two performed alike job for the up as they did for the down stage. Some six or eight passengers tumbled out at the word of command, and were also relieved of their valuables. Wells, Fargo's box being rifled. When the "gentlemanly" road agents had got all that was worth taking that they could find, the passengers were ordered to get in their respective coaches and "git" and they got. Previous to the coaches leaving, the highwaymen returned Capt. Gordon his watch, as also that of Mr. Solomon, and gave them a few dollars to pay for their breakfast. Here are two men, their faces concealed by silk handkerchiefs, capture two stages containing some twelve or fifteen persons, and coolly proceed to rob them, without any show of resistance. This class of highwaymen have inspired travelers with such dread that the order to "hold up your hands," is sufficient to appal the stoutest traveling heart, and every knight of the road has an easy victory.

Until travelers go heavily armed, with a determination to fight when molested on the highway, and shoot down these marauders, just so long will two men be able to master fifteen. It is about time that the bugbear, "stage robbers," ceased to paralyze strong men.

(Arizona Silver Belt of Sept. 9, 1882)

Globe is the gateway to the luxuriant grass-covered Tonto Basin, historical home of certain Apache tribes. While the Apaches hold no more love for the Globe townsmen than other settlers, there are surprisingly few incidents of bloodshed between the two races. Globe, however, does not escape entirely and has at least one false alarm.

Frontiersmen, as do their eastern relatives, fear three things: storms, floods, and fire. Against these three, guns, knives, and fists are useless. Though Globe escapes the ravages of tornadoes and floods, she faces the menace of fire.

This settlement does not even support a hook and ladder company. So if a spark is whipped by the breeze into a raging conflagration, no volunteer firemen will run through the streets, dragging behind them their small tank of water on a cart. Merchants are aware of the ever-present danger and act accordingly. "An adjunct to Pascoe's bucket brigade can be seen on top of his hotel. He has a number of barrels filled with water in order to have it handy in case of fire." Even water is a problem as it must be obtained at two public wells. To transport the water from the well to a house or store, Chinese laborers are paid 10 cents for every 10 gallons they haul.

Globe's worst fears are realized on a spring day in 1885.

LURID BLAZES

GLOBE Visited for the First Time by a Destructive Fire

A Scene of Ruin and Dismay

Six Buildings Gutted — Heavy Losses — Only One Building Insured

At 3 o'clock on Thursday morning the people of Globe were startled from their slumbers by the ringing of the church bell and cries of fire and in a few minutes after the first alarm was sounded the whole community was astir and the wildest excitement prevailed. Flames were seen bursting from the roof of the Pascoe House, leaping high into the air and running with lightening rapidity over the dry shingles, carrying destruction to the adjoining buildings. It was a scene to appal the stoutest heart, but strong arms and clear heads were not wanting to begin the work of salvage and endeavor to check the progress of the flames . . .

The heat in front of the burning buildings on Broad street was so great that the houses on the opposite side of the street, more than 100 feet distant, were badly scorched and were with difficulty saved from the devouring flames.

In the rear of the fire the scene was one of intense excitement and activity. Twenty-five or more men worked with desperation tearing down the dry fences and outbuildings which lined the alley and threatened to communicate the flames to the residence on the west side of the block. Others were busily engaged covering threatened buildings with wet blankets and drenching them with water, and it was a great relief to those who had worked almost without hope, when it was seen that their efforts had been successful.

By five o'clock the fire was well under control, and the

crowds of weary people who had worked so hard sought their homes, leaving a few to keep guard over the smouldering ruins.

The origin of the fire is in doubt and probably will never be known. It was discovered by Mrs. J. Hyndman, proprietress of the hotel, who was awakened by a report which sounded like the explosion of a lamp. She arose and hastily proceeded to room 21, on the second floor, at the northwestern corner of the building, and upon opening the door found the apartment completely filled with fire. The flames, bursting out, forced Mrs. Hyndman to retreat, but although terrified, she did not loose her presence of mind and the first impulse and desire of the noble woman was to save the lives of the guests under her roof. Running through the hall, she knocked at every door, uttering cries of warning. The flames followed rapidly in her wake, and in a very few minutes the whole building, which was a light frame structure, was one mass of flames. A majority of the guests had barely time to escape from the building and could save none of their effects. It was not until Mrs. Hyndman had succeeded in arousing everybody that she thought of a large sum of money (between $800 and $1,000) which she had secreted in her room and she was about to run the gaunlet of the flames in an endeavor to secure the treasure, when bystanders realizing the danger of such an attempt prevented her from again entering the burning structure.

A few moments after the discovery of the fire in the interior by Mrs. Hyndman, John Murphy, Tom Montgomery and others who were walking south on Broad street, saw the flames issuing from the roof and at once sounded the alarm.

We cannot give an accurate estimate of the losses, but they will approximate $28,000, divided as follows: J. Hyndman, $11,000; ARIZONA SILVER BELT; $10,000, F. W. Westmeyer, $3,000; Alex Love, $1,200; Alonzo Bailey, $1,000; W. E. Spence, $600; G. Bosche $500; J. D. McCabe $400; J. C. Ramsdell (Pascoe House restaurant) $400.

(*Arizona Silver Belt* of April 4, 1885)

While having a reporter's factual manner of writing, Editor Hackney realizes that it is the small sidelights of tragedy that make for the human interest side of the news. The fire is the major story; but, the stories of individuals and their losses are scattered throughout the paper.

> Mr. and Mrs. Benbrook by great exertion succeeded in holding the fire at bay and thus saved their new residence.
>
> The dirt roof saved the interior of the SILVER BELT editorial office, although it was considerable damaged.
>
> Jerry Hyndman raked out about $80 from the debris of the Pascoe House yesterday.
>
> A highly prized inmate of the SILVER BELT editorial office, "the cat" was saved, which is a matter of congratulation.
>
> Phoenix like we shall rise from the ashes

While Globe lies choking from the still smoking wreckage, Judge Hackney seeks to prevent still another and perhaps more destructive blaze. Dynamite is a popular fire-fighting weapon on the frontier. In the beginning, sticks of the explosive were borrowed from the nearby mines. Then, in advance of the fire, men created a path through stores and homes by exploding them. When the fire met this lane of man-made destruction, it died from lack of combustible material. So Editor Hackney advocates the purchase of a more modern type of explosive to be used in case of future fires.

The rebuilding begins. Fire-defying adobe structures replace the wooden buildings so recently destroyed. New merchandise from New Mexico arrives by wagon train. Bronzed arms and willing bodies inject new life into Globe as the wreckage is slowly cleared away.

The *Silver Belt,* though heavily damaged by the blaze, continues publication. Forced to move the paper to a new location after the destruction of the old printing plant, Editor Hackney thanks his neighbors for their assistance.

Almost without exception every person in Globe is the friend of the editor. Hackney, to them, is a patriarch, as dependable as the hills upon which Globe sprawls and from which

120

she draws her money; money in the form of silver, gold and copper.

Editor Hackney often sits in front of the *Silver Belt* office, tilts his chair back against the wall and watches the mining town as it goes about the job of living. "Fanning his wrinkled old visage, and snorting like a porpoise," Judge Hackney becomes an institution in Globe and a colorful character on the frontier.

Globe's editor has never lifted a gun against a man, has never indulged in bitter attacks against fellow journalists, and has never joined in the popular "sport" of demanding the scalp of every Indian. Yet, Hackney is known as a fighting editor. He wages a different kind of fight. A seldom-used jail, peals of the church bell, the laughter of vaudeville players, a new hospital, and the sound of violins at a dance vouch for Editor Hackney's success.

For many years the old judge will battle to civilize the country he has helped others to conquer. A pioneer writes what ought to be Editor Hackney's epitaph: "A Grand old man (who) wields a pen dipped in vitriol against humbugery and fraud."

---

1 John J. Valentine, president of Wells, Fargo & Co.

"Judge Lynch supreme"

... we shall ever wage war on corruption and wrongdoers ... — James Reilly

A deputy sheriff's badge clings to the soft folds of a shirt. Its
wearer — a tall, rather slender man with sun-bronzed features
and gray-flecked temples — turns his back on the Colorado River
and seeks the scant shade offered by the front veranda of a local
saloon.

Though christened James Reilly, he is often called O'Reilly
by fellow Arizonians. After all, don't all good Irish names begin
with O, and wasn't it Ireland that heard his first wail on an
autumn day in 1830? The Arizona Territory first glimpsed

123

James Reilly in the uniform of the U. S. Army. Having served 10 years with Company C, 8th U. S. Infantry, Private Reilly's last duty was to escort a U. S. topographical expedition through Arizona. At the completion of this mission he returned to Texas to receive his honorable discharge.

Reilly at first thought the freighting business a good venture. The Indians must have agreed with him for they promptly made off with all his mules. Undaunted, the Irishman bought 18 more teams and hired 21 Mexican teamsters. The Indians waited until they were sure Reilly had purchased all the stock he needed. Then, a lightning raid. The Indians again left Reilly without a mule. Disgusted, Reilly moves to Mexico where he becomes a farm owner and operator of a flour mill.

Moving to Arizona in 1869, Reilly engages in the mercantile and hotel business in Yuma. Here he becomes a deputy sheriff in 1875. Having studied law in his spare hours, he now plans to leave the sheriff's office and seek the office of district attorney of Yuma County. A member of the bar, Reilly depends on his quick wit to compensate for his lack of formal legal training.

Reilly believes that the law is to defend as well as to prosecute. To aid him in his attack against political corruption, Reilly founds the *Yuma Expositor*. The paper will be devoted to "the exposition of the official fraud, oppression and corruption in this Territory. . . ." Reilly promises that the *Expositor* will always be "Democratic in politics, but will shield no Democrat on account of his Democracy. . ."

Some might call Reilly a muckraker. He makes strong charges against those suspected of corruption and then uses his legal authority as district attorney to bring about the suspect's downfall. For his efforts, Reilly is denounced as a "vile, libelous, dirty, low down, contemptible, profane, indecent polluter. . . ." Others in the Territory defend him, maintaining that the crusading Irishman is "dignified and manly" and "devoted to the service of the honest people of Arizona."

Having completed his term as district attorney, Reilly moves his paper to Phoenix in the central portion of Arizona. Phoenix is a relatively new community, located near the banks of the Salt River. In the midst of the great Salt River Valley, which stretches east and west for some 50 miles and north and south for 22 miles, Phoenix is an oasis in the desert. To the land clings desert life: giant saguaro cactus, mesquite and palo verde trees, brushy greasewood, numerous cacti, and the ever-feared rattlesnake.

Renting an office for $40 a month, Jim Reilly again issues his newspaper, now called the *Territorial Expositor*. Though Phoenix already supports one newspaper, the *Salt River Valley Herald*, Reilly hopes there will be room for his own Democratic organ because the *Herald* is Republican. With these thoughts, Reilly addresses his new neighbors.

SALUTATORY

Today we issue the first number of the Expositor in its new field of labor, and as it shall be our endeavor to build up a paper that will be of substantial benefit to Arizona and Arizonians, we hope our attempt in the undertaking will meet with the approval of all who feel an interest in the development of the Territory and who believe that fair and impartial advertising of its resources will hasten the march of progress . . .

Low, vulgar abuse will never find a place in these columns, and though we shall ever wage war upon corruption and wrongdoers, and do all in our power to sustain principles of right and justice, we do not believe that personal vituperation will in any way tend to root out the corrupt nor advance the cause of truth and purity.

The Expositor will labor for and in the interest of the Democracy, *(sic)* as long as that party remains true to its principles and its supremacy is necessary to the happiness and prosperity of the whole country.

(*Territorial Expositor* of June 6, 1879)

The *Expositor* seems to thrive in Phoenix, the town of contrasts. While maintaining that it is purely an "American" town, the community includes many Mexicans, some friendly Indians, and a few Chinese. Before long, racial clashes between the Americans and Mexicans will spill blood in the dirt-packed streets.

Phoenix as a settlement is a newcomer in the Territory when compared to the time-weathered Spanish towns of Tubac and Tucson. Yet it was inhabited at the time of Christ by the prehistoric Hohokams.[1] These peace-loving people were farmers in the great valley. With a stick they dug holes in the parched ground into which they dropped kernels of corn. This enterprising Hohokam culture began a series of canals which stretched many miles from the Salt River to their numerous fields. Digging with bare hands and sticks, they performed an engineering miracle. Some 300 miles of canals watered more than 200,000 acres of fields to support the vast population. Not until World War II would the white men put a greater area under cultivation in the valley.

The valley was undoubtedly seen in the early 1800's by fur trappers, men in search of precious beaver skins. However, a John Smith was the first white man to live in the valley. Establishing a crude ranch and farm, Smith in 1876 was visited by an ex-Confederate soldier named Jack Swilling. The visionary Swilling noted the outlines of the prehistoric canals. He envisioned the valley as an agricultural paradise, if water from the Salt River could be used for irrigation. The banks of the river were nearly on the same level as the valley floor so this plan seemed feasible.

Having organized the Swilling Canal Company, and obtained men from other settled communities in Arizona, Swilling returned to the future site of Phoenix. The men depended on their muscles and shovels to dig the first ditch. There wasn't enough money to pay for horse feed! The men survived on scanty rations of bread, beans and coffee, but the canal was finished.

The naming of the new settlement on the banks of the river proved something of a problem. Swilling wanted to name the town "Stonewall," in honor of the famous Confederate general. Among the ditch diggers was an adventurous and educated Englishman, "Lord" Darrel Duppa. Duppa was consulted. Noting the remains of an extensive prehistoric settlement in the valley, Duppa suggested the name of Phoenix, for the mythical sacred bird of the Egyptians. "Lord" Duppa prophesied: "A city will rise Phoenix-like, new and more beautiful from these ashes of the past." So Phoenix was christened.

The town was a little slow in rising, for in 1870 there were only 240 inhabitants. The settlers planted cottonwood trees which thrived in the arid climate. These shade trees cut a green

126

swath through the dull brown desert. Phoenix appeared to be, and was, a virtual oasis.

By 1879, when Reilly moves to Phoenix, the community is prospering. It has every appearance of a peaceful community, lacking the harsh lines of a mining camp and the rowdiness of a cow town. Editor Reilly loses little time in voicing his view of the town.

PHOENIX

We are not yet sufficiently acquainted with this town and county to be able to speak understandingly of all its various business interests and capacity of development, for the valley of Salt River is a very large one, of which we have not had time to examine one-fourth. And therefore will merely attempt a slight sketch of the town of Phoenix, which is about one mile north of Salt River; has a population of about 1,300, of nearly all races. The American or Anglo-Saxon predominating, and the Mexican ranking next in number.

We count 15 general merchantile (*sic*) establishments in this town, great and small, about six of which carry stocks well up in the tens of thousands. There are two blacksmiths and wagon making establishments, two wheelwrights, nine carpenter shops, one hotel, (perhaps lodging house is a better name) four restaurants, two private boarding houses, three lumber yards, two stores, one medical dispensary, two breweries, two furniture and cabinet-making establishments, two livery and sale stables and a large number of feed corrals, three bakeries, one auction house, one painter and two tinsmiths; besides there are several stone masons and bricklayers as well as dressmakers, two saddler shops, eleven lawyers, and six doctors. In the way of saloons and beer houses Phoenix is quite up to most frontier towns. We counted thirteen of these establishments and may have missed one or two.

And now for the moral and educational side of the town: Phoenix has a public school, with an average attendance of 103 pupils, under the superintendence of Mr. Smith, principal, who appears to be competent and attentive, assisted by Mrs. Cox and Miss Winn, who appear to be two very competent and amiable ladies. In visiting the school we did not dare to essay an examination of the

127

pupils least we might betray our own ignorance of those neglected arts, reading, writing and spelling; but from the exercises we witnessed, we are satisfied that the senior class could teach us a good deal in elocution, mathematics and geography.

And now we come to the subject on which we are always delicate and diffident — religion. The people of Phoenix have two churches—one a commodious and roomy adobe building on the southwest corner of Center and Monroe streets, in which Rev. Mr. Hedgpeth of the Methdist *(sic)* Church South presides, assisted by Rev. Mr. Wiley, and a temporary shade fenced with stakes on the southwest corner of Court House block, in which Rev. Mr. Meyer of the Presbyterian Church preaches on Sundays to a respectable congregation. There is no Catholic Church, but the Rev. Father Becker of Prescott, and Rev. Father Le Clerc of Florence occasionally visit Phoenix and hold divine service at the residence of Don Jesus Otero on Washington street.

In reference to the sign of progress in Phoenix, there are now in course of construction several large and commodious buildings, notably the brick building of Irvine & Co., corner Washington and Montezuma streets; those of Steinacher & Goodrich, brick front, on Washington street, opposite the plaza; the brick building of Talheimer & Luke, opposite the plaza; the private residences (brick) of Mr. J. Lutgerding and Mr. Swain, and the residence *(sic)* of Mr. Peralta. Besides those enumerated, there are many unpretentious buildings on the outskirts of the town in various stages of construction. We find that the older residents of Phoenix begin to put on style and discard adobe in favor of brick as a building material, and, in fact, few except those who are as poor and unpretentious as ourselves, talk or think of adobe . . .

(Territorial Expositor of May 9, 1879)

Having gained a reputation in Yuma for crusading against political skulduggery, Reilly chooses to ignore the political scene in Phoenix. He might entertain thoughts of continuing his crusade but that is before Phoenix becomes a city of death. Only a few weeks after Editor Reilly's arrival, Phoenix sheds her gloves of innocence to show her bloody hands.

128

Stage robberies have been frequent but the "Saber-Slasher" brings the first real violence to the town. Sunday horse races through the main street have always been an important part of the social life in Phoenix. However, on a Sunday in June, the race turns from a gala event into one of horror. Editor Reilly reports:

RUNNING A MUCK

Last Sunday was a lively day in Phoenix. The streets were crowded with strangers and people from the country surrounding; the saloons sold whiskey straight as fast as they could dish it out and in the afternoon horseracing in the principal street of the town was indulged in. Taking it all in all, it was a Sunday for an intelligent Christian community to be proud of. But, unfortunately while everything was going off so pleasantly, and betting on the scrub stock running high, a Mexican named Jesus Carrillo mounted on a horse and armed with a saber, dashed through the crowd, cutting right and left, wounded several men, and made it seek a place of safety quicker than, perhaps was compatible with its dignity. After the sudden dispersement, this modern Quixote, seeing he could win no more laurels unless he dismounted and did combat on foot, rode leisurely out of town, followed at long range by a shower of stones from that portion of the crowd which first ventured forth from secure retreat. As soon as arms could be procured for there was not a weapon in all the crowd assembled on the street, the "race horses" were mounted and the Mexican pursued by officers and citizens eager for his blood. While the chase grew hot and fierce, one of the officers deemed it best to come back and start again in a buggy. But, sad to relate, the axles (he forgot to grease 'em) grew so hot as the buggy sped like lightning over the level roads, that even this ingenious and praise worthy effort proved futile, and Carrillo considers himself a hero, and lives to tell how he on a Sunday charged through a crowd of three hundred men (not to mention race horses) in Washington street, Phoenix, severely wounded three of them and escaped unhurt . . .

(*Territorial Expositor* of June 6, 1879)

With the cry of the "Saber-Slasher" — "Death to the Americans" — still ringing in their ears, the townsmen demand action. Phoenix's constable, Henry Garfias, takes up the chase. One of Arizona's most outstanding lawmen, Garfias follows his quarry into Mexico. Editor Reilly reports, "Much credit is due Henry Garfias, constable, and Jesus Vasquez for their capture of Jesus Romero, the desperado who severely cut three men in a crowd of 300 in the streets of Phoenix, some three weeks ago. But for the energy and courage displayed by Mssrs. Garfias and Vasquez, Romero would still be at large."

As for the "Saber-Slasher," the wily outlaw manages to remain in the news.

Jesus Romero, that "fish from the Ures River," who diverted himself by breaking the heads of Sabbath breakers, on the 1st of this month, in Phoenix, is now in jail. He was caught up and brought back by our good fishermen Constable Henry Garfias and Jesus Vasquez. He (Romero) was tried day before yesterday, found guilty and sentenced to six months in the county jail. We have heard some people express dissatisfaction at this sentence, and say it was too small, others think it wrong to punish a man for clearing our streets of a Sabbath day nuisance. We have not got any opinion on the subject ourselves. Opinions are dangerous things, and we don't cultivate them.

(*Territorial Expositor* of June 27, 1879)

Reilly next reports that Romero is feigning insanity to keep from being put to work by the sheriff. Romero makes one bold break for freedom. Wielding a mesquite club, he attacks an attorney and the jailer. A hurried shot is fired and Romero tumbles to the floor. The Mexican population doesn't believe that Romero was killed in self-defense as is claimed by the jailer.

Knives and old-fashioned horse pistols appear on the belts of Mexicans who gather in an ever-growing crowd. Several citizens believe that the angry mob is going to demand "an eye for an eye." Messengers hurry over the darkened desert. Ranchers seize their shotguns and hurry to join the merchants of Phoenix. A Vigilante Committee must be organized.

130

Vigilantes are no novelty to the West. Names of the members remain a secret, although the townspeople have a general idea of the identity of those who take the law into their own hands. Many Vigilantes are the most outstanding leaders of the town. Others are of questionable reputation, masking their activities behind mob action in the name of law. In any respect, the power of the Vigilante Committee is a potent force in bringing law to the frontier. The Vigilantes are too often pictured as grim executioners, who hang all their victims from the nearest tree. This is not true. Unfortunately, in some areas the power of the group is sometimes used to rid a town of those persons who do not agree with the majority.

However, at this time Phoenix has good reason to organize a Vigilante Committee. The valley town has witnessed nine deaths within a few days. Then there are those numerous acts of bullying and molestation that plague the valley town. Editor Reilly sees little hope for the civilizing of a community in which a man does not respect the rights of another.

Though not married, the Irish editor is shocked when he learns of outrages committed against "defenseless" women. What will become of Phoenix?

PURELY LOCAL

Every once in a while we hear complaints of the unchristian, ungentlemanly and unkind behavior of certain men (we will not say *gentlemen* until they prove their right to the title) towards ladies who for any cause are without natural protectors. Sometimes this behavior is indulged in towards ladies who are destitute of good sense, and perhaps of good character; but even then such conduct is extremely reprehensible and marks the man who is guilty of it as neither a christian, a gentleman, nor a good citizen. Foolish or even scandalous conduct on the part of a woman is no justification to a man for behaving towards her in an inconsiderate, indelicate or unkind manner. It is enough for him that he can keep away from all ladies of a certain class, if he so desires. But this want of consideration is still more offensive, injurious to the good name of a community, and more likely to produce serious results when practiced towards ladies of exemplary character and conduct, who have the misfortune to be poor and whose natural protector may be absent . . . We have now in our mind's eye one case in point, and we say to the dark-featured cur, beware, least you have your dark hide flayed off your ugly carcass.

(*Territorial Expositor* of Aug. 29, 1879)

Any hopes of even temporary order in the town are shattered by two short announcements in the *Expositor.*

The Coroner is the busiest man in town. He has been busy holding inquests since Wednesday morning.

MORE CRIMES — MORE MURDER — A man named McCluskey, who, it it said, was driven from Prescott a short time ago, and has been laying around Phoenix drunk and idle for more than a week, cut, with a knife, in the abdomen, John LeBar, a well known and highly esteemed citizen of this town, in front of the saloon of Brown & Daniels at about 12 o'clock last night. The act was unprovoked, and it is feared LeBar will not recover.

(*Territorial Expositor* of Aug. 22, 1879)

The genial LeBar, a saloon keeper, had refused to serve liquor to a man named McCluskey. The ruffian then went and obtained a long butcher knife with which he fatally wounded LeBar. This killing further enraged the townspeople because the previous week a prominent farmer had been brutally murdered from ambush.

The victim was Luke Monihan, brother of Phoenix's late mayor. While driving home in a wagon at dusk, the farmer had been shot in the back by a man named Keller. The murderer, hidden along the roadside in sagebrush, had had words with the farmer previously and chose to end the trouble by ambushing Monihan. Without a driver, the steady farm horses traveled the well-known route home, coming to a halt before the door of the house. The victim's wife found the body and sounded the alert. Keller's grudge was well known and Indian trackers followed his footsteps from the site of the ambush to his house. Arrested, Keller was hurriedly locked in the Phoenix jail.

So while farmers ride across the sun-bleached desert to Phoenix to join the proposed Vigilante Committee, the murderers Keller and McCluskey sit behind bars. The first rose tinges of dawn reveal the ever-milling crowd of Mexicans. Several hundred of their ponies are tied to the huge cottonwood trees that surround the plaza.

A few hours later, the now organized Vigilantes ride past the plaza. Some 100 men, heavily armed, carefully eye the restless crowd. All become silent. Now is not the time for talk. The Vigilantes ride past the mob to the small adobe courthouse about a block away. Dismounting, they enter the jail. Only the jailer faces them; all the law officers, knowing what is about to take place, have made themselves scarce. The jailer makes a token effort to resist handing over the jail keys but is helpless before so many Vigilantes.

Other criminals are behind bars but the law and order committee seize only the murderers, Keller and McCluskey. The committee then takes its prisoners to the plaza. Those restless Mexicans must watch the coming event as a warning of what will happen to them if they get any ideas.

A wagon is obtained. Keller is forced into the wooden vehicle. "Have anything to say?" asks the captain of the Vigilantes. Noting the noose drooping from the limb of a cottonwood tree, Keller is satisfied to admit his guilt, without attempting to defend himself. A sudden flick of the reins leaves the confessed murderer standing on air.

The wagon is again wheeled around to the adjoining tree. Placed in the vehicle of death, McCluskey tells the assembled crowd that whiskey caused his downfall and that they should profit from his hanging. As the wagon starts to move, McCluskey jumps. His weight, however, pulls down the elastic limb. With his toes touching the ground, the man undergoes a death by strangulation rather than dying quickly of a broken neck. The onlookers make no move. Tough Vigilantes lose their hurriedly eaten breakfasts as McCluskey, eyes bulging in a purple face, chokes to death.

The drama is not yet over. Two Mexican merchants have been seized from the mob and are now forced to climb into the wagon. These two men have been crusading against the whites, attempting to start a "race" war. The quaking men are promised

133

that they will dangle like the murderers just hung if they ever again try to incite a mob. The cowed merchants are finally released and the threat of a Mexican insurrection is a thing of the past.

The unofficial lawmen undertake one more task before disbanding. All suspected ruffians are rounded up, given a canteen of water, and ordered to get out of the county — or else. They need little urging.

The missing sheriff finally appears from hiding to make an announcement. Editor Reilly prints the sheriff's statement and then adds a little editorial comment.

> Sheriff Thomas has a notice in this issue to all idle persons, having no visible means of support, to leave Phoenix within two days or they will be dealt with according to law. This town is becoming very unhealthy for hoodlums, and we think they had better heed the warning.
>
> (*Territorial Expositor* of August 22, 1879)

The editor gives no screaming headlines to the activity of the Vigilante Committee. While not giving much space to the lynching, Reilly interjects his own opinion into the actual facts.

JUDGE LYNCH SUPREME

> At 10 A.M. to-day about 300 men gathered on Washington street in this town, and as though moved by machinery, marched together to the jail, interviewed the jailor, and took out two prisoners — John Keller and McClosky, *(sic)* and after giving them about ten minutes to prepare for death marched them with a rope about the neck of each to the Plaza and hanged them each to a cottonwood limb. The whole was done so quietly and without any apparent excitement that no attempt was made to prevent this; for the few who would have been glad to stem the torrent were so hopelessly in the minority and so devoid of local influence, and the quiet determination of the crowd was so apparent, that any effort to prevent the consumation of their wishes was plainly not only useless, but dangerous in the last degree. We never approve these acts of violence

and cannot now, for there is no reason given by the advocates of lynch law that convinces our mind, and we fear that all such acts give to the opponents of human liberty their greatest arguments against popular government . . .

Even if a citizen disagrees with the action of the Vigilantes, he seldom expresses his opinion verbally. Editor Reilly explains why it is wisest to keep one's own counsel.

OUR EXCUSE

Some of our readers, particularly those who have known us a long time, have no doubt been surprised that in our last issue we failed to condemn, in the manner deserved, the acts of those men who hanged the murderers, Keller and McClosky (sic). If we were disposed to conceal our cowardice behind spacious excuses we could offer many and, to the minds of most men, good reasons for having contented ourselves with an expression of disapproval and regret. But we don't choose to do so. The only valid reason we can offer for failing to oppose the hanging before it was done, and to denounce it afterwards, consists in what is called prudence, fear of consequence, or cowardice.

The "committee" was so overwhelmingly a majority of the men in town and they were so quiet and determined . . .

"We waive the quantum o' the sin,
The hazard o' concealing;
But, oh! it hardens a' within,
And petrifies the feeling."

But now that the hot blood of these men has had time to cool, now that they have had time to reflect on what they have done, we sincerely hope that they will each determine to do his duty in the future as juror and as elector; that they will each discountenance and condemn the practices by which courts and juries, as well as legislatures, are managed and controlled; that they will hereafter combine for a good purpose — that of making and enforcing good laws which will be sufficient to punish and suppress crimes and criminals and to secure all in the enjoyment of life, liberty and property.

(*Territorial Expositor* of August 29, 1879)

135

Some of the more self-righteous citizens of Phoenix disagree with the editor. They want to bring the lynchers to trial as an example, while increasing their own political prestige. Reilly's contempt for lynch law is only exceeded by his wrath at the proposed actions of these "good" citizens.

THE LATEST PHASE OF THE
"LAW AND ORDER" DEVELOPMENT

It is now generally said that a few influential politicians of Phoenix are devoting their influence, as well with the District Judge as with their friends and fellow citizens, to the end of having the participants in the hanging of Keller and McClosky (sic) indicted by the Grand Jury, at the approaching term of the District Court. It is also said that these men say the District Judge is with them. And this, by the bye, is one of the first and most powerful causes of our hearty contempt for the Judge — that he will always allow parties or intended parties to actions, as well as attorneys and politicians, to approach, toady, buzz, and even dictate to him out of court; so that the saying, "the Judge is with you," "the Judge is against you," "the Judge says so," are common expressions, as well on questions pending in court as on questions not yet brought into court. And even lawyers, or men who pass for such, tell their clients "the judge is with us," "the judge is all right . . ."

We also think the men who desired to make political capital by hanging Keller and McClosky (sic), have by this time discovered that they have made a woeful mistake, and we think that those men who now seek to influence Judge and jury, for the purpose of singling out a few men (even though they may not be good ones) to be punished for a crime committed by all, or nearly all, the people of Phoenix, will wake up to find that all popularity gained by such means, evaporates like dew before an August sun. If any one have a case to bring before the grand jury, he must and should be heard by that body; but how any man who was present on the 22d day of August and failed to express his opposition to the act then being done, or, what was worse, left town purposely to avoid being present, can now have the cheek to use his influence with Judge and jurors, to indict men for a crime of which they themselves

136

are not innocent, we cannot understand, and if our advice is worth attention, we would say: Mind your own business; let the Judge and Grand Jury do their duty without any buzzing from you: the "law and order" business stinks already too much, and won't bear stirring up — for if the guilty are to be punished, we will have to go to New York for jurors; we know of only one man (the jailer) in Phoenix who can escape indictment.

(*Territorial Expositor* of September 19, 1879)

Reilly's crusading paper does not let the townspeople forget the recent lynching. Reilly, as do many other early editors, places the responsibility for maintaining order on the citizens of the community. Reilly humorously captions his editorial:

PHOENIX AS A CENTER OF CIVILIZATION

. . . Phoenix and Maricopa county are now coming to the front. Four stage robberies within three months; seven homicides within a week — four of these in town, one seven miles from town, one on the Gila and one at Seymour. And to this a general license to kill stage robbers with $500 bonus per scalp, and none but constitutional growlers will deny that we are progressing fast. True, two of these homicides in Phoenix were not of the regular order. They were the work of a "Law and Order Committee" and we are told that these latter homicides were not only deserved, but were good, useful and necessary. A few captious individuals, among them ourself, may ask; Where did the "Law and Order Committee" get their warrant for hanging Keller and McClosky? (*sic*) if Keller was a cold-blooded murderer — and this nobody denies — how could he without wealth, friends or influence, cheat the hangman? Would not the same evidence that satisfied the Committee, be equally convincing to a Jury? Do cold-blooded murderers like Keller ever succeed in entirely defying the laws? As for McClosky, (*sic*) some people will be apt to attribute his butcherly act to the abusive practice of indiscriminate selling of whiskey; they will point out that men like McClosky (*sic*) are always found at and about saloons waiting for some man who wants a drink to come along, in order that they may "ring in for a dose of rot;"

137

and may even say that saloon-keepers, in their hunt for
the almighty dollar, not only tolerate but even encourage
such men to lay around and "stand in," so as to avoid
"taking a shingle off the house." These dissatisfied men
may go further and inquire if the members of the "Law
and Order Committee" would have been so prompt if they
had to do with rich, respectable and influential murderers;
they may ask if these men, or some of them, are not themselves in a measure to blame for the state of affairs which
rendered their "Law and Order Committee" necessary
— if they have always discountenanced and condemned —
corruption, fraud and venality in our legislative, executive
and judicial offices, and if they have not rather tried to
influence legislators and judges for their own personal
ends or for those of their friends and relatives? They may
ask if the frequency with which criminals of all kinds escape punishment, is not due, in a large degree, to the increasing corruption and contempt of all law found in our
legislators and judges, and for which the people themselves are responsible. For sound-thinking and far-seeing
men say, and with good reason, that law-makers, judges
and other officers never become corrupt unless the people
are sufficiently so to make corruption in office profitable.
                    (*Territorial Expositor* of Aug. 29, 1879)

The movement to have the Vigilante leaders brought to trial
for the "murder" of Keller and McCluskey gains momentum.
While condemning the action, Reilly berates those who would
make a few persons the scapegoats for a crime committed by all
Phoenicians.

The turmoil caused by the lynchings finally subsides when
the leaders of the law and order group are brought before the
grand jury which refuses to indict them. Reilly, a lawyer, questions the judge's instruction to the jury. The editor has little respect for the judge and never misses an opportunity to say so.

Judge Porter's charge to the Grand Jury, in the matter
of the recent lynching case in Phoenix, was peculiar. He
denounced the affair as a cowardly murder, and told the
jury that if they deemed it best for the good of the community to let the matter rest, they were at liberty to do

so. Telling a community, that was so largely represented as this was in that affair that they are all cowardly murderers, and in the same breath informing members of a Grand Jury that it is optional with them as to whether they inquire into a "cowardly murder" or not, is certainly queer jurisprudence.

(Territorial Expositor of Oct. 17, 1879)

The rebuked judge is not the only one who might be questioned for his interpretations of the law. West of the Pecos River much of the law exists in name only. In too many places the judge is frequently appointed because he can write, which is more than can be said for some of his neighbors. Arizona supports such a person in "Judge" Meyer.

Meyer, a pharmacist, is elected judge because of his honest reputation. Never noted for mercy, Meyer allows testimony only if it serves to convict the accused. Peering over spectacles, the judge, whenever a question of law arises, consults his only two reference books, "Materia Medica" and, "Household Medicine." Court opens when the judge looks down on the prisoner, points his finger at the man and shouts, *"Tu eres bagabundo."*[2] The only excuse for the hearing is to determine how long the prisoner will have to spend on the chain gang.

After receiving a sentence to the local chain gang, one loafer questions, (*sic*) "Jedge, isn't thet a r-a-a-ther tough dose to give t' poor fellow that knowed your grandfadder?"

"Ha! you knowed my grandfaddy; vere abouts, mine frient, you know him?" queries the pill-dispensing judge.

"Wa'al, Jedge, it's jest like this. Th' las' time I seed the old gent was on th' Isthmus o' Panama; he war a-swingin' by his tail from th' limbs of a cocoanut tree, a-gatherin' o' cocanuts, 'n_____."

"Dare; dat vill do, mine frient, dat vill do. I gifts anodder two viks mit der shane gang fur gontembt ov goort; how you like dat?"

Even less than this poor prisoner do the lawyers like to appear before Judge Meyer. The man is unreasonable. He knows nothing of law. But if you wish to stay in practice you must defend your client in court. One such lawyer, hearing his client about to be sentenced to the chain gang, complains;

"My client objects to being tried by this Court on the ground of prejudice, and demands a trial by jury."

139

"Py a shury!" exclaims the judge. "Phwat is dat shury?"
"He insists that he be tried by his peers."
"Oh, he does, does he? Vell, I sentence him to two weeks in de shain gang, and I sentence you to von week for disrespect of de Court. Now, how do you like dat trial by shury?"
So into the chain gang go both client and lawyer.

Though this is a crude form of justice it proves effective. The fledgling territorial government enacts one law after another in an attempt to bring order to the untamed country. While the lawmakers are well-meaning men, their inexperience results in some strange legislation. One of their most recent enactments draws the ridicule of Editor Reilly.

A PREMIUM ON CRIME

Our patriotic legislature adjourned last February, and our equally patriotic Governor went on a mission to that Republican high court at Washington and has not yet returned, and common people like ourselves supposed that there was no more fame for Arizona — at least not just now. But we had counted "with out our host." Our noble and public-spirited acting Governor comes to the rescue, and offers a reward of $500 per head for killing stage robbers. None of our Legislatures, not even our last, has displayed so much patriotism. Legislatures have merely allowed the Governor to offer a reward for the apprehension of criminals at large. All this, of course, suits the "respectable" press.***Now here is a fine chance for enterprising "dead brokes." Just plan a stage robbery, get some weak-minded, impecunious and disheartened wretch, point out to him how easily the thing can be done and how much booty can be obtained — after the pattern of the Mantle-Pierson affair —. Give him a loaded gun, but, to avoid mistakes, stop the tubes or load with soap; tell him exactly when the stage leaves town; jump into the stage yourself, well armed, just before its departure, and if you cannot manage the rest and get yourself $500 and a big name, don't ask us for any more advice, for we don't think you can be fit for much, any how.

(*Territorial Expositor* of Aug. 22, 1879)

Any paper depends for its existence upon advertising income

from merchants. Unfortunately, most advertisers believe that since a paper exists on their money it should print only what is favorable to the merchants. The problem has existed since the first newspaper advertisement appeared in England in 1647.

There is no attempt to assassinate the Irish editor; Phoenix merchants merely withdraw their advertising. This coupled with the printer's refusal to set type for any more inflammatory editorials, forces the virtual closing of the *Expositor*. Reilly disgustedly writes, ". . . a diminished subscription list and a diminished advertising patronage will bring to terms the most bull-headed editor that ever put his name at the head of a newspaper. . . ."

Though Reilly is forced to close the paper, his crusade is successful, for never again will Phoenix endure the reign of terror that gripped the town in the summer of 1879. News items of shootings and death are replaced by these comments.

Do we need a city government?

Phoenix has been rather quiet this week. No cuttings or shootings and not quite as much drunkenness and noise as last week.

Messrs. Law and Order, we don't know their other names, had a difficulty in Phoenix on Sunday. Not wishing to disturb the quiet of the town, they retired to the rural shades north of the city, and a bout of fisticuffs settled the matter. Let us have peace.

Prescott has a theatre; but Phoenix has a water cart.

Mr. Fuson, whose horses were stolen last week, as reported in the EXPOSITOR, is still in hot pursuit of the thieves. He tracked them to Fort McDowell, where he found they had already sold or exchanged one of the horses, and had headed for New Mexico. We hope Mr. Fuson will catch them.

Phoenix has fifteen stores where they sell general merchandise and only fifteen saloons. In western towns, generally, there are two of the latter to one of the former.

Phoenix is now the most orderly town we know of.

No longer will it be necessary for a few close friends to stand with guns behind a barricade in the printing plant to protect Reilly while he writes.

With $45 in his pocket, Reilly contemplates a trip to the new boomtown of Tombstone in southern Arizona. Here he will gain fame and wealth as a lawyer. Prior to his departure, the immigrant editor cannot resist one last jibe:

"Ain't it about time for another stage robbery?"

---

1 Prehistoric Indians whose name in the modern Pima Indian language means "The Ancient Ones."
2 "You are a bum."

142

ℭ𝔥𝔢 𝔈𝔫𝔱𝔢𝔯𝔭𝔯𝔦𝔰𝔢.

Vol. I   PHŒNIX, ARIZONA, SATURDAY, AUGUST 20, 1898.   No 95

ONVENTION ADJOURNS

fter Two and a Half Days' Session.

UCCESS ASSURED

Cobb, Nolin, Hunter, who reported the following named parties be declared the county central committee. Peoria and Glendale—B E Chute.

Alhambra and Johnstone—W C Dawes.

Gila Bend and Lower Gila Bend—Ed E Caruthers.

Cave Creek—W T Linville. Wickenburg, Vulture Sanzo Domingo—R W Baxter. Agua Caliente—F W Baxter. Orme—Chas Pendergast. Alma—J A Stewart. Madison—J B Whitton.

ONLY FOUR MONITORS

Fit For Service In The South.

WE WILL WAIT

duty. Battleships and cruisers will be relieved from that station.

The Porto Rican Tariff.

Washington, August 20.—The war department has promulgated tariff rates for Porto Rico. The rate is the Spanish minimum tariff rates heretofore enforced for Cuba.

The Arizona to Sail.

San Francisco, August 20.—The Arizona, with the troops already designated, will depart on Sunday, as scheduled. Army officials have believe that all the soldiers now gathered in this city will be dispatched to the Philippines as preserve order there.

Need No More Troops.

Washington, August 20.—Gen...

MOVING SLOWLY.

Peace Negotiations Are Prolonged.

POOR OLD SPAIN

shirt. It will permit the American people to approach the rainpaign of 1900 with unbiased judgment. This state of affairs will be of inestimable benefit to the advocates of silver, because they are right. Arizona Bulletin.

At The Churches.

Rev. Goodman, of the Southern Illinois conference, will preach at the First M. E. church Sunday morning at 11 o'clock. Epworth League in evening at 7 o'clock; leader, Dr. Pratt. Subject, "The Duty of Cheerfulness."

At the Baptist church Sunday school at 9 a. m., and Young People's meeting at 7 p. m.

GREATEST DAY

"... Prison shall never be your portion."

A man has to be a good fighter to be a good editor . . . . — Rollin C. Brown

THE RAILROAD HERE

Its Value to Tucson — Some Hints for the Future.

. . . About this time the railroad began to reach into and over the Colorado desert . . . Throughout the land the railway time-cards and advertisements said rich Arizona was connected with the world at large by rail. Leading newspapers then sent out their correspondents. Without the road they would not have done so. Their letters were favorable. The railway kept coming this way and

143

capitalists, too. The company's advertisements kept speaking most highly of Arizona's natural wealth and so did the big newspapers abroad, and as a consequence men of means and enterprise came more frequently and invested more largely. The road kept coming apace. It crossed the Colorado. It brought freights and passengers quicker, easier and cheaper . . . The company asked indirect help from the Territory. The good influences already exerted induced the Legislature to exempt it from taxation for six years . . . The railroad was bringing the Territory and its people from obscurity and despondency to prominence and prosperity.

These facts apply to the Territory at large. Let us consider them in connection with Tucson, in which they are true and border on the marvelous.

Tucson lost the capital and it went where the largest Government patronage had been controlled. Real estate became depressed and vigorous advertising of improved and well rented property brought no buyers. Under Tucson's loss and Prescott's gain the latter town grew rapidly. Although its prosperity was mainly due to accidents, but for the iron horse coming this way it would have continued above that of Tucson. The long and rough stage rides to Prescott and easy and shortening ones here, turned the tide of wealth and enterprise to Tucson, and the latter now leads ahead so much that a comparsion is needless, and would be almost cruel to those whose adversity (as was their prosperity) is largely due to accidents. The railway could have passed a mile or so outside of Tucson on a little shorter route of cheaper construction and built a town of its own. The people here had acted fairly towards the company, and the latter said, give us just the ground we need to do our business in and pass through Tucson and through it we'll go. The people here agreed to do it and have done it, and the company sent their agents to patiently assist in rightly doing it. Good faith has been kept on both sides. Tucson's prosperity is simply amazing in consequence. Real estate that was and otherwise would have been quite worthless, is now ready sale at from two to ten times its highest market price before the absolute fixing of this railway condition. Already capitalists are coming in special and private cars, and only last week they put a million dollars earned elsewhere into Pima

County enterprises, of which Tucson is the commercial moneyed center. It is safe to say the approaching railway has brought us millions of money, (*sic*) cheapened supplies and given immense value to hitherto valueless property; and what may we not expect from its actual operation here? By continued friendly conduct toward this company, the latter's benefits will continue and grow; turn hostile, and it is not in human nature to continue them. Hamper it with municipal restrictions, press it to pay taxes in face of the agreed exemption, and the home station, the shops, the fine buildings, the hotel and powerful influence not tending so certain in our favor, may still not be ours . . . and in the new and practical phase of railroading here, Tucson could hardly fail to reap great benefit by adopting and maintaining a liberal policy with the Southern Pacific Company. Plant the good seed now and nourish it prudently, and it will bring forth an hundred fold.

(*Arizona Citizen* of March 15, 1880)

After three years of confusion, steel rails finally creep from Yuma northward to Tucson. *The Commercial Bulletin* in New York City comments, "The building of this road will greatly stimulate mining enterprises in that great interior country." A territorial paper proclaims: "The vitalizing power of steam infuses new energy into the merchants, new hope into the miner, brings comfort to the farmer, and sends the product of flocks and herds to busy lands in the hum of human industry."

The pattern of frontier living changes with the arrival of the railroad. Eastern products, standards, and ideas can more readily infiltrate the West. Cultural and economic changes also may be noted in the East as a result of this closer contact between the frontier and the settled eastern states.

While sweating men strip to their waists to drive steel spikes with heavy mauls into the ever-lengthening line of railroad ties, Tucson citizens learn:

RAILROAD ITEMS

'Tis now the 3rd of the month, and the 20th those who are not fond of stage riding will be able to take the cars at our depot. Some of the tallest tracklaying ever

145

seen in this country will be done in our vicinity in a few days. The rails will be on hand in a short time, and they will be put down so fast when they arrive, that the train will find it a hard matter to keep up with them.

(*Arizona Citizen* of March 2, 1880)

Editor Rollin C. Brown of the *Arizona Citizen* has good reason to believe that many will welcome the luxury of railroad travel. He has traveled from San Diego to Tucson by stage! Of the trip, he says, "We were six nights and five days traveling continually. It was not hard for we soon got used to it. I slept well in the coach in spite of the fact that it was loaded with public documents and there was no room for my feet, but I was young then and could double them up."

Son of a newspaperman, Brown was born in Rushville, Indiana in the fall of 1844. The Civil War found him a member of the 124th Infantry, Indiana Regulars. "I was in the service for two years, took part in several battles and was on Sherman's march to the sea . . ."

At the war's end, Brown traveled to San Francisco where he worked as a typesetter on the *Chronicle* and *Bulletin*. Blinded in one eye while still a youth, he gained his knowledge and experience in his father's newspaper office. A wiry five-foot seven, Brown invariably wore a tailor-made suit, square-toed shoes, a black string tie and dilapidated Stetson. Upon leaving his job in San Francisco, Brown traveled by steamer to San Diego, where he caught the stage for Tucson.

Though it had once been the seat of the territorial government, "Tucson is as foreign a town as if it were in Haiti instead of within our own boundaries. The language, dress, funeral processions, religious ceremonies, feasts, dances, games, joys, perils, griefs and tribulations of its population are something not to be looked for in the region east of the Missouri river. The general appearance of the place gives one the impression that it had originally been a hill, which, owing to an unexpected but just visitation of Providence, had been struck with lightning. The only objects which meet the eye are dilapidated bake ovens, old sheds, broken pottery, dead horses, tumbled-down corrals, live dogs, drunken Indians, mules, pigs and naked children."

146

Editor Brown has been a resident of Tucson and staff member of the *Citizen* for seven years when the railroad approaches. Assuming the editorship in January of 1880, he reports the progress of the railroad in his daily paper. Tucson plans a celebration to honor the coming of the rails, but how different it will be from the one which marked the opening of the Arizona and New Mexico Stage Company. Then, Editor Brown reported, "the line met a hearty welcome on its first entrance to Tucson, with its six-horse coach, the messenger with his bugle announcing his entrance as he came down Main street to their office. . . . Several hundred people gathered to welcome the new line. As the coach drew up, the crowd gave a cheer as the passengers alighted. The sight was pleasing with six fine horses fitted with Concord harness. The coach was handsomely painted and upholstered."

St. Patrick's Day marks the arrival of the first train and the jubilant editor announces:

COMPLETED AT LAST

The Railroad Within the City Limits of Tucson.

We have delayed until the last hour before going to press to be able to give a full and complete description of the laying of the last rail, and as we write the construction men are rapidly nearing the site of the Depot. This afternoon, Engine No. 41, with a train consisting of two water, thirteen box, thirty-nine flat and eleven construction cars came up to the then terminus and was greeted with cheers by a large crowd who had all day been on the ground witnessing the operations. The event we have all so long looked for has transpired, and our citizens, as well as the people of the entire Territory, are to be congratulated.

(*Arizona Citizen* of March 17, 1880)

The arrival of the long-desired railroad is the signal for a general celebration. Not depending on the spontaneous feelings of the citizens, the city fathers announce:

147

PROGRAMME OF EXERCISES

A salute of 38 guns will be fired under military orders as the train reaches the City limits; after which music by the brass band will welcome the visitors.

The Mayor and Council, with the Committee of Reception, will receive the officers of the Railroad Company, and their guests.

William S. Oury, Esq., will deliver an address of Welcome at the train.

Don Estevan Ochoa will present a Silver Spike to the President of the Railroad Company.

The officers and guests will be conducted to the Park Hall, where the Committee of Invitation will receive them.

The Banquet to follow immediately.

Toasts will conclude the Banquet.

The Ball will open at 8 o'clock.

Citizens are urgently requested, by the Mayor and Council, to decorate their houses, and to illuminate them at night.

Some 1,200 dance to the music of the 6th Cavalry Band of Fort Lowell at the ball marking the end of the official program. Charles Crocker, president of the Southern Pacific, is the guest of honor at the affair held in a colorfully decorated and brilliantly lighted Park Hall.

The high point of the day, however, comes at the banquet. The mayor of Tucson, acting in his official capacity, has sent telegrams announcing the arrival of the railroad to the president of the United States, Governor Fremont of the Arizona Territory, and mayors of several cities in California. Then a member of the welcoming committee decides that a wire should be sent to the pope. Here history and legend merge but this wire is written:

148

Tucson, Arizona, March 17, 1880

To His Holiness, the Pope of Rome, Italy. The mayor of Tucson begs the honor of reminding Your Holiness that this ancient and honorable pueblo was founded by the Spaniards under the sanction of the church more than three centuries ago, and to inform Your Holiness that a railroad from San Francisco, California, now connects us with the Christian world.

(signed) R. N. Leatherwood, Mayor.

Asking your benediction, J. B. Salpointe, Vic. Ap.

The footnote of the Catholic bishop of the area gives additional merit to the telegram. According to the story, however, the messenger charged with delivering the wire takes a few too many drinks. The bewildered telegraph operator on seeing the drunk, thinks it is a joke and fears to send the message. But what will they tell the mayor who is expecting to read the reply to the distinguished guests at the banquet?

The drunken messenger, the telegraph operator, and a few enterprising but tipsy citizens soon solve the dilemma. Why not just make up a reply? No one will know the difference.

The "reply" is first read by the mayor at the banquet. To his embarrassment and the delight of the audience the hoax has not been discovered previously. This reply from the pope is to become one of the most amusing anecdotes of Arizona history.

His Holiness the Pope acknowledges with appreciation receipt of your telegram informing him that the ancient city of Tucson at last has been connected by rail with the outside world and sends his benediction, but for his own satisfaction would ask, where in hell is Tucson?

(signed) ANTONELLI

While bringing new life to the city, the railroad does not dim a long-standing fight between Editor Brown and the editor of the opposition paper, the *Arizona Daily Star*. Only a few weeks after the arrival of the locomotive the *Star's* editor brings a libel suit against Brown.

Brown is placed under a $3,000 bond and the case is given

149

to the grand jury. Of the long-existing editorial feud, Brown says, ". . . the feeling between the Star and The Citizen is terrible. We are always fighting and sometimes it goes so far that we want to kill each other. . . . I've been shot at and attacked with a six-shooter and with a cane. The worst lick I ever received was from a gun butt wielded by a man that I had discharged from the paper. That's the blow that caused this scar over my eye. But that is part of an editor's life. A man has to be a good fighter to be a good editor."

Grandson of an Irish revolutionist, Editor Brown decides to do his fighting in some other section of Arizona; so, in 1887, he issues the *Arizona Enterprise* from Florence.

Lying on the banks of the Gila River and some 60 miles north of Tucson, Florence was founded in 1866 by an Indian agent, Levi Ruggles. Ruggles claims that his title to the townsite comes from a former homesteader by "deed of mouth." The homesteader dies of smallpox and no one disputes Ruggles' title. Opening a store to serve the numerous neighboring mines, Ruggles succeeds financially and his adobe home becomes the showplace of Florence.

The discovery and eventual working of numerous silver mines near Florence brings prosperity to the town. A wandering California newspaperman describes "the town of Florence as containing about 1,500 inhabitants, about evenly distributed between Americans, Mexicans and Spaniards, and yet retaining all the evidences of its Mexican origin. The streets are laid out wide and straight, shaded on each side by a row of fine cottonwood trees, and at their roots along each sidewalk is a babbling stream of running water, thus reminding us of Salt Lake City in its general appearance.

"Many buildings of adobe brick are now being erected, and the streets present a lively and thriving appearance. Two hotels are in the full tide of success — and have good accommodations for the officials and courts . . . A good and well arranged post office is conveniently located on the main street, which is also used for the stage office and the express office of Wells, Fargo & Co. . . . The buildings are all built of adobe, as lumber is very high, and has to be hauled all the way from Prescott, a distance of nearly 200 miles. Like other southern frontier villages, the

150

buildings are only one-story high, generally having a wide porch or veranda surrounding them."

It is in this town that R. C. Brown once again enters the newspaper field. He goes into partnership with George W. Brown (no relation) who is also an ex-staff member of the *Citizen* in Tucson. Born in New York, George is 43, the same age as his co-editor.

The *Arizona Enterprise* has no opposition. Prospects for an advertising income are good for "there are three flouring mills in or near the town, a school-house with one hundred pupils, a Catholic church, several stores, a smelting furnace, a brewery, two hotels, several restaurants, six physicians and . . . a U. S. land office."

Peons, earning a dollar a day and their keep, dig the numerous irrigation ditches from the river to the fields. While grains and alfalfa are the principal crops, the area also raises the produce that is needed by the various outlying mines and the mountain mining city of Globe.

Though agricultural settlements generally escape the rowdiness and violence of railroad or mining towns, Florence receives an early baptism in blood. One of the first to die is a discharged soldier who becomes abusive after too many drinks . . .

A man doesn't necessarily die every time a gun is fired. Yet, there are always those who swagger the streets in imitation of fictional gunmen. These imitation "tough men" hasten the graying of any sheriff's hair and give the town many a restless night of sleep. These bullies seldom call on a man to draw, but content themselves with shooting out windows or bottles off the bar. Their actions are still annoying and dangerous so Editors Brown give them this warning.

> There is a great deal of unnecessary and careless shooting of fire-arms prevalent in town and steps should be taken to have the practice stopped before some person is injured. It often happens that a bullet goes singing through the trees and it is only by the merest chance that no one is hurt. The practice is a dangerous one and unless it is stopped some one will surely be injured.
> (*Arizona Enterprise* of June 8, 1889)

It is not too long before someone is hurt! Two well-known

151

Florence citizens cease their war of words and decide to settle it with guns. The editors carefully chronicle the battle and then explain the events which lead up to the shooting.

A DOUBLE TRAGEDY

An Impromptu Duel with Fatal Results

*Josephus Phy and Ex-Sheriff Gabriel Meet
in Deadly Encounter — One is Killed and
the other Mortally Wounded.*

About eight o'clock Thursday night the people on Main street were suddenly startled by the loud reports of pistol shots in rapid succession proceeding from the Tunnel saloon . . . when two struggling forms came through the screen doors into the street, still firing at each other, and one fell on the street and the other staggered down the sidewalk towards the Florence Hotel, the fact was recognized that a fearful tragedy had been enacted in the semi-darkness that surrounded the entrance of the Tunnel saloon.

Eleven shots were fired, and the echo of the last had scarcely died away ere dozens of people had gathered about the prostrate form of Josephus Phy, a well known resident of this place, who was evidently badly wounded, but was still flourishing a keen bowie knife in a threatening manner that for a short time repelled the friendly offices tendered him.

He was carried to the stage corral where Dr. Harvey examined his wounds. One shot had passed through his left thigh, utterly shattering both bones; another shot had passed through the front portion of his abdomen . . . The last wound occasioned internal hemorrhage and, although everything possible was done to relieve his sufferings, he died at half past twelve o'clock the same night, four and one-half hours after receiving the shots.

The other party to the tragedy ex-Sheriff Gabriel, had proceeded down Main street after the shooting, to the entrance of the O. K. livery stable, where he fell. He was assisted into a room where the blood from his wounds was staunched until a doctor could be summoned from Sacaton, 18 miles distant. Dr. Sabin reached town about half past one o'clock yesterday morning and found Mr. Gabriel bearing up heroically under his severe wounds. It was found that one shot had entered his left side, very close to the heart, and had come out below the left shoulder blade, causing a dangerous wound. The second shot had entered the right groin and come out low down and close to the spine, also making a dangerous wound. He rested quite easily however, and yesterday felt very cheerful and hopeful, and Dr. Sabin said that, although the chances were against recovery, there is a possibility for him surviving the dreadful wounds . . .

THE CAUSES

The beginning of the bad feeling existing between the two men was a very insignificant occurence dating back nearly three years ago, when Sheriff Gabriel discharged Phy as deputy sheriff. The latter took away a satchel belonging to Gabriel, and when asked for it grew very indignant. He had a room over the sheriff's office which he refused to vacate when ordered to do so by Sheriff Gabriel, and the board of supervisors at a subsequent meeting had him evicted. This led to some unnecessary talk against Gabriel.

Later on Phy became a candidate for sheriff and a remark attributed to him by Tom Montgomery brought about the scandalous assault upon the latter by Phy at Casa Grande and, as Gabriel figured in it in an official way and placed Phy under arrest, this added fuel to the flames and engendered much evil gossip. The avowed intention of Phy to become a candidate for sheriff this fall brought forth the antagonisms natural to such events and he was told that Gabriel, who is popular with the voters in spite of all his faults, would also run for that office and beat him. Harassed by the prospect of such formidable opposition and stung by the jibes met with among his acquaintances, he became unduly excited, and some are charitable enough to express a belief that he had become mentally unbalanced. Upon the day of the tragedy he was unusually excited and every one expected trouble if they should meet. No one believes that Mr. Gabriel sought the difficulty, but rather avoided it, and since the fact has become known that he had several times passively submitted to abuse from Phy, without marked resentment, public comment has been more reserved than is usual in such events . . .

The deceased, Josephus Phy, was a native of Missouri, aged 54 years. He was well known in Tucson and Phoenix, where he has resided, and to the people of Pinal county. He leaves a brother and sister, living in Pinal, but no family of his own.

His funeral took place at three o'clock yesterday afternoon, the Masonic burial service being read at the grave . . .

(*Arizona Enterprise* of June 2, 1888)

The Phy-Gabriel duel is the only shooting of any importance that the two editors will report. Rather, they are occupied with reporting one series of robberies after another . . . One of the most daring and notorious of these is the Wham robbery . . .

Major J. W. Wham, paymaster of the U. S. Army, is en route to Fort Thomas on the Gila River. Transporting an Army payroll of some $26,000 in gold and silver in a wagon, Wham is escorted by 11 Negro soldiers. As the party nears Cedar Springs, site of many battles with the Indians, they find the small pass blocked by a boulder . . . As the soldiers lay aside their guns to move the rock, they are met by a fusillade of bullets. Hiding behind whatever cover they can find, the Negro troops soon discover that the major is in full flight. Lacking an officer, these men flee too, leaving behind the payroll and five of their wounded.

The deserting major finds himself in disgrace. The gold, though, has long since been packed into gunnysacks and thrown onto horses by the robbers. The soldiers at Fort Thomas do without their pay as the military authorities scour the countryside for the highwaymen. Editors Brown interject their opinions.

The robbery of Paymaster Wham at Cedar Springs by a gang of highwaymen, is one of those unfortunate circumstances liable to occur in any country where a large sum of money can tempt human cupidity, and it will be freely used by the eastern press to demonstrate a state of frontier lawlessness that has no equal on the continent. In common with all good citizens we greatly deplore the perpetration of such a great crime, and particularly so be-

154

cause of the loss of life attending it. Just such crimes have been committed in other portions of the country and we do not hesitate to express our belief that not a single citizen of Arizona was connected with its perpetration. Some of them were undoubtedly familiar with the topography of that portion of the country and were cognizant of the movements of the paymaster, but we believe time will demonstrate the fact that none of them are other than adventurers of no settle place of abode — the outcasts of eastern cities in hiding from pursuit and plying their nefarious vocation whenever a favorable opportunity presents itself. They probably rob a bank in one state; hold up a railroad train in another; stop a stage coach and commit any and all sorts of crimes when opportunity is presented with the most exact impartiality as to geographical locality. They are birds of prey and if they are not caught in the stern chase that is now in progress, they will flit away and be lost to public view for a time, only to reappear unexpectedly in other portions of the country to pluck whomsoever they will with money in his possession.

(*Arizona Enterprise* of May 18, 1889)

Unfortunately, the citizens of Arizona are not quite so innocent as the Browns hope. Eight popular Gila Valley farmers and stockmen are arrested but four are released for lack of evidence. The remainder are indicted by the grand jury and bound over for trial in November.

In late November, the defendants are finally brought to trial. Some 33 days are consumed in hearing the testimony of 165 witnesses, most of whom testify for the defense. The major's cowardly desertion and the bad feeling towards the inefficient military lead most of the citizens to join the defendants' camp. The defendants are finally acquitted but it takes a special act of Congress to remove from the major financial responsibility for the loss. The gold? Who knows? It may still lie hidden in some remote cranny.

Though the territorial government still offers a reward of $500 for the capture of every road bandit, many continue to prowl through the sparsely settled country. Nor are their activities confined to stagecoaches.

EXPRESS ROBBERY

Wednesday night's west bound passenger train on the Southern Pacific road was held up by five train robbers near Papago station, fifteen miles east of Tucson, close to the scene of the former hold up. The gravel switch had been turned and the engine, cab and a few cars were derailed. The robbers fired many shots, but no one was hurt. The engineer, Jas. Guthrie and fireman R. T. Bradford, jumped down the embankment and escaped. The robbers then blew open the express car with a dymanite (sic) cartridge and beat messenger Smith over the head and compelled him to open the safe. Route agent Grant was also in the car. How much money was taken no one seems to know, but it is estimated that from $3000 to $5000 was taken. The mail car was also entered, but nothing was disturbed . . .

(Arizona Enterprise of Aug. 13, 1887)

Though a few of the road agents are eventually caught and hung, or sentenced to long prison terms, holdups are just as frequent. Stages carry a "shotgun guard" only when a bullion shipment or valuable merchandise is on board. The solitary driver, traveling through long stretches of uninhabited country, has little choice but to yield to the demanding gun of the bandit.

The area near Florence is the scene of many holdups as it is on the route from the capital city of Prescott to the large commercial center of Tucson. Therefore the rough and unguarded terrain around the farming settlement is the perfect site for any attempts to earn easy money. The local paper reports still another robbery.

THE STAGE HELD UP

Wednesday's down stage for Casa Grande was held up by two Mexicans six miles this side of its destination and all the mail and express matter taken. The robbers cut two of the traces, but the driver, Nelson Caplett managed to improvise substitutes for them and, being without passengers or load, he dashed into Casa Grande at the top of the horses' speed to give the alarm. The news was at once telegraphed to Florence and pursuit was organized at each

156

place; that from Casa Grande found the empty express box and mail sacks on the trail of the robbers.

The guilty parties are well known here and at Tempe, in which direction they went, and the officers of the latter place were communicated with by telegraph to look out for their arrival there, where they have relatives living.

It is not known how much money was taken. There was no registered mail from Florence and but one package from Pinal. It is not known what the through Globe pouch contained. The express was not a bonanza, but several packages of merchandise were taken. It is estimated that they obtained about $500 in money.

This robbery occurred just one year from the first of a series of similar crimes, the stage on Tuesday, October 2, 1888, having been robbed by three Mexicans who were never caught. On Thursday, November 22, 1888, the stage was again robbed, it is believed by the same parties, and on the following day it was again robbed, this time by an American who gave the name of Henry Miller, and is now serving a term of twelve years in the penitentary for his crime.

The present instance possesses the same features as the former robberies by Mexicans, and their flight towards Tempe suggests that they belong to a band of outlaws that ply their nefarious calling in various portions of southern Arizona.

The government offers a standing reward of $1,000 for the arrest and conviction of mail robbers, in addition to which the express company offers a reward and the territory will probably offer an additional bounty for their apprehension — sufficient to induce the most determined search for them . . .

(*Arizona Enterprise* of Oct. 5, 1889)

Why doesn't someone put a stop to all these holdups? Many Florence citizens ask the same question. But how much can a sheriff with one or two deputies do against numerous individual bandits and against the organized gangs who command the trails? The sheriff, however, does make an attempt as evidenced by these comments in the newspaper.

The road agents that took in the Casa Grande stage

last Tuesday were not only novices in the "profession," but they evidently were in the peculiar attitude of Mr. Micawber, and the stage chanced to be the something that "turned up" at that critical moment. They were not disguised, but were strangers — likely a part of the late pilgrims from Sonora whose chivalric valor suddenly oozed out of their heels when the conscription order was issued in their land of God and Liberty, while the country of the gringos presented a better field for their talents. They likely acted upon a sudden impulse and trusted to luck to escape the pursuit that would certainly follow.

(Arizona Enterprise of Oct. 12, 1888)

The job of protecting the stagecoaches is further complicated by Indians. Though many of the hostiles have been rounded up by the military and placed on reservations, a few outlaw bands still exist. Then, too, some of the young braves become bored with the quiet life on the reservation. Small groups of the "captives" frequently slip away to hunt up excitement. And what could be more exciting or rewarding than attacking a coach.

Probably the most infamous attack on a coach in the Southwest is the Wickenburg Massacre. The driver and six passengers left Wickenburg, Arizona on what appeared to be a routine trip. Fred W. Loring, a prominent Easterner and recent graduate of Harvard, chose to ride on top with the driver. Another passenger was Miss Sheppard, "whose charms found a ready market" in Arizona.

Indians, though, lay in wait. Hidden in underbrush in the bottom of a canyon through which the stagecoach had to pass, these renegades from a nearby reservation gave the coach no warning. The stage driver's cry, "Apaches! Apaches!" mingled with the Indians' first volley. The driver and two passengers were killed outright. With the stage being fired upon from three sides, Miss Sheppard and a male companion managed to jump from the protected side of the coach. Though the woman in her flight received a flesh wound, the attackers were too busy with the remaining passengers to halt the escape. The two survivors then walked the nine miles back to Wickenburg to give the alarm.

Two parties of citizens responded to the appeal and hurried

158

to the scene of the attack. There they found the bodies of the remaining passengers. Loring, an ex-correspondent for the *Appleton's Journal,* had been shot twice, run through the chest with a lance and finally scalped. When news of his fate reached the East, papers there began demanding that "the Apache must be treated with less Bible, and more sword." One of the civilian scouting parties escorted the bodies back to Wickenburg while the second group took up the trail of the murderers.

At first there was some speculation that the massacre was the handiwork of Mexican bandits rather than that of the Apaches. The trail of the ambushing party, however, led straight to the Camp Date Creek Reservation, home of the Apache-Mohave Indians. After the guilt of the Indians had been established, General George Crook and his army assumed control.

Crook entered the camp of the hostiles and had a visit with their chief. These two were old friends and few words were wasted. The chief knew the guilty parties of his band. Crook watched silently as the old man cut a plug of tobacco into eight pieces. The chief then went through his encampment, handing out the tobacco squares to certain warriors. Following the movements of the chief were Crook and his soldiers. Eight warriors held the squares while the soldiers closed around them. Crook drew his pistol and killed Ochocama, leader of the murdering war party. Other shots rang throughout the encampment and the remaining seven guilty Indians lay dying, the tobacco squares still in their hands. The Wickenburg Massacre was avenged.

It is such a tragedy as this that prompts the early journalist to write:

INDIANS

DISARM the Apaches and make their lives the forfeit of being found off their reservation without a pass and a more docile and submissive set of cutthroats will be hard to find.

(Arizona Enterprise of Aug. 18, 1888)

Perhaps the Indians don't read Editors Brown's editorials. At least, Ski-Be-Nan-Ted, or the "Apache Kid," isn't afraid of the fate that awaits renegades. Before his downfall, the Kid had been a top sergeant of the Apache Scouts who were a part of the U. S. Army. Highly regarded for his loyalty and courage by the Army officers, the Kid soon learned the white man's ways and his language.

There are several versions of how the Kid got into difficulty. Some say that his father was murdered. Apache custom demands that the oldest son of the injured family seek vengeance. Sergeant Kid was sent to arrest the murderer; but, following the custom of his tribe, he killed his father's slayer. Fearing punishment from the white men for breaking the American law, the Kid got himself drunk and in this state returned to the chief of scouts' camp. Others maintain that the Kid was ordered to take a group of Apache scouts into the back country to destroy an illegal Indian still. Instead of following orders, the scouts went on a drunk that lasted over a week.

Regardless of the cause of the Kid's downfall, he and his men were captured by troops and later tried for mutiny. Though given long terms in a federal prison, the men were soon pardoned by President Grover Cleveland. Then the erring scouts were tried by a civil court in Globe and sentenced to seven years each in the territorial prison at Yuma.

The Kid and other prisoners begin the trip to the prison by Concord stage. That fateful journey is reported by Editors Brown.

KILLED BY APACHES

The Sheriff of Gila County Overpowered
By His Prisoners.

*A Tragedy that Nearly Precipitated an Outbreak on the
San Carlos Reservation.*

On Friday morning of last week Sheriff Glenn Reynolds, of Gila county, started from Globe with eight Apache Indians and one Mexican, prisoners sentenced to various terms in the pententiary, for Yuma. The Indians were named in commitment as Hale, Sayes, Bach e-on-nal, Bithejabethishlscean, Kid . . . W. A. Holmes accompanied the sheriff as guard and Eugene Middleton, proprietor of the Florence and Globe stage line, drove the four-horse team that conveyed them down, while sheriff Reynolds rode his horse as far as Riverside. They reached the latter station in due season without any event of special importance and set out for Florence about four o'clock Saturday morning. An hour later they reached the big wash nearly five miles this side of Riverside and the sheriff ordered six of the Indians to walk up the steep grade. They were handcuffed in pairs and, strange to relate, were preceded by the sheriff on foot, his horse having been left at Riverside, and were followed by the guard. Both the sheriff and guard wore heavy overcoats and gloves, the morning being quite cold as well as dark, and the wagon containing two remaining Indians and Mr. Middleton, went on a little in advance of the sheriff.

Suddenly the Indians nearest the sheriff and guard gave a wild whoop and with their free arms grapled the officers and held them while the others took away the guns and shot both. Holmes was probably killed first and with his own gun, the bullet passing directly through his heart and coming out below his right arm.

Sheriff Reynolds was next shot with the rifle and afterwards received a charge of buckshot from his own gun through his head, instantly killing him. The wretches then struck his face several times with the muzzle of the gun in token of their hatred of the man, and then beat his head with a sharp stone.

The firing caused Mr. Middleton to stop his horses and look back out of the side of the coach just in time to receive a bullet in his right cheek which, as afterwards learned, cut around the back of his neck and came out of the opposite side, inflicting a very severe but not necessarily fatal wound. The shock caused Mr. Middleton to fall from the coach and almost immediately the Indians were upon him. While still retaining full consciousness, he feigned death and the savages were content with taking off his overcoat and robbing him of his watch and money. They likewise robbed the sheriff and guard and also took their arms and ammunition and fled.

In the meantime the Mexican ran for dear life. He subsequently got one of the stage horses and rode it as far as it could carry him and then made his way to the stone house at the Buttes and surrendered himself more dead than alive, to Mr. Charles White who happened to be there and who brought him to Florence.

After the departure of the Indians from the scene of

161

the tragedy, Mr. Middleton succeeded in getting upon his feet and, covered with blood and begrimed with dirt, he started upon the back track for Riverside to give the alarm. A messenger was at once dispatched to Globe and a telegram from that place was the first tidings received here of the tragedy. Later on the mail was brought in by the regular stage driver and the news was confirmed . . .

The sheriff's posse soon found the trail and followed it across the river at Zellweger's ranch and over mountains and across canyons, occassionally finding fragments of the effects of the dead men that had been cast away by savages, until they found the troops had taken up the trail, when they returned to Florence.

The military acted with surprising promptness and as soon as the news of the emunte (sic) reached San Carlos, troops were ordered from Fort McDowell, Fort Grant, Camp Thomas, Fort Lowell and Huachuca and at last accounts an ample force of soldiers and thirty Indian scouts were following the fugitives towards the White Mountains, on the reservation, and were hourly gaining upon them. There is scarcely a doubt that they will be captured and turned over to the authorities of this county to answer for their latest terrible crime . . .

Sheriff Glenn Reynolds had been a resident of Gila county nearly four years, and came from Texas. He was engaged in the stock business in Tonto Basin with a man named Connors and his popularity was attested by his election last fall over two opposing candidates. He was about thirty-five years of age and leaves a wife and three children. He was a brave officer and his daring bordered on recklessness. It is believed that his self-reliance led him into unnecessary danger which the desperate Indians quickly took advantage of.

W. A. Holmes, the guard, had been a resident of Globe for many years and was one of the most prominent democratic politicians of Gila county . . .

Mr. Eugene Middleton, who now lies at the residence of Mr. W. P. Bamrick in this city, is a young man of push and energy and has the mail contract between Globe and Florence. His brother was killed by Indians on Salt River in 1882 and at the same time a sister narrowly escaped death at their hands. His delivery from death was almost miraculous, and can be attributed only to his cool nerve and presence of mind, favored by the haste of the Indians to avoid pursuit. His wounds are very serious, but it is now believed that he will recover.

(Arizona Enterprise of Nov. 9, 1889)

Apache scouts, U. S. Cavalry, and sheriff's posses scour the countryside for the renegades. The manhunters in particular want the Apache Kid whom they correctly believe plotted and led the escape.

The Kid eludes the search parties though his fellow convicts are not so fortunate. Killing ranchers for their horses and murdering miners for their food, the Kid rides a trail of death. He finally seeks a place of refuge deep in the Sierra Madre mountains of Old Mexico. However, the Kid, a full-blooded Apache, returns on frequent raids into Arizona. When the loyal Apache Scouts lead the army in its chase for the murderer, the Kid splits his vengeance between the whites and the Apaches. To both settler and Indian, the name of the Kid becomes a thing of terror.

A reward of $5,000 for the capture of the Kid is offered by the Territory. Still the renegade continues to kill unsuspecting whites while stealing an occassional Apache squaw from her family's wickiup. If the squaw becomes sick or refuses to accompany the outlaw scout, she forfeits her life. Dead squaws cannot betray the Kid to the Army.

For over 25 years men will report that they have seen the Apache Kid but that he has eluded them. While the never-ending search for the Apache Kid continues, the Florence editors also find themselves in trouble with the law.

As with R. C. Brown's first brush with the law in Tucson, the editors are again faced with a libel suit. The suit of criminal libel against the editors is the outcome of a long and bitter battle waged with territorial Governor L. C. Hughes and his administration. The editors, unfrightened by the impending action, continue to fight with:

IN CONTEMPT

Boss Cameron Must Not Be
Criticized by the Press

The Enterprise Selected as
a Target for His Wrath —
Proceedings in the Court for Contempt

The publication in last week's ENTERPRISE of articles referring to the indictment found against its publishers for libel, and other items regarding Brewster Cameron, resulted in the arraingment of R. C. and G. W. Brown for contempt of court, last Tuesday.

Francis J. Heney, an attorney . . . said . . . R. C. and G. W. Brown published . . . certain libelous articles intended to filify, degrade and defame the said court and it officers and to bring them into contempt and evidently calculated to obstruct the administration of justice therein.

The following is the publication made editorially in THE ENTERPRISE on July 21, 1892, upon which the bill was found:

It is rumored that an effort is being made for the removal of Brewster Cameron from the clerkship of the District court. When he was appointed to that position there was a strong protest against it unavailingly made, and at that time THE ENTERPRISE pointed out the grave impropriety of a person having so much prospective litigation being placed so close to the councils of the court, but the compact remained unbroken.

Upon the authority of a gentleman in position to know the facts, who received the information direct from Major Cecil Clay, Chief Clerk of the Department of Justice, it seems that a protest came from that department against the appointment of Cameron as Clerk, based upon his record while employed there. Among the many things charged of him was that he mutilated and abstracted pages of some of the records of the Department and committed many of lesser sins, any of which should have caused his dismissal in disgrace. Attorney General Miller was aware of these offences and objected to Cameron's appointment, but finally gave way to the influence brought to bear upon him. If Brewster Cameron was really guilty of these grave charges, where his offences were liable at any time to come

164

to the knowledge of his superiors, what might be expected of him where his interests are at stake, in a position where he holds unlimited sway? The very suggestion is sufficient to arouse the suspicion of every litigant that this evil hand has in some manner jeopardized his cause. At the last moment of his active career as Clerk, these land grant cases are suddenly sprung upon unsuspecting settlers, and if his evil deeds live after him, there can be no conjecture of the possible manipulation of records and documents that may come up to confront these men who are defending their homes and all they have on earth. That such a man — assuming that these charges are true, and which, from their scource can admit of no doubt — can be kept in so responsible an office for such a length of time he has been retained, is beyond the comprehension of all decent people, and its evil influence cannot but environ the sacred ermine with suspicions that we sincerely hope may be nothing more grave.

THE ENTERPRISE is able to produce the authority upon which the above article was written, and if given an opportunity, will do so with a pleasure that will somewhat astonish the Cameron clan.

It is talked freely upon the streets of Tucson that Brewster Cameron has dominated grand juries where his interests were involved and that plain testimony against the Camerons has been ignored which, in cases of other persons would have sent them to Yuma.

It is also stated that in the case of S. L. Parks, against whom an indictment was found upon testimony of the Camerons, and who furnished an appearance bond last week, was threatened by the Camerons to be "put behind the bars." True enough, late Saturday evening the bond had mysteriously disappeared from Clerk Cameron's office, and Mr. Parks was re-arrested and placed in jail where, owing to the lateness of the hour preventing the procuring of a new bond, he remained until Monday morning, when the original bond came to light and he was released.

This is the Cameron that comes very near running both political parties, wants a good share of the earth and all the possessions thereof belonging to the industrious people who have toiled hard for their homes, has a reputation of getting juries that bend the supple hinges of the knee to his will; has more litigation in the court in which he holds a very important position than any other man in the county, and yet there can be found a grand jury of sufficient verdancy to believe that he can be libeled!

(*Arizona Enterprise* of Nov. 27, 1892)

The Browns are tried in the district court and found guilty as charged. The editors are then sentenced to one day in the Yuma penitentiary. Now a stay in the county jail has been the fate of more than one pioneering editor but a sentence to the penitentiary means the loss of citizenship rights. The bewildered editors, though, enjoy the support of the people and at least one territorial offiicial.

Office of
Superintendent Territorial Prison,
of Arizona

M. McInernay,
Superintendent
Messrs. G. W. and R. C. Brown,
Tucson, Arizona

Gentlemen:

It is with feelings of the keenest regrets, that I have learned of the penalty which has been imposed upon you and in additions to tendering you my sincere sympathy, desire to assure you, that should it become necessary for you to be temporarily residents of Yuma, the half of my residence shall be open for your occupancy and while regretting its occasion, will nevertheless welcome your visit. With kindest regards and the compliments of the season, I remain

Yours very truly
(signed)   M. McInernay

The inside of the Prison shall never be your portion.

In the meantime other territorial editors have joined in the defense of the Browns. After a meeting of the recently formed Arizona Editorial Association, the irate editors make a call on the governor. A demand is made that the governor grant a pardon to the Browns before they serve their sentence. Now the governor has received his share of criticism from the Browns' paper so this executive is content to see the editors behind bars. Seeing that their request will receive no attention, the incensed editors make a few threats.

Himself a former editor, the governor begins to listen to "reason." Thinking perhaps of the next election and deciding that he should maintain the good will of the working press, Hughes sends the following telegram.

Phoenix, Arizona, April 22, 1893

To: George W. and R. C. Brown,

Tucson

I have this day granted an unconditional pardon to George W. and R. C. Brown.

L. C. Hughes, Governor

TOMBSTONE PROSPECTOR.

VOL. VII.   TOMBSTONE ARIZONA, TUESDAY EVENING MAY 2 1893   NO 228

TOMBSTONE PROSPECTOR
City and County Official Paper

PUBLISHED EVERY EVENING
(EXCEPT SUNDAY)
S. C. BAGG, Editor and Proprietor.
OFFICE:
Fremont St., Opposite City Hall.

OFFICIAL DIRECTORY.

Pioneer Store

Cor. 5th and Fremont Sts.

JOB HOEFLER, Prop.

— DEALER IN —

General Merchandise

— AGENT FOR IMPROVED —

Agricultural Implements and
the Celebrated] Turbine
Wind-Mills.

A BIG BATTLE.

Navajos and Cowboys Have
a Fearful Fight on the
San Juan.

Evans and Sontag Rob
Stage—The "World's Fair—
Revolutionists Rampant—
Another Broken Bank—A
Saloon Row.

"The crowning infamy!"

"The day has gone by when the press can be gagged.
— Stanley C. Bagg

"All you're gonna find is your Tombstone," shout the soldiers as the tall, gaunt prospector leads his pack-laden burro through the gates of the army post.

Shoulder-length, gray-black hair, a matted beard, and tattered clothes complete the picture of Ed. Schieffelin. Ignoring the prophecy of the soldiers, he trudges toward the San Pedro Valley. Born in Pennsylvania, Schieffelin has spent most of his life panning for gold and silver in California, Oregon, Idaho, Nevada, and now Arizona. Still in his 30's, he hopes to make his big strike.

169

South of the San Pedro River, the valley floor is covered with sagebrush and other scrubby desert vegetation. The rolling country gives way to bare mountains within a few miles and it is on the treeless foothills that the prospector begins his search. Because this part of the Territory is unsettled and is the domain of the Apaches, no one expects the prospector to find anything but his grave.

Constantly on the alert for Indian war parties, Schieffelin finds his silver strike in 1877. Remembering the soldiers' warning, the prospector calls his mine Tombstone. Then Al Schieffelin, a brother of the prospector, and an assayer friend join the venture. Still "looking for stones," Ed finds another rich deposit of silver-bearing ore. "You're a lucky cuss," exclaims the admiring brother. Ed is. For the Lucky Cuss, as the mine comes to be named, proves to be one of the richest in all of the Territory.

A townsite is laid out in 1879 and is incorporated two years later as Tombstone. The city becomes a hell-hole over night. Prospectors and miners from the played-out gold fields of California and even from Australia rush to the scene. Into this town on the foothills of the Mule Mountains pour thousands of men. Gamblers from notorious Dodge City, Kansas, migrate en masse to the boom camp. A tax on saloons and dance halls is collected for the support of the proposed school. Miners give their patronage to numerous brothels in the town's sprawling red-light district. This then is Tombstone, which for notoriety will equal or even surpass those other "wide-open" frontier towns of Dodge City, Wichita, and Virginia City.

During the tumultuous 80's, Tombstone never lacks excitement. Playing a major role in the community is Nellie Cashman, proprietress of the Russ House, a boardinghouse for miners. An Irish immigrant, Miss Cashman soon becomes the driving force for the erection of churches, care of the sick, founding of theatres, and general care of the needy. While most of Tombstone's women ply a questionable trade, Nellie Cashman enjoys an "unimpeachable reputation." Often called "the miner's angel," she is recognized as a civic leader and commands the respect of all the men in the town.

For all of her activities she gains the most commendation for her part in the hanging of the participants of the "Bisbee Massacre." Four men have been sentenced to death on the gallows

170

for their killing of four Bisbee citizens during a holdup. The execution is set for a spring day in 1884. Noting the lack of seating space near the gallows, an enterprising promoter erects a grandstand and begins to peddle tickets for the spectacle. Miss Cashman considers the scheme a disgrace to the town. Enlisting the support of her numerous miner friends, she marches an army, armed with axes, to the grandstand. "Tear it down, boys," she commands. The boys not only make kindling wood out of the structure but run the promotor out of town. The execution assumes a semblance of dignity and is conducted without fanfare.

At the height of the silver boom, Stanley C. Bagg settles in the roaring mining camp. A shade over 30, Bagg comes to the Territory from his hometown of Detroit, Michigan, by way of California. A former student at the University of Michigan, Bagg is neither a saddle tramp nor a miner. Looking for a chance to go into business, Bagg finds himself being offered the job of editing a newspaper. The about-to-be editor says:

"One evening while strolling along Allen street I was hailed by James Reilly to 'Come on in and have something.' Once inside I found Andy Ritter, Joe Pascholy, James Reilly (ex-editor of the *Expositor in Phoenix*) and myself lined up along the rail of Martin Costello's Anheuser-Busch subsidiary.

"After becoming socially inclined I was told that a newspaper was to be launched in Tombstone to combat the powerful group which ruled the roost at the court house. The result of the conference was that a plant was purchased with the money subscribed by the four above mentioned citizens and was leased to Jimmy Nash for one dollar a month. But Jimmy made a poor job of combating and the paper was thrown back on its sponsors. Again I was approached, and I was told this time that The Prospector was going to die, but that if I would run it I could have the other interests at fifty cents on the dollar. So I have the other interests at fifty cents on the dollar. So I tossed my hat into the ring."

The rumble of a press is no new sound to Bagg, as his father was founder of the Detroit *Tribune*. However. the *Tombstone Epitaph* is the established paper in the town and offers competition. Numerous other papers have been born in Tombstone only to fall prey to financial ruin. The same fate seems to await Bagg's paper, the *Tombstone Prospector*.

171

The *Prospector* is published daily except Sunday. The Sunday funny papers are still unknown so no readers object to the editor's taking one day a week off.

Few, if any, early newspapers can survive financially on the income received from advertisers. To supplement their meager incomes, the journalists do job printing for local businesses. One of the most lucrative of this type is the printing for the county. The endless forms and notices insure their printer a goodly amount of work and profit. Now the county is supposed to let all the work go to the printer who makes the lowest bid. Editor Bagg submits his bid for this work. This is where his difficulties begin.

"The county job printing is the velvet of the business at this time. So I placed my bid before the supervisors. The Epitaph was the other bidder. Although my bid was less than half that of my rival, the contract was awarded to The Epitaph. I commenced suit to enjoin the supervisors from awarding the contract.

"The hearing is before Judge Barnes, a resident of Illinois, who had just been appointed district judge for the southern district of Arizona. He decides that the board of supervisors is within its rights and that it is not compelled to let the contract to the lowest bidder."

Bagg doesn't take his defeat in court without a protest. "I criticize this decision editorially in a humorous vein and am arrested and taken before the court and declared in contempt and sentenced to pay $300 or spend 300 days in jail." Bagg refuses to pay the fine, choosing to go to jail in the hopes of gaining public support.

Some confusion now clouds the record. Though the name of a Mr. Peck appears as editor of the *Tombstone Epitaph,* and Bagg is the editor of the *Prospector,* the following editorial is found in the *Epitaph*:

THE CROWNING INFAMY!

The Editor of the Epitaph is Thrown into
Jail for Daring to Defend his Rights
as an American Citizen

The latest news in relation to the persecution against
S. C. Bagg for daring to express his opinion of the actions

of Judge Barnes and the county ring which has flourished and fattened off the people's money during the past year, will be a startling revelation to the people of Arizona, who in the past have submitted to many outrages, but never before has the right of free speech and free press been denied them. It has remained for a lawyer from the interior of Illinois to construe the laws so as to deprive them of the most sacred priveleges granted by the Constitution of our country. In his inaugural address Thomas Jefferson, the author of the Declaration of Independence, said: "Freedom of the press; freedom of person under the protection of habeas corpus; and trial by juries impartially selected — these principles form the bright constellation which has gone before us, and guided our steps through an age of revolution and reformation."

We doubt whether this case has a parallel in modern jurisprudence, a case where the proprietor and editor of a newspaper is fined and imprisoned without trial by jury for exposing corruption of public officers, who betrayed the trust imposed upon them by the people for their own personal gain and aggrandisement. It is an established principle in law that the acts of public officials are subject to criticism, whether it be orally or through the medium of the press. Deny the people of this right and you throw open the doors to corruption without check or hinderance upon those whom they have elected to serve them. A man who betrays a trust in private life loses the respect of his fellowmen, but doubly heineous if the act in (sic) one who wilfully and maliciously betrays both private and public trusts. In such case it is not only the right but the absolute duty of the press to expose the evil doer in his unlawful acts, to hold him up to the scorn of the public, and insist upon his punishment for the laws he has violated and the trusts he has ignored . . .

(*Tombstone Epitaph* of July 27, 188-)

Turning the *Prospector* over to his printers, Bagg walks over to the jail to serve his 300-day sentence. He doesn't consider the matter very seriously for he later says: "I went to jail with the thought that I soon would get out without difficulty. But I was wrong. I soon discovered that I was hog-tied. My attorney, Colonel William Herring told me that any attorney who took the case could never practice successfully afterward in Judge Barnes' court. Other attorneys told me the same thing. Sheriff Slaughter, a personal friend of mine, declined to let me sleep in his office as Barnes had instructed him to lock me up and treat me like other criminals.

"That night as I rolled in my blankets on the hard floor I took an oath that I would unhorse the doers of the outrage if I died in the process."

Friends of the editor however are working for his release. Two cronies make the rounds of business houses, collecting money to pay the editor's fine. Citizens willingly contribute, for ". . . S. C. Bagg has been making a fight for clean government in Cochise county and has been thrown in jail for so doing. . . ."

Though the editor is released after spending only three days in jail, he turns his energies toward unseating the Democratically controlled government of the county. He says, "I have been a life-long Democrat and as much as I dislike to do it, I turn over the editorial columns of my paper to the Republican central committee. The wound caused by my incarceration is festering, and I feel the end justified by means." (sic)

As an election is approaching, Bagg has every opportunity to put his plans into action. "I gather a mass of testimony against the powerful interests at the court house and give it publicity plus." The campaign is successful, for Bagg gleefully writes, "At the election every man of the bunch who had gloated over my incarceration is put out of office. Judge Barnes remains and I make his political life such a burden for him to carry that he writes Delegate Marcus A. Smith, at Washington, asking him to use his influence to have me stop my criticism."

The Judge doesn't receive much aid from the delegate. Instead, Smith forwards the letter to Editor Bagg with this notation on it: "Do as you see fit." This is all the encouragement that Bagg needs and in the coming years he needles the judge at every opportunity.

Since Bagg's trouble began when the *Tombstone Epitaph* received the county's job printing, the editor decides to buy this opposition paper. That will prevent any future debates as to who gets the county's business.

Now editor of both the *Epitaph* and the *Prospector,* Bagg continues his crusade against the present territorial officials.

174

Other editors have criticized the officials, including Governor Hughes, calling them "Patronage peddlers, land grant sharks, assassins and looters." For such writing as this, J. O. Dunbar and J. H. McClintock of the *Gazette* in Phoenix soon find themselves indicted for criminal libel. Bagg offers this encouragement to his fellow journalists.

A FELLOW FEELING

The editor of the Gazette (in Phoenix) has the sympathy of the editor of the PROSPECTOR in the hours of his illness. He is suffering from a painful attack of neuralgia in the face, brought on, no doubt, by contact with the death-dealing atmosphere of a dungeon. A fellow feeling makes us wondrous kind.

For six years the PROSPECTOR man (Bagg) has been suffering from an acute attack of gout, brought on by overindulgence in prison fare while confined in the bastile of Cochise county.

John, we have a common enemy to fight. We were both placed there by the same agent. When your neuralgia and our gout troubles us most we are apt to think thoughts not complimentary to Judge Barnes. Although he used a different method of getting you in the toils than he did us, you "got thar just the same." . . .

(*Tombstone Epitath* of Nov. 12, 1893)

Politicians are not the only ones who heap abuse upon editors. Bagg suggests:

Any citizen who feels himself aggrieved at a publisher of a newspaper for a wrong, whether real or imaginary, has the courts open to him for redress. No fair newspaper man will object to such a course on the part of any citizen. It is far preferable to the plan of going for the editor with a club or sandbagging him on his way home from prayer meeting.

(*Tombstone Epitaph* of Nov. 5, 1893)

The troubles encountered by an editor are endless. Bagg believes, though, that most of his problems and those of the community will be solved if Arizona can become a state. Territorial government allows too much room for corruption and mismanagement. So when a convention meets in 1891 to draw up a constitution for the proposed state of Arizona, Bagg's paper is filled with enthusiastic comments.

Statehood for New Mexico means statehood for Arizona. By barking incessantly at the heels of Congress it will eventually take us in to get rid of us.

We hear of many statehood mass meetings but no anti-statehood demonstration has yet been made. The anti-constitution men are at work though in a quiet way.

It will be the question of statehood for Arizona, and not the adoption or rejection of a constitution, at the polis (sic) next december.

Arizona will be the 45th state in the union. This is authentic.

Though the citizens of the Arizona Territory vote overwhelmingly for the proposed constitution, there are many stumbling blocks. Utah is admitted as the 45th state, followed in a few years by Oklahoma and New Mexico. Other constitutional conventions are called but Arizona still remains a territory. Numerous obstacles must be overcome and even the chaplain of one of the conventions becomes apprehensive and prays, ". . . Lord, we hope that President Taft will not turn down the Constitution for a little thing like the initiative and referendum; Lord, don't let him be so narrow and partisan as to refuse us self-government." It will take 21 years for Arizona to be admitted to the Union as the 48th state, on February 14, 1912.

While the fight for Arizona statehood drags on slowly, the Tombstone editor turns his attention to local affairs. The people must be economically stable or Arizona will always remain a territory. Though Tombstone is the center of mining operations, news items in the *Prospector* show that it is rapidly becoming an agricultural center.

A large load of peaches was brought in from Berner's ranch Tuesday night and was bought by Frank Wolcott.

176

H. Kimball came up from Fairbanks today, bringing a load of new potatoes.

Forty pound, Arizona-grown watermelons are now common in the Tucson market.

In Phenix, (*sic*) a good family watermelon, large enough for five persons, is now sold for ten cents.

A rancher from Gila Bend brought in today a couple hundred pounds of Muscat grapes. They are large, juicy, and finely flavored. Wolcott purchased the bulk of the load.

The second crop of strawberries are coming in in good quantities from the Huachuca mountains.

Quite a number of residents of St. David came up today, bringing with them fruit and vegetables, chickens and eggs.

Peaches ten inches in circumference and at the same time of delicate flavor, is the kind of fruit Tombstone soil and climate can produce, as was demonstrated by Commissioner Swain who placed some choice ones on our table this morning.

Several loads of wheat were brought up from the river yesterday and disposed of to our merchants.

W. T. Fowler came in from Lesis' Springs Saturday evening bringing a load of hay for Dr. Holcombe.

H. C. Herrick had about 70 acres of waving wheat on his Fairbank ranch this season and has just completed cutting ten acres to be threshed and milled. The balance was cut for hay.

Southeastern Arizona has been the scene of farming activity for thousands of years. The food-gathering prehistoric Indians known as the Cochise culture are believed to have inhabited the region as early as 10,000 years ago. These people, however, were not farmers but lived on nuts, herbs, and native plants. The Hohokam, another prehistoric culture, were the first to cultivate plants and irrigate the land. At the time of Christ they were planting fields of corn, beans, cotton, and native tobacco. For unknown reasons these people abandoned the area after some six centuries.

Some of the earliest white farmers in this locality did not plant crops but, rather, cut native hay which they sold to the Army for horse feed. Where the prehistoric Indians' lives depended on a constant source of water, white farmers face a greater danger in the warring Apaches. The Indians usually emerge victorious whenever white and red man meet for they know the terrain and have the element of surprise on their side. King Woolsey, though, is one farmer who beats the Apache at his own game.

By trickery, Woolsey has killed almost 100 of these Indians. Nor do the Apaches fare very well in open warfare against this man. One such attack is made on Woolsey while he and two hired hands are taking a wagonload of hay to an Army post. A writer of the day gives this version of the fight.

"They have but one gun with them which by good luck rather than precaution is charged with buck-shot. In emerging from the bushes, where the road approaches the point of the sand hill, a terrific yell bursts upon them, and in a moment the Apaches spring up from their ambush and charge upon them like so many devils incarnate.

"Woolsey says: 'Hold the mules, boys, and give me the gun!' which they do with great coolness.

"The Indians wheel about and dodge, but keep shooting their arrows with such fearful dexterity that Woolsey thinks it advisable to give them a load of buckshot. The distance is too great, and no damage is done. At this the savages renew their diabolical yells; closer and closer they crowd, the brave little handful of whites standing coolly by the wagon and mules, ready to sell their lives as dearly as possible.

"The leader of the Apaches, a warrior of gigantic stature and hideous features, rushes forward brandishing his warclub, and calls upon his men to follow. Woolsey waits until the chief has approached within 20 paces, when he discharges the other barrel of his gun. Down tumbles the yelling savage, with a hole through his head. In the panic and confusion that follows, it is deemed advisable, as there is no more ammunition, to cut loose the mules and retire to the station. Here they procure additional forces and arm themselves. Returning as soon as possible to the

178

scene of the conflict, they find that the cowardly wretches who had attempted to murder them have fled, not even taking time to destroy the wagon. The chief lays just where he had fallen, stiff and stark, as peaceable an Indian as one could wish to meet of a summer's afternoon.

"Woolsey and his party determine to make a conspicuous mark of the dead chief, from which marauding Indians might take warning. They drag it to the nearest mesquite tree and hang it up by the neck, leaving the feet to dangle about a yard from the ground."[1]

If the pioneer farmer is beset with difficulty, even more so is the rancher. While the rancher is troubled, too, by lack of water and attacks by the Indians, he has the additional worry of protecting his property from rustlers. Ranching, though, can be profitable, as illustrated by these two items in the Tombstone paper.

> Cattlemen in the Oaks and Willows near Prescott, who have been rounding up beef steers for shipment to Kansas, have had to stop on account of the railroad tie-up. The Perrin Cattle company had rounded up 500 head and started for the railroad. Prices offered were $8, $12, and $16 for yearlings, two-year-olds and three-year-olds.

> The outlook for good stock and plenty in Arizona was never better than at present. The increase this year will be very nearly 100 per cent. There is hardly a cow on the ranges but that is accompanied by a bouncing, frisky calf.

One of the earliest and certainly most persistent ranchers in the area is Pete Kitchen. According to the historian, Dr. Lockwood, "Kitchen is a rough charcoal sketch of a civilized man — a sort of connecting link between savagery and civilization. He is about five feet ten inches in height, spare, erect, and even when verging toward old age physically fit. He is of florid complexion with eyes of grayish blue. Usually he wears a broadbrimmed sombrero, and instead of an overcoat, a Mexican serape."

This indomitable rancher remains at a time when "ranch after ranch is desolated by fire, robbery, and murder. Here are fields with torndown fences; houses burned or racked to pieces by violence, the walls cast about in heaps over the once-pleasant

179

homes; everywhere ruin, grim and ghastly with associations of sudden death."

Kitchen's continued operation of his ranch is not due to any fault of the Apaches. They do their best. A newspaper account gives some reasons for the rancher's success. "The Apaches have endeavored to take his place many times — one partner, and all his neighbors, have been murdered, and last summer his boy was killed within gunshot of his door. Instead of being frightened or discouraged by those bold and numerous attacks, he seems only the more determined to stand his ground and take his chances. The Indians have learned to their sorrow that in him they have no insignificant foe. He never travels the same route twice in succession, and he always sleeps with one eye open; therefore, ambushes and surprises do not win on him worth a cent."

Hogs rather than cattle roam the vast Kitchen ranch. There is a large demand in the Southwest for bacon and ham and Kitchen's hams are famous from Texas to the Pacific coast. To operate the ranch and the business, Kitchen establishes a virtual one-family community.

An early visitor to the homestead has this to say. "Pete Kitchen's 'ranch' has all the airs of a feudal castle in the days of chivalry. Pete Kitchen has probably had more contests with Indians than any other settler in America . . .

"Approaching Pete Kitchen's ranch, one finds himself in a fertile valley, with a small hillock near one extremity. Upon the summit of this has been built the house from which no effort of the Apaches has ever succeeded in driving our friend. There is a sentinel posted on the roof, there is another out in the "cienaga" with the stock, and the men ploughing in the bottom are obliged to carry rifles, cocked and loaded, swung to the plough handle. Every man and boy is armed with one or two revolvers on hip.

"Everything speaks of a land of warfare and bloodshed. The title of 'Dark and Bloody Ground' never fairly belonged to Kentucky. Kentucky never was anything except a Sunday-school convention in comparison with Arizona, every mile of whose surface could tell its tale of horror were the stones and gravel, the sagebrush and mescal, the mesquite and the yucca, only endowed with speech for one brief hour.

180

"Within the hospitable walls of the Kitchen home the traveller is made to feel perfectly at ease. If food is not already on the fire, some of the women set about the preparation of the savory and spicy stews for which the Mexicans are deservedly famous, and others knead the dough and pat into shape the paper-like tortillas with which to eat the juicy frijoles or dip up the tempting chile colorado. There are women carding, spinning, sewing — doing the thousand and one duties of domestic life in a great ranch, which has its own blacksmith, saddler, and wagon-maker, and all other officials needed to keep the machinery running smoothly.

"Between Pete Kitchen and the Apaches a ceaseless war is waged, with the advantages not all on the side of Kitchen. His employees are killed and wounded, his stock driven away, his pigs filled with arrows, making the suffering quadrupeds look like perambulating pin-cushions — everything that can be thought of to drive him away; but there he stays, unconquered and unconquerable."[2]

When ranchers are of Kitchen's caliber they'll tackle almost anything or anybody. Lawyers and "fancy words," however, are two things which give them trouble. A dispute over water rights is taken to court and this is where the uneducated ranchers, are stumped. They must have water to stay alive, yet the court will not give them an answer. Confused, the ranchers seek the advice of Editor Bagg in Tombstone. The journalist takes up their fight and angrily demands action.

The ranchers along the San Pedro river are anxiously awaiting for Judge Barnes to render his decision in the water cases. He has certainly had ample time to make up his mind which way he wants to jump, and the people who have their all dependant upon his ruling have a right to know where they stand . . . Judge Barnes, render a decision if you have a spark of manhood in you, and relieve these settlers from the uncertainity hovering over their homes, which the law of decency, common sense and justice demands and has a right to expect from one who took an oath to "do unto others as he would that others should to unto him."

(*Tombstone Prospector* of July 13, 1889)

While protecting their scanty water supply, the pioneer ranchers must also fight for their grassland. Though cattle from one ranch sometimes wander into a neighbor's territory, there is almost no conflict. Throughout the history of the frontier, discord between ranchers is insignificant when compared to the violent conflicts between cattlemen and sheep owners.

The old question of cattle vs. sheep explodes in all its fury with the Pleasant Valley War of Arizona. The war finally evolves as a blood feud and for cruelty and violence it equals or surpasses the war in Lincoln County, New Mexico, the sheep and cattle wars of Wyoming, and the well-known Hatfield-McCoy feud of Kentucky and West Virginia.

The two leading factions of the Pleasant Valley feud are the Graham and Tewksbury families. A slight animosity between the two is fanned into a hellish war when the Tewksburys drive sheep over the forested Mogollon Rim and into Pleasant Valley. Though both these families own cattle ranches in the valley, the Grahams, ex-Iowa farmers, decide to fight rather than let the valley's luxuriant range grass be destroyed by sheep. Other ranchers in the valley join forces with the Grahams against former Bostonian Tewksbury and his three sons.

The most barbaric incident of the five-year feud is the Grahams' attack on the Tewksbury ranch. On a fall morning in 1887, the attackers strike without warning. John Tewksbury Jr. and his partner, William Jacobs, are caught in the open at the onset of the attack. Running for the safety of the ranch house, they are gunned down just short of their goal.

Within the shelter of the ranch house are John Tewksbury Sr., his wife, two sons, an infant, and possibly a fourth man. From the ferocity of the attack it seems that the Grahams are intent on wiping out the Tewksburys "to the last man." While steady bursts of gunfire break the morning silence, a herd of hogs root around the bodies of the two fallen men. The Tewskbury men dare not leave the cabin to save their dead from the jaws of the hogs for the cattlemen will not grant a burial truce.

Then above the sound of shooting rises a woman's scream. In a moment, Mrs. Tewksbury steps through the ranch door, a shovel in hand. Silence drops like a blanket over the mountainside as the ambushers cease fire. Killing men is one thing but frontier chivalry demands that a woman must never be harmed.

182

Swinging her shovel, this woman drives the hogs from her son's body and that of his comrade. She hurriedly scoops out a shallow grave and rolls the men into it. Her mission completed, she returns to the besieged cabin and the battle is renewed. The defenders of the cabin are finally rescued from an almost certain death by the unexpected arrival of a sheriff's posse.

By the close of the war some 27 men have been killed and seven others wounded. The Graham family suffers the heaviest casualties, with Tom Graham the only survivor. Then Tom's wife persuades him to leave Pleasant Valley, for the Tewksburys make almost daily attempts to kill the last of the Grahams. Tom and his wife establish a new ranch just a few miles from Phoenix. Hating the years of manhunting during the war, he no longer wears a gun.

His peaceful life is short-lived for he is cut down from ambush in August of 1892. The ex-leader of the cattlemen, however, lives long enough to identify his assassins as Edward Tewksbury and his brother-in-law, John Rhodes. Sickened by the renewal of the feud, ranchers and citizens throughout the Territory demand justice.

The accused men are arrested. Angry citizens attempt to lynch Rhodes but their efforts are thwarted by quick-thinking law officers. After a lengthy trial, Tewksbury is found guilty of first degree murder but escapes punishment on a legal technicality. Though Rhodes is given a preliminary hearing, there is no indication of his ever being brought to trial.

The territorial papers have a field day during the preliminary hearings. The widow of the slain man provides the drama. When witnesses to the crime identify Rhodes as the killer, Mrs. Graham draws a hidden revolver which belonged to her husband. Pressing the gun into Rhodes' back, she pulls the trigger. The gun misfires and before she can fire again startled officials seize the weapon.

The trials also provide the journalists with an opportunity to offer a lot of advice. The pros and cons of the case are debated more loudly perhaps by the editors than the lawyers. The *Tucson Citizen* is particularly guilty of trial by newspaper. Growing tired of all the editorializing on the subject, Tombstone Editor Bagg has just one comment on the subject.

183

The Tucson Citizen has tried Rhodes, who is charged
with killing Graham and acquitted him.
(*Tombstone Prospector* of Aug. 18, 1892)

While the Tewksburys and Grahams were feuding in the
northern part of the Territory, Tombstone, too, has been fighting for its life. Though the population of the town has increased
to 1,875 by 1890 compared to 973 at the census of 1880, Tombstone seems to be fighting a losing battle. Hoping the future
will brighten, citizens remain and there is little change in community life as evidenced by these items in the *Prospector*.

Skating at the rink to-night.

Yom Kipper today. Its observation was general among
the Jewish residents of Tombstone.

During the week past, many improvements of a permanent nature have been arranged for the Can Can Res-
taurant. Everything in and around the house which has a
fault, has been or is to be made perfect. The management
(*sic*) are always ready to give their customers a good share
of improved accommodations which is in in (*sic*) turn ap-
preciated. To-morrow being Sunday, a most sumptuous re-
past has been arranged for those who dine out on that day.
The choicest of fowl, of meats and vegetables, and in fact
much more than the home market supplies, will be supplied. No extra price is charged at this house on these
occasions.

There will be an examination of teachers on Monday
night.

Do not neglect to Attend the Thomas concert to-
morrow night. The rawhide band will furnish the music
and is alone well worth going to hear.

The Thomas concert to-morrow night at Schieffelin
hall will be a local affair which cannot fail to be appre-
ciated by the Tombstone public. There is no town in the
territory which can furnish such an array of vocal and instrumental talent as can Tombstone, and our people have
never been backward in supporting their efforts by their
presence and commendation.

The failure to obtain a railroad is one cause for the town's gloom. Editor Bagg of the *Prospector* had led the fight and many were the enthusiastic articles in his paper.

The editor's best efforts are not enough and his pet project is defeated. He realizes that Tombstone is about to become a cow camp rather that the "queen city of Arizona." Bagg's opponents on the issue receive full credit for their victory in this editorial.

VICTORY

But not for the People.

The Back Sliders and Old Fogies Defeat The Railroad Project.

Ever since the railroad to Bisbee was talked of there has been an uncertainty as to whether it would come through Tombstone or sidetrack it. The latter has been accomplished through the machination of combined capitol, which would have been endangered by the advancement of civilization in the shape of a railroad to Tombstone.

News was received yesterday from Mr. Ben Williams, Supt. of the Copper Queen mines, that the managers of the railroad enterprises had decided owing to the increased cost of building the road by way of Tombstone, and the small amount subscribed by the people to build the road by the river route. The road will be commenced immediately and finished into Bisbee by October 30th.

We congratulate the people of Bisbee and Fairbanks on their good fortune in securing the great advantages which will accrue to them by the building of the road.

(*Tombstone Prospector* of June 23, 1888)

Following the defeat of the railroad, the town is plunged still further into despair by news of water in the mines. An unusual season of heavy rains combines with a twist of fate to fill the numerous mine shafts with water. With the town depending so heavily on mining for economic prosperity, Editor Bagg reprints an editorial from another territorial paper and captions it:

FULL OF TRUTH

If the proper pumping machinery be put in the Tombstone mines that town will enjoy an era of permanent
prosperity never before known to Cochise county. Millions
have been taken out but millions yet remain in the deeper
workings and will be unearthed, we hope, in the near
future. In no country under the sun, outside of Arizona,
would such known richness be allowed to lie year in and
year out, without an effort being made for its extraction.
We sincerely trust that the new movement in that direction will speedly materialize. — *Citizen*.

(Tombstone Prospector of Sept. 11, 1891)

Pumps are tried but the muddy water oozes back into the
tunnels as fast as the motors syphon it out. Tombstone becomes
only a shell of its former self. Even Editor Bagg is discouraged
and plans to sell out. Shortly before leaving with his wife and
son for California, Bagg receives news of an old friend. Bagg
gleefully writes:

TAKING HIS MEDICINE
Ex-Judge Barnes Goes Behind
the Bars for Ten Days for
Contempt of Court.

A telegram received at this office last night announced
the commitment of W. H. Barnes to jail in Tucson for a
term of ten days for contempt of court.

Upon receipt of this news the editor of the **PROSPECTOR**
sent the following dispatch of sympathy:

> W. H. Barnes, County jail Tucson.
> Are you thar, Mariority?
> (signed) S. C. Bagg

---

1 Brown, J. Ross; *A Tour Through Arizona 1864*, (reprinted, Tucson, Arizona
Silhouettes, 1951).
2 Bourke, John G; op. cit.

"White chief of the Apaches"

No tombstone is complete without its epitaph. . . . — John
P. Clum

THE RETURN OF THE OLD NAN-TAN

A few years ago, at Rice, on the San Carlos Indian
reservation, an aged Apache buck was jogging along on
horseback. An elderly American called to him across a
distance of about 100 yards, addressing the rider as "Sneezer," at the same time motioning him to approach.

The old buck looked puzzled. A younger Indian yelled
— "Nan-Tan Be-Tun — ee-kiay!" — and a riderless horse
was left behind as the old buck sprang to the ground,

187

running, to throw himself into the arms of his old nan-tan of more than a half century.

John P. Clum, first civilian Indian agent at San Carlos, from 1874 to 1877, had come back to see his old pals and to chat with them in the Apache dialect after an absence of 52 years. The meeting with Sneezer was the first of a number of affectionate encounters with old Indians that day. The ordinary stolidity of Apache countenances changed and smiles wreathed happy faces . . .

The custom of using descriptive nomenclature, as practiced by Indians, led the Apaches at San Carlos to designate a prematurely bald young agent, in the middle of the '70's, as "the boss with the white brow" — Nan-Tan Be-Tun-ee-kiay.

On this visit in the fall of 1929 to the scenes of his early life in Arizona, John Clum relives many episodes of that life. It seems only yesterday and not 55 years ago that he first entered the Territory.

Born of Holland Dutch parents, Clum spent his boyhood days on a farm in the Hudson River Valley in New York. Finishing his studies at a military academy, the 18-year-old youth entered Rutgers College. Here he plunged into studies, yet devoted time to outdoor sports as well. Football was the rage of Rutgers, and Clum managed to be on the team when it clashed with the Princeton squad for the first time. No one remembers the score but it is believed that this game was the third intercollegiate football clash in the United States.

Clum's chief desire while a freshman at Rutgers was to become an oarsman. Freshmen were not allowed on the varsity crew, so the blond, six-footer organized a freshman crew.

Unfortunately, Clum became a victim of rheumatism from exposure to bad weather. Since he had been working in the summertime as a farm hand to pay for his college, the rheumatism prevented any further farm work and put an end to his college career after his sophomore year. Though his parents hoped he would become a minister, history planned otherwise.

Clum's first job is with the meteorological service of the United States.[1] Appointed an observer-sergeant in the U. S. Signal Corps, he is sent to Santa Fe, New Mexico in 1871. He travels by railroad to the end of the tracks at Kit Carson, Colorado. Completing the last 300 miles of his trip by stagecoach, Clum reaches Santa Fe just a few days after celebrating his 20th birthday.

His stay in the Old Pueblo is almost uneventful, though Clum, prematurely bald and 21 does manage to become the unofficial governor of New Mexico. It all comes about when the real governor is called to Washington on official business. Clum's official actions seem to be limited to moving into the "Governor's Palace" and receiving the salutes of the populace.

In 1873 Clum receives an offer that is destined to bring him to Arizona. The Dutch Reformed Church, which has assumed the responsibility for Apache welfare, asks Clum, a member of the church, to become Indian agent at the San Carlos Reservation in Arizona. Clum takes his time in considering the matter, for the last agent barely escaped with his life and the Indians are reported in a state of open warfare.

Possessing a seemingly limitless amount of courage and humor, Clum takes the job. The most he can lose in Arizona is his life, and what Apache can scalp a bald man? Selecting the most accessible route from Santa Fe to Arizona at the time, Clum backtracks to St. Louis where he catches the train for San Francisco. He travels by steamship from the Bay City to San Diego, thence by stagecoach to Tucson. From here it is only a 125-mile horseback ride to the San Carlos Reservation.

Some might call Clum an idealist, while others might attribute his optimism to the inexperience of youth. He feels that the Apaches have been ill-treated, and that understanding coupled with honesty will bring an end to the Indian problem. The new agent is shocked by the official record of white and Indian contact. The government in the last nine years has spent $38,000,000 to subdue the Apaches, yet has been able to "exterminate" less than 100 of them. Such things as the Johnson Massacre, the betrayal of Cochise, the treacherous death of Mangas Coloradas, and the Camp Grant Massacre have taught the Indians that it doesn't pay to trust the white man. No wonder the Apaches are again on the warpath.

With such thoughts the new agent arrives at San Carlos. The building housing the agency headquarters is constructed of poles and mud. The roof is of mud. "Low ceiling, paneless holes in walls for windows, doors of canvas tacked on frames of poles, with hinges of rope, or strips of leather from the leg of some

189

discarded boot, and a dirt floor," make the place look even more disreputable. The few pieces of furniture in the room have been crudely constructed from discarded army packing boxes.

The new agent doesn't take time to fix up the agency but chooses to call for a big smoke. Several days later some 700 Apaches gather for the powwow at which this latest agent will talk.

After the preliminary formality of smoking in silence, the conference proceeds. The suspicious Indians can hardly believe their ears when Clum announces that he is forming an Indian police, establishing an Indian court with Apaches as judges, and building a jail to be guarded by Apaches. The Indians begin to snap out of their former apathy and even obey Clum's order to surrender all their weapons. Perhaps, here is a white man who can be trusted.

Though most of the violent Apache warfare has ceased by the time Clum becomes agent, the hills are still filled with renegade bands of Apaches, and even those on reservations do pretty much as they please.

Clum's program calls for discipline, self-government, and fair dealing. Such ideas are unheard of in the West and the citizens put up a howl of protest. The very idea of trouble-making savages being arrested by Apache police and tried by an Apache court, even though Clum is the chief justice of that body! The man is crazy!

Though Clum's whole approach is revolutionary, he quickly wins the confidence of the Indians. At first, the police force is composed of four men. Finding it difficult to pronounce their Apache names, Clum gives them nicknames, "Sneezer," "Goody-Goody," and "Nosey." The fourth officer, Tauelclyee, won't stand for such nonsense and Clum struggles along with the Apache name.

The policemen soon report an illegal Apache moonshine party in the neighboring hills. This is a definite violation of reservation law. Clum's faith in his police is quickly justified when he leads them on a midnight raid against the lawbreakers. Eleven prisoners are taken and returned to the agency head-quarters under guard by native police. The accused are found guilty by the court and are sentenced to 15 days hard labor by their fellow Apaches. The prisoners begin their sentence under the watchful eyes of Apache guards. Any doubting Indians now know that Agent Clum means business.

An agent is supposed to keep under control the Indians placed in his charge. This is his sole job. Clum, however, is so successful that he is called upon to lead his ever-growing band of native policemen against white outlaws in the region and against bands of renegade Apaches that the Army hasn't been able to capture. Seven hundred Apaches were under Clum's charge when he first became agent at San Carlos but within four years he is the white chief of some 5,000.

Five bands of the Apache nation are now on the San Carlos Reservation. Though these tribes have all fought against the whites, there has always been considerable hostility between the individual tribes as well. Their great chiefs — Cochise, Mangas Coloradas and others — who might keep order between the bands are now dead. In spite of these obstacles, Clum, with the aid of his Indian police, manages to keep order. The agent's biggest task, however, still lies ahead of him.

It is standard procedure on the frontier to have the military forces guard all reservations. Troops, however, are withdrawn from San Carlos — Clum's police maintain perfect order. Outside the reservation, several bands of renegade Apaches are still murdering and plundering. Citizens of Arizona demand action. Since the military has been unable to capture or kill the warring Apaches, the Territorial Legislature of Arizona appropriates $10,000 and authorizes the governor to organize a state militia of 60 men for this purpose.

The governor doesn't call on ranchers and miners but turns to Agent Clum. Can 60 Apache policemen be spared to serve as militiamen? Clum consults with his men. The Apache lawmen and Clum agree to the plan, providing the Apache chief of police is their commanding officer. Governor Safford readily agrees, and so it is that Apache policemen form the first Arizona National Guard.

Since the renegades forage in Arizona, but flee into Old Mexico when pursued, the militia meets with little success. As state troops they cannot invade a foreign country. Something must be done. Again the aid of Clum is sought.

Word has been received that Geronimo, war chief of the Chiricahuas, and his band are raiding in New Mexico. Will

Clum and his policemen try to capture this renegade and his band? Though some 5,000 U. S. troops have been in the field against Geronimo and his 100 warriors, the wily chief seems to rob, plunder, and murder at will. The agent agrees to pursue the outlaw band but requests the return of the Apaches in the militia. He will need all the men he can get for such an attempt.

On a March morning in 1877, Clum and 100 of his policemen start for Silver City, New Mexico. The men are on foot and their goal is 400 miles away. Such a march is an undertaking in itself. Before the campaign is completed, Clum and his men have not only placed Geronimo and his subchiefs in irons, and taken into custody his band of 300, but also have effected the surrender of Chief Victorio and his band of 400. This has been accomplished by the diplomacy of the agent and the skillfulness of his police. Not one belligerent nor policemen has been wounded or killed in the process. (Ed. Note: The reader will find a detailed account of the above action in *Apache Agent* by Woodworth Clum.)

Clum, as per his instructions, starts back for the San Carlos Reservation with his shackled prisoners and their 800 followers. The march is again made on foot and the trip is further complicated by an outbreak of smallpox. The 25-year-old agent, however, reaches the reservation without letting a prisoner escape. Geronimo and the other ringleaders are placed in the guardhouse.

Unfortunately, politics wrecks most of the good work that Clum has so painstakingly built up. Geronimo, for some unknown reason, is released and will again strike terror into the hearts of Arizona citizens before old age makes him want to surrender. Then it will be on his own terms because Agent Clum will be the only white man to "capture" the murderer.

In hopes of promoting better understanding between white man and red, Clum takes his police to the nation's capital. Nor are citizens of Arizona neglected in the indoctrination program. In the excellent biography of Clum, *Apache Agent,* is an account of a stopover in Tucson. Since Clum and his 54 policemen are preparing to go in pursuit of renegade Apaches, they are armed for war.

Agent Clum says: "A committee of Tucson's leading businessmen comes to me with a request for an Apache war dance. I

192

consult my Indians, and find them not only willing, but enthusiastic. A load of firewood is hauled to the center of the old military plaza. As soon as it is dark, the campfire is kindled. Under a full moon, spectators file into the plaza by hundreds, until we have an audience of 3,000. Appear the actors, 35 redskins stripped to their waists, bodies and faces hideous with smears of warpaint: fantastic headgear; bearing lances and shields, bows and arrows, or rifles, according to the act assigned. Redskin chanters; musicians with tom-toms. First comes the 'instigation scene,' in which one lithe dancer performs gracefully with lance and shield. Gradually the number of participants increases, until the campfire is circled by a score of wildly gesticulating Apaches, of ferocious aspects. The night air is vibrant with blood-curdling warhoops. The committee had expressed its desire for a realistic spectacle, and when I observe the audience gradually retreating from the lunging, howling Apaches, I suspect that the presentation is becoming a bit too realistic. Chief Justice French edges his way to my side.

" 'Clum,' he urges, 'hadn't you better stop this before the Indians get beyond your control?'

"Adopting somewhat the style of John Paul Jones, I reply:

" 'Judge, we have just begun to dance.'

"Now we approach the climax, for which our audience is wholly unprepared. None of the citizens knew that I had supplied *blank* cartridges for each rifle in the custody of this apparently frantic bunch of savages. Suddenly comes the sharp crack of a rifle, keen, clear, above the din of the dance. This is the signal for a chorus of super-yells; then the fusillade — nerve-racking explosions from 20 additional rifles, fired in volleys, in rapid succession. Meanwhile, the vocal efforts and athletic contortions of our redskin entertainers approach the peak of noise and confusion. To the spectators it looks as if these unleashed Apaches are running amuck. Fortunately, the old military plaza affords ample exits for our audience, and the audience literally takes to its heels. Soon we have the entire plaza to ourselves. For 10 or 15 minutes we perform, alone in our glory. But as we have arranged a full programme of events, we decide to go through with it. The show ends with a final salvo from the rifles.

"Then my redskin actors transform themselves immediately into well-trained, decorous Apache scouts. The company forms

193

at 'attention.' I thank them on behalf of the departed audience, and dismiss them. Of course, we all have a good laugh over the timidity of the citizens. By this time, the citizens, who have been watching the finale from behind adobe walls and deep shadows in the distance, conclude we are safe and sane, return by groups to the plaza, and congratulate us on our very vivid and realistic portrayal. We are in Tucson several days, and so pleased are the citizens with the general deportment of my company of Apaches, that they raise a purse by popular subscription and supply my Indians with uniforms of white pants, red shirts, and obsolete army hats."

Clum proves that white and Indian can live in peace. The Army, however, decides that soldiers will again guard the reservation. Clum protests, because the Apache has been self-governing at San Carlos for the two years since the withdrawal of the troops. Again, this is a question of politics rather than policy. Preferring not to wait to see his work undone, Agent Clum brings his career to an abrupt end by resigning.

On his trip to Washington, Clum had married and Mrs. Clum had returned with him to the agency. After bidding his Apache friends farewell, Culm takes his bride of a few months to Tucson. The trip is made by buckboard.

No longer an agent of the government, Clum believes that the people should know of the political double-crossing which exists. If the Apaches are mistreated, they will flee the reservations and the war will start all over again. Now the best way to reach the people is through the newspaper, so Clum purchases the *Arizona Citizen* in November of 1877. Making his paper a daily, the first in the Territory, Editor Clum spends the next three years in denouncing corruption in the Army and government.

Then news of a silver strike at Tombstone reaches Tucson. Editor Clum decides to survey the mushrooming tent city. Wagons are pouring into the town in an endless flow, hundreds of tents are being pitched by their silver-hungry owners, and thousands of men claw the earth for her riches. Realizing that Tombstone may even exceed Tucson for size within a few months, Clum decides to sell the *Citizen* and open a paper in Tombstone. He writes:

Having decided upon the establishment of a newspaper

at Tombstone, the next important question for determination was the date of its appearance. After due consideration, May 1, 1880, was fixed upon as the Epitaph's natal day, with an issue of four pages of seven columns each. In view of the conditions prevailing at Tombstone I realized that the greatest problem confronting me was the matter of suitable building in which to house the new printing plant. Nevertheless inspired with the superior grade of optimism and confidence that often lures the young and robust into unforseen difficulties, I tackled the job.

Forthwith telegrams were dispatched to San Francisco ordering a Washington hand newspaper press — that old reliable friend of the pioneer publisher — type, cases, ink, etc., and a supply of printpaper. Then I boarded the stage for Tombstone (my home was still in Tucson) for the purpose of arranging for a building of some sort. There was no building available. Thereupon I purchased the lot on the north side of Fremont street and west of Fourth street, where the Epitaph was until recently located. But the building boom seemed to mock all my efforts for the erection of a suitable shelter for our plant.

PLANT RUSHED IN

It was then about the first of April. My equipment and supplies were at the end of the railroad and would be in Tombstone in a few days. In this extremity, and being greatly worried, I got very busy and, finally, was fortunate enough to contract for the immediate erection on our lot of a light skeleton frame measuring 20 by 40 feet. Hastening to Tucson I purchased sufficient heavy canvas to serve as a roof and walls for this temporary structure, and had this canvas sewed to fit the dimensions of the frame in course of construction. Rushing back to Tombstone, this canvas was then stretched over and around the frame and — PRESTO — before one might say "Jack Robinson" the Epitaph was provided with a shelter against the day of its birth.

When Friday morning dawned only two pages of the paper were off the press. The remaining two pages were still "in course of construction." Furthermore there still loomed hours of tedious and fatiguing "press work," menacing our strenuous efforts with defeat. But the gang was game, and every fellow "tightened his cinch" as the

195

saying goes, and settled down on the home-stretch with a grim determination that inspired all with the assurance that whatever might be the odds against us, we would achieve that which we had set out to accomplish.

Thus we trudged on all day Friday, and when the sable curtain of the night fell upon our canvas home we simply lighted those dear old kerosene lamps — and still trudged on. And when we had toiled diligently past the hour of mid-night we realized that we had no moments for sleep if we were to DEFEAT defeat.

PAPER BORN MAY 1, 1880

The dawn of Saturday saw the gang still on the job — worn and weary — but cheerful and smiling for the GOAL WAS IN SIGHT. But as yet there was not rest for the weary. Not yet, but soon. It was not until late in the afternoon of Saturday, May 1, 1880, that brave old Tom Sorrin (for it was he who served as pressman) took from the press the first impression of the last two pages of the issue — thus actually bringing into existence THE TOMBSTONE EPITAPH . . .

(Tombtone Epitaph of May 1, 1880)

At first, the *Epitaph* has three editors. Clum isn't taking any chances in case he is killed or disabled by some citizen on the rampage. Even though the town is "wide-open," Clum brings his wife and two-year-old son to the city. But tragedy strikes the Clums late in 1880. A week after giving birth to a baby girl, Mrs. Clum dies. The stricken editor buries his wife in "Boot Hill," the town's only cemetery.

The *Weekly Epitaph* becomes a daily newspaper after a few months. The town can certainly support a daily, for its population is already 7,000 and growing by the month. Money is comparatively free since miners usually receive $4 per day and shaft men $6. Jobs are always available in one of the 3,000 mining locations.

The *Epitaph* is not without opposition because the *Nugget* was the town's first paper. Clum is soon drawn into conflict with the opposition editor because of local politics. The cowboys and ranchers around Tombstone receive the *Nugget's* sup-

196

port while Clum joins forces with the business and mining interests of Tombstone.

At this time the town and surrounding countryside are being terrorized by gangs of lawless men. Hardly a day passes without a murder, theft, or scene of brutality. To combat these ruffians, a Law and Order League has been organized by the town's businessmen. Clum, a member of the Vigilantes, is nominated for mayor in the impending election. Though his opponent is backed by the *Nugget,* Clum is elected.

Using his power and authority as mayor and his prestige as editor, Clum begins a crusade to rid the town of its lawless element. Clum believes that most of the violence can be laid at the feet of gun-happy cowboys and a few renegade ranchers. He minces few words on these men, terming them gangsters, rustlers, and murderers. The *Nugget,* however, disagrees. The suspects aren't bad boys, just a bunch of cowboys having a little fun.

Knowing that two can play the same game, Clum readily identifies the perpetrator of each new crime as a cowboy, until the word becomes synonymous with outlaw throughout the entire Southwest. Every incident is carefully reported by the editor, even to the printing of any item from a neighboring paper.

AN INTERRUPTED BREAKFAST

Report comes to us of a fresh outrage perpetrated by the cow-boys in Sonora. Early last Monday morning a party of sixteen Mexicans from the interior of Sonora on their way to this Territory to purchase goods and carrying $4000 for that purpose, stopped at a curve in the road at Los Animas, near Fronteras, to prepare their frugal breakfast. While busily engaged preparing their tortillas they were saluted with music of twenty rifles fired by cowboys who lay in ambush awaiting them. The Mexicans took this as an invitation to leave and did not stand on the order of their going but left all their mules and pack saddles in which they carried their money for the purchase of goods. When they stopped running they were at Fronteras and their party was four short. The missing men are supposed to have been killed. The citizens of Babispe and troops are after the cow-boys and are disposed to take

197

summary vengeance if they overtake them. — Tucson Citizen.

A gentleman arrived in Tombstone yesterday, it is said, who verifies the above story, however, we have not seen him and cannot vouch for the truth of the report.

(Tombstone Epitaph of Aug. 5, 1881)

While the cowboys occasionally sojourn south of the border, their headquarters and chief place of operation is Tombstone. The columns of the *Epitaph* are filled with such stories as this.

THE MURDERING COW-BOYS

More Depredations by the "Rustlers" —
An Attempt to Steal Cattle Frustrated —
Three Mexicans Attacked and Robbed.

News was brought to town yesterday of further depredations by a party of five men, who are supposed to belong to the gang of outlaws infesting this county, calling themselves "Rustlers." They are principally from western Texas and Lincoln county, New Mexico, from whence they have been driven by an outraged community and now seem to have found the place they long have sought, where they can commit their depredations without fear of arrest. For a long time this gang have confined themselves and their operations to the east of Tombstone and along the line of Sonora, but seeing no steps were taken for their arrest they have become emboldened to take up their haunts and perpetrate their depredations nearer the center of business and population. About half past three on Friday morning the son of Mr. Henning, who runs a milk ranch about three miles above Charleston, on the San Pedro, suspecting something wrong among the cows, which run on the bottom below the house, aroused the two Mexican herders and a party of campers — ten in number, also Mexicans — and started down, when they found a couple of cow-boys gathering up the herd. Henning and his party being in the majority, frightened them off and saved the stock. About 10:30 that same day a party of four gentlemen who were coming to Tombstone, saw a couple of suspicious characters, who left the road when they saw the carriage and

198

rode about forty rods towards the river, heading then upstream until they were a safe distance past the carriage, when they rode back to the travelled road again. Both were armed with rifles in leather cases and were well mounted. One a large man on powerful bay horse, and the other a medium-sized man on a dark sorrel horse with a white face. Shortly after passing these men the party in the carriage met three Mexicans, who had a quantity of packages tied upon their saddles going up the San Pedro also. This party proved to be three of General Pesquelra's men from the Cananae, who had been in Tombstone and were taking out some supplies with them, as also $1000 in gold and Mexican silver for the General. When the latter party got above Hereford and half way to Ochoaville, they were set upon by a party of the cow-boys, who fired, mortally wounding one of the Mexicans and killing one of the horses. They took a rifle and one package of goods and it is supposed killed the one who had the money, as he had not up to last evening, been seen or heard from since the encounter. It is said that the Mexican who escaped, recognized one of the bandits having seen him in Tombstone the day before . . .

It remains to be seen how much longer such damnable acts as the Fronteres massacre and the San Pedro murders shall go unpunished.

(*Tombstone Epitaph* of Aug. 13, 1881)

By an unrelenting crusade, Clum hopes to arouse the citizens to action. Arizona is not the only place troubled by outlaws. New Mexico had them but she has rid herself of them! The notorious Lincoln County war there has ended all organized crime. This range war had pitted honest ranchers against the rustlers and outlaws. Though both sides attracted or hired gunfighters, the ranchers were victorious. It is only a few days ago that Billy the Kid, notorious leader of the outlaws, was killed by Sheriff Pat Garrett.

Clum takes advantage of a news item telling of the death of the Kid, who at 21 had shot a man for each year of his life, to plead that the honest men in Tombstone take action against the outlaws in southern Arizona.

OUR COW-BOYS

A dark menacing cloud has been lifted from the portals of many a home in Southern New Mexico, by the death of the Kid. Now, if the governers of the legislatures of Arizona and New Mexico would bestir themselves and institute a determined, vigorous pursuit of the remaining desperadoes in their prospective territories, and never, never give up the hunt until they have meted out justice, the peaceable citizens throughout the southwest will feel thankful, the section will be free of the odium which has been attached to it for so many years, and settlers will flock in greater numbers, when they know there is security to life and property. — (El Paso Herald.)

In all such calculations the Governor of Arizona must not be counted on. His mining and lottery speculations require his undivided attention in the East. It is a well-known fact that in the southeastern part of this county there is a band of desperadoes variously estimated at from fifty to one hundred men, whose crimes have merited the severest penalties, and yet, we hear of no effort for their capture. It is true their depredations have been committed principally upon citizens of our sister Republic (Mexico), but that is no reason why they should go unpunished. If the officers of the law cannot enforce the law, they would turn over the responsibility to more willing hands. The Herald further says:

The order-loving element surely rises above the lawless, as it always has done and always will do, and crushes it. Sometimes the revolution comes by slow but relentless pursuit, the outlaw sinking one here and one there into bloody graves. But frequently, when crime follows in rapid succession, the outraged lovers of peace arise in their might and crush the malefactor with tremendous force. This is certainly, in many ways, a commendable method of dealing with murderous bands of men. It accomplishes speedily that end which will surely be accomplished some time. In some parts of Texas and New Merico, as well as in other States and Territories, the sudden revolution has been effected, and in not one of these parts, we fully believe, has the dangerous class even attempted to gain the ascendency; in fact, all Western Texas is now nearly entirely free of this element, the desperadoes having been either killed or driven westward. Eastern and Central New Mexico are now beginning to breathe more freely. "Commitees of Safety," honest men banded together, to rid the country of murderers and robbers, have been of incalculable service in that Territory during the past year . . .

(Tombstone Epitaph of Aug. 13, 1881)

New outrages draw only laughter from the Nugget. In fact, it is so noticeable that this paper is nothing but a mouthpiece for the outlaws that the Nugget is known throughout the West as "The Cow-boys Organ." While the Nugget chuckles over the boys' "pranks," Mayor Clum takes action.

Wyatt Earp, who has been working in town as a shotgun guard for Wells, Fargo & Co., is the new deputy U. S. marshal. When a vacancy occurs in the city marshal's office, Clum, within his authority as mayor, appoints Virgil Earp, a brother of Wyatt. Virgil in turn appoints his brother, Morgan, as a deputy. Within days the three brothers take over the job of taming the town.

Wyatt, an ex-member of the police force in Wichita and former city marshal, is responsible for maintaining order within Tombstone; while the United States marshal acts whenever there is interference with the mails. Since this usually occurs at stagecoach robberies, Wyatt soon finds himself in conflict with Sheriff Behan who has jurisdiction over all crimes in the district.

The tension is further heightened between the sheriff and the Earp brothers, because the sheriff is a Democrat as is the territorial government. Wyatt Earp is a Republican and was appointed to his office by the national administration, which is Republican. Then, the Earps are supported by the Epitaph whereas Sheriff Behan is too friendly with the outlaws and their mouthpiece, the Nugget, according to Editor Clum.

As the town begins to take sides, choosing either the cowboy faction or the Law and Order League, the Earps start enforcing the law. The Epitaph prints many items like this.

Officer Bronk trotted Jose Luce before Recorder Wallace yesterday, charging him with the offense of carrying concealed weapons. Luce pleaded guilty and was let off with a fine of $10, which is paid.

Thanks to an act of the territorial legislature in 1875, men can no longer draw a gun without fear of punishment. The law provides that any person found guilty of pulling a pistol, gun, dirk-knife, or other deadly weapon on another party will be fined a minimum of $100 or one month in jail or both. However, the law does not forbid the *carrying* of weapons. Most towns, though, have a local ordinance against carrying *concealed* weapons.

The *Epitaph* of October 26th, 1881, carries this item.

> Another accidental shot disturbed the usual quiet of the city last evening just about sundown. It was in the office of the O. K. corral and caused by some one carelessly handling a loaded rifle. If this thing continues some one will get hurt yet.

When writing this simple news item, Editor Clum has little idea of the violence that is to explode on this day. The 26th of October will go down as the bloodiest day in Tombstone history.

This day begins peaceful enough, although a drunken cowboy is roaming the streets, threatening to kill Marshal Wyatt Earp on sight. The cowboy is Ike Clanton, believed to be a leading figure in one of the area's most active outlaw gangs. Clanton, as do the rest of the outlaws, has every reason to kill Wyatt and his brothers, for these lawmen since coming into office have relentlessly pursued the outlaws, killing a few and throwing others into jail.

In his ravings, Clanton also threatens to get Doc Holliday, a consumptive-ridden ex-dentist, who is Wyatt's closest friend. Hearing of the cowboy's threats, Wyatt, Virgil, and Morgan Earp seek out the drunk.

Virgil finds Clanton in the middle of Allen Street. But before the cowboy can bring his Winchester into play, Virgil draws his six gun and cracks it against Clanton's skull. Slumping to the dirt street, Clanton is seized by Virgil and unceremoniously dragged off to court. Virgil is quickly joined by Wyatt and Morgan, as there is trouble in the air.

A crowd of spectators pours into the courtroom. Many have witnessed Clanton's submission. One spectator gives this version of the events which follow, although his story is not substantiated.

202

"During the examination Ike is sitting quietly in front of the Judge, when all at once he turns toward Earp and says: 'You fellows haven't given me my show at all today. You've treated me like a dog.' The words are hardly out of his mouth, when one of the Earps — I'm not sure which of them — walked over and offered him a Henry rifle, saying at the same time: 'Here take this; you can have all the show you want right now.' You should see that crowd light out just then. In less than half a minute everybody is about a block away. I run with the crowd, but as no shooting is heard, in a short time we all go back again, when we find that Ike has refused to take the gun. But I tell you, pard, that is the worst scared crowd I ever saw."

Clanton is fined and turned loose. Realizing that a showdown is imminent, the Law and Order League meet. The citizens offer to back the Earps in the coming fight but Wyatt rejects the offer. A general gunfight on the streets will certainly cost the lives of townspeople. Businessmen are a poor match for professional killers. Editor Clum and the other Vigilantes content themselves with deputizing Doc Holliday, and Wyatt and Morgan Earp as city marshals.

Small incidents punctuate the late morning hours but there is no open conflict. Noon comes and passes without the sound of battle. Then — gunfire! Late diners at the Rockway Oyster House drop their fried chicken lunch in their haste to see what has happened. A sweet potato slides off an overturned plate and is squashed by a running boot.

Details of the battle between the lawmen and the cowboys are found in the *Epitaph*. Not only does editor Clum give a blow by blow description of the fight but he carefully lists all the events leading up to the gun duel.

YESTERDAY'S TRAGEDY

Three Men Hurled into
Eternity in the
Duration of a Moment

*The Causes that Led to the
Sad Affair*

Stormy as were the early days of Tombstone, nothing ever occurred equal to the event of yesterday. Since the retirement of Ben Sippy as marshal and the appointment of V. W. Earp to fill the vacancy, the town has been noted for its quietness and good order. The fractious and formerly much dreaded cow-boys when they came to town were upon their good behavior, and no unseemly brawls were indulged in, and it was hoped by our citizens that no more such deed would occur as led to the killing of Marshal White one year ago. It seems that this quiet state of affairs was but the calm that precedes the storm that burst in all its fury yesterday, with this difference in results, that the lightning's bolt struck in a different quarter than the one that fell one year ago. This time it struck with its full and awful force upon those who heretofore, have made the good name of this country a byword and a reproach, instead of upon some officer in the discharge of his duty or a peaceable and unoffending citizen.

THE PROXIMATE CAUSE.

Since the arrest of Stilwell and Spence, for the robbery of the Bisbee stage, there have been oft repeated threats conveyed to the Earp Brothers — Virgil, Morgan and Wyatt — that the friends of the accused, or in other words, the cow-boys, would get even with them for the part they had taken in the pursuit and arrest of Stilwell and Spence. The active part the Earps have always taken in going after stage robbers, beginning with the one last spring where Budd Philpot lost his life, and the more recent one near Contention, has made them exceedingly obnoxious with the bad element of the country, and put their lives in jeopardy every month.

Sometime Tuesday Ike Clanton came into town, and during the evening had some little talk with Doc Holliday and Marshal Earp, but nothing that caused either to suspect, further than their general knowledge of the man and the threats that had previously been conveyed to the Marshal that the gang intended to clean out the Earps, that he was thirsting for blood at this time, with one exception, and that was that Clanton had told the Marshal, in answer to a question, that the McLowrys were in Sonora. Shortly after this occurred some one came to the Marshal and told him the McLowrys had been seen a short time before, just below town. Marshal Earp . . . staid (*sic*) all

204

night and added to the police force his brother Morgan and Holliday. The night passed without any disturbance whatever, and at sunrise he went home and retired to rest and sleep. A short time afterward one of his brothers came to his house and told him that Clanton was hunting him, with threats of shooting him on sight. He discredited the report and did not get out of bed. It was not long before another of his brothers came down and told him the same thing, whereupon he got up, dressed and went with his brother Morgan uptown. They walked up Allen Street to Fifth, crossed over to Fremont and down to Fourth, where upon turning up Fourth toward Allen, they came upon Clanton, with a Winchester rifle in his hand and a revolver on his hip. The Marshal walked up to him, grabbed the rifle and hit him a blow at the same time on the head, stunning him so that he was able to disarm him without further trouble. He marched Clanton off to the police court, where he entered complaint against him for carrying deadly weapons, and the court fined Clanton $25 and costs, making $27.50 altogether. This occurrence must have been about 1 o'clock in the afternoon.

THE AFTER-OCCURRENCE

Close upon the heels of this came the finale, which is best told in the words of R. F. Coleman, who was an eyewitness from the beginning to the end. Mr. Coleman says: "I was in the O. K. Corral at 2:30 p.m. when I saw the two Clanton's (Oke and Bill), and the two McLowry boys (Frank and Tom), in earnest conversation across the street, in Dunbar's corral. I went up the street and notified Sheriff Behan, and told him it was my opinion they meant trouble and that it was his duty, as Sheriff, to go and disarm them; I told him they had gone to the West End Corral. I then went and saw Marshal Virgil Earp, and notified him to the same effect. I then met Billy Allen, and we walked through the O. K. Corral, about fifty yards behind the Sheriff. On reaching Fremont street I saw Virgil Earp, Wyatt Earp, Morgan Earp and Doc Holliday, in the center of the street, all armed. I had reached Baver's meat market. Johnny Behan had just left the cowboys, after having a conversation with them. I went along to Fly's photograph gallery, when I heard Virgil Earp say,

"Give up your arms, or throw up your arms." There was some reply made by Frank McLowry, but at the same moment there were two shots fired simultaneously by Doc Holliday and Frank McLowry, when the firing became general, over thirty shots being fired. Tom McLowry fell first, but raised and fired again before he died. Bill Clanton fell next, and raised to fire again when Mr. Fly took his revolver from him. Frank McLowry ran a few rods and fell. Morgan Earp was shot through and fell. Doc Holliday was hit in the left hip, but kept on firing. Virgil Earp was hit in the third or fourth fire in the leg, which staggered him, but he kept up his effective work. Wyatt Earp stood up and fired in rapid succession, as cool as a cucumber, and was not hit. Doc Holliday was as calm as if at target practice, and fired rapidly. After the firing was over Sheriff Behan went up to Wyatt Earp and said, "I'll have to arrest you." Wyatt replied, "I won't be arrested today; I am right here and am not going away. You have deceived me; you told me those men were disarmed; I went to disarm them."

This ends Mr. Coleman's story, which in the most essential particulars has been confirmed by others. Marshal Earp says that he and his party met the Clantons and McLowrys in the alleyway by the McDonald place; he called to them to throw up their hands, that he had come to disarm them. Instantaneously Bill Clanton and one of the McLowrys fired, and then it became general. Mr. Earp says that it was the first shot from Frank McLowry that hit him. In other particulars his statement does not materially differ from the statement above given. Ike Clanton was not armed and ran across to Allen street and took refuge in the dance house there. The two McLowrys and Bill Clanton all died within a few minutes after being shot. The Marshal was shot through the calf of the right leg, the ball going clear through. His brother Morgan was shot through the shoulders, the ball entering the point of the the right shoulder blade, following across the back, shattering off a piece of one of the vertebrae and passing out the left shoulder in about the same position that entered the right. This wound is dangerous but not necessarily fatal, and Virgil's is far more painful than dangerous. Doc Holliday was hit upon the scabbard of his pistol, the leather breaking the force of the ball, so that no material damage was done other than to make him limp a little in his walk.

Dr. Mathews impaneled a coroner's jury, who went and viewed the bodies as they lay in the cabin in the rear of Dunbar's livery stables on Fifth street, and then adjourned until 10 o'clock this morning.

THE ALARM GIVEN

The moment that word of the shooting reached the Vizina and Tough Nut mines the whistles blew a shrill signal, and the miners came to the surface, armed themselves, and poured into town like an invading army. A few moments served to bring out all the better portions of the citizens, thoroughly armed and ready for any emergency. Precautions were immediately taken to preserve law and order, even if they had to fight for it. A guard of ten men were stationed around the county jail, and extra policemen put on for the night.

THE EARP BROTHERS JUSTIFIED

The feeling among the best class of our citizens is that the Marshal was entirely justifiable in his efforts to disarm these men, and that being fired upon they had to defend themselves, which they did most bravely . . .

(*Tombstone Epitaph* of Oct. 27, 1881)

The hastily empaneled coroner's jury deliberates twice before bringing in a verdict that the McLowry brothers and William Clanton were killed by wounds inflicted by the Earps and Doc Holliday. This jury, however, does not commit itself as to whether the killings were justified.

While Morgan and Virgil Earp are still confined to bed because of their wounds, the dead cowboys are buried. The *Epitaph* gives the latest interment in "Boot Hill" only passing notice.

The Law and Order League of the town fully expects an all-out attack on the Earps and Holliday by the cowboys. There is even talk of calling for federal troops to protect the town from the vengeance of the outlaws. The cowboys, however, plan to make their fight in court. There is no use to make another open attempt on the marshals; they are too handy with their guns.

Following this new line of attack, the cowboys see that warrants are sworn out for the arrest of the Earps and Holliday. This action nets little for the outlaws, as the peace officers are examined before Justice Spicer and found not guilty. For this decision Judge Wells Spicer earns the hatred of the cowboys.

Editor Clum adds his name to the growing list of men marked for death by the outlaws. As mayor, he is the leading force behind the organization of the Vigilantes. As editor, he now pleads that more active support be given to the Vigilante organization.

THE PUBLIC SAFETY

We have been passing through a period common to the experience of all frontier cities. The eager desire for success among our merchants and business men, made them for a time unmindful of their duty and responsibility in securing a careful administration of the laws. At the same time there has been attracted to this locality a class of men whose continued infractions of the law in other places had finally compelled them to flee from justice.

The penalties of the law have few terrors to restrain men of the class referred to, and this condition arises from the weak and tardy enforcement of such penalties. Realizing these facts and conditions, an organization has been perfected in this county, composed of men of character and determination, of men who have brought their means and business experience among us to earn an honest livelihood, or amass a fortune by steady, persistent industry. Urged by considerations of public welfare and personal securing, these gentlemen have firmly united, and express their unalterable determination to pursue and punish criminals of all classes until our community is placed upon a sound footing. To accomplish this result, they propose to see that officials charged with an enforcement of the laws perform their duty unflinchingly, or make room for better men. The organization is built up in no sense in defiance of the law, but to secure to the people the fundamental principle of government, namely, PROTECTION — protection to life and property. The organization has the men and the means, and if need be the weapons, at its command to accomplish its object, and the cattle thieves and desperadoes of classes may as well understand first as last that their day for successful operations in Cochise county, and immunity from punishment, has gone by.

The mineral resources of our country have already awakened the astonishment of the world. Our success and development have been extremely rapid. Our mining men and businessmen generally have displayed remarkable conservatism, and in order that our county should be permitted promptly to realize the benefits to be derived from the vast elements of wealth embosomed in the hills and mountains, capital must be made secure in our midst and all causes which are operative to prostrate business to any degree must be removed.

To accomplish this result every man who hopes to make an honest dollar among us must at once make his decision to stamp out crime and wrong doing of every description. We congratulate our people that the organization referred to is in the hands of sterling men, of unflinching courage and ample resources.

(Tombstone Epitaph of Oct. 28, 1881)

This editorial seems to have the desired effect for the Vigilantes become an important force not only in Tombstone but also in surrounding areas.

One of the most important rendezvous of the rustlers is Galeyville in the Chiricahua mountains. Though the camp is only a few miles from Tombstone, the mountains act as an effective barrier to law enforcement. Outlaws, though, now learn that this once inaccessible haven of theirs is no longer a sanctuary. Editor Clum reports:

MORE GOOD COW-BOYS

Lynching of Five Rustlers at Shakspeare.

A gentleman who came in from Galeyville last evening informed an EPITAPH reporter that the report was current and universally believed in that place that five rustlers turned up their toes to the daisies in the neighborhood of Shakspeare last week. It seems that they came in to take the town, and a deputy sheriff of Grant county ordered them to lay down their arms, which they refused to do. The citizens came to the rescue, disarmed the party

209

and hung them all. The names of the victims or any further particulars could not be learned.

Charles Rodig, who lives six miles from Tombstone on the Turquois road, was in Galeyville looking after a horse which had been stolen a few days previous. Upon inquiry he found that the horse had been there, but that the thief had skipped with it, being notified, as was reported, by the deputy sheriff that the owner was looking after his property. Mr. Rodig laid the case before several of the leading citizens, who held a meeting and investigated the matter, and gave the deputy sheriff three hours to leave town. It is needless to say he left, as the citizens are well organized and determined. If this report is true it does not speak well for Sheriff Behan's judgment in the selection of his deputies.

(*Weekly Epitaph* of Dec. 19, 1881)

As the holiday season approaches Editor Clum decides to leave for Washington D. C. After his wife's death, Clum had placed his infant son in the care of the boy's grandparents, living in the nation's capital. The editor decides to spend the holidays with his family and accordingly catches the evening stage on December 14.

Clum has received numerous veiled and open threats against his life for leading the fight against the outlaws. Thinking that the cowboys will not try to assassinate him openly, Clum doesn't take the warnings too seriously. He soon learns otherwise.

As we go to press this morning, we learn through the kindness of Mr. Samdom, one of Sandy Bob's drivers, that an attempt was made to stop the stage last evening, about three and a half miles out of town, just below Male — lm's wells. Simultenously with the command to stop the coach, came a volley of shots, evidently aimed at the horses for the purpose of disabling them thus stopping the coach.

It could not be discovered in the darkness from whence the shots came, or how many men were engaged in the assault. The horses were frightened at the firing and started off on a dead run, continuing their flight for about half a mile, when one of the lead horses fell dead, having been wounded by the highwaymen, and the coach proceeded on

210

without him. The robbers did not overtake the coach, and nothing more was heard of them. The only casualties to the passengers were a slight wound on the leg received by "Whistling Dick," and the disappearance of Mayor Clum, who was on his way to Tucson.

As near as could be ascertained, Mr. Clum was on the outside, and either fell or jumped off during the shooting. As nothing has been heard of him at the present writing — 2:30 a.m. — the gravest apprehensions are felt regarding his safety; as unless he had been killed or wounded by the fusilade, it would seem that he must have reported himself by this time.

This information was obtained by Sandy Bob's driver when he met Kinnear's coach on his way in last night.

Arrangements are now being made to send out a party in quest of the missing Mayor.

(Weekly Epitaph of Dec. 19, 1881)

Though the worst is feared for the safety of the editor and Mayor, the *Epitaph* announces:

A DARK DEED

Full Particulars of the
Last Attempt upon the Benson Stage.

The Narratives of Two Pursuing Parties

MAYOR CLUM SAFE

The announcement in yesterday's EPITAPH of the attack upon the coach night before last threw the city into the wildest excitement, and the gravest apprehensions were felt for Mayor Clum. As before stated, upon receipt of the news a party started out about 3 a.m. to obtain some tidings of the missing mayor, among whom were Sheriff Behan and C. D. Reppy. The sheriff and Mr. Reppy started first and arrived at Contention between 4 and 5 o'clock, where they learned from Mr. Dunham, of Philadelphia, who was on the stage the first particulars of the affair. The six-horse coach, driven by Jimmy Harrington, and the bullion wagon, driven by "Whistling Dick," had just left Malcolm's water station, which is the last house

211

on the road to Contention, and only about four miles from Tombstone, and were bowling along at a rapid gait, when the order to "Halt!" was given from the roadside, and almost simultaneously a volley was fired into them. The off leader of the coach was struck in the neck, and all the horses became unmanageable. Dick was hit in the calf of the leg, receiving a painful flesh wound, but kept his seat and his wagon right side up. The horses ran about half a mile, when the wounded one weakened and fell from loss of blood. Mr. Clum, with the assistance of other passengers, cut the leaders loose, and on they went, it being the general impression that all the passengers were aboard. Mr. Clum had been riding on the inside, and he was missed, but it was supposed by his fellow passengers that he had taken a seat on the outside, consequently his absence was not detected until the arrival of the coach at Contention. Upon learning this, Messrs. Behan and Reppy started for Tombstone, and upon arriving at the place where the attack was made, examined the locality carefully, but no trace of the missing man was found. In the meantime,

The Second Party

which had left Tombstone about 4 a.m., upon arriving at Malcolm's Station, learned that two teamsters in camp with their wagons at that point, had not only heard the noise of their shooting, but could distinctly see the flash, the attack having been made about the apex of the first rise beyond. Continuing down the road about a half-mile beyond the attacking point, by the light of a match, two large pools of blood were found on the right, where the off leader had given out, and after wandering several hundred rods to the right of the road, marking his trail by his ebbing life, had already fallen a prey to the skulking coyote. Not being able to discover any trail, the party proceeded on to Contention, where from Mr. Dunham it was learned that after assisting in releasing the wounded leader, it was supposed by the passengers that Mr. Clum had either taken a seat with the driver or on the bullion wagon, while it was rationally presumed by the driver that he was inside, and his absence was not ascertained until arriving at Contention. Just after leaving Mr. Dunham it was stated that Mr. C. had been heard of at the Grand Central mill, whither the party proceeded, and learned that the mayor had taken the ore road to the mill, from whence, after resting he had gone by saddle to Benson, arriving between 7 and 8 o'clock.

As the teamsters at Malcom's (*sic*) and Mr. Dunham both state that the flashes seemed to come from both sides of the road, and as the wound received by the bullion driver, as well as the death-shot of a faithful leader that had done service ever since the establishment of the line, were made by revolvers, it does not, to say the least, have the semblance of an organized intent to rob the stage, as no rifle cartridge shells could be found on the ground, and all parties claim that there were from fifteen to twenty shots fired in quick succession . . .

Whether this affair was a brutal attempt at assassination or a bungling effort to rob the stage, the passengers and drivers had a narrow escape from death amidst the whistling bullets, and it is hardly presumable that the most ignorant Hottentot or brutal Apache would be so callous and unjust, in the meagre light of yesterday mornings's (*sic*) news, as to attempt to ridicule any person who was upon the coach. This was reserved for yesterday morning's Nugget, and when this is said the utmost dregs of possibility have been reached.

(*Tombstone Epitaph* of Dec. 15, 1881)

The story of Clum's flight seems to tickle the funny bone of the *Nugget's* editor who belittles the whole affair. Tombstone residents think differently and take the *Nugget* editor to task.

THE COW-BOY ORGAN

EDITOR EPITAPH: Please allow me a little space to express my views of the course pursued by the Nuggett on the cow-boy question, and particularly on the attempted murder of J. P. Clum. And here first allow me to say that this letter has been read to many of our best and leading citizens, who heartily endorse every word of it.

For a journal to make sport of, and publish articles intended to be funny on such an affair as the attempted assassination of the mayor of a city, is truly an outrage upon decency, and an insult to the intelligence of the com-

213

munity. They make a joke of it, and publish their slurs; but good citizens cannot look at it in that light. It is well known that no bullion goes out in the wagon on that day; neither does Kinnear's light stage carry mail or express. In fact, it was well known that the stage that night had no treasure or valuables on board. Why, then, the attempt to stop it that night; and that, too, so near to town? The fact of firing about fifteen shots into the stage, and the exclamation which two of the passengers heard them make of, "Be sure and get the old bald-headed son of a b——," explains it all! They were assassins seeking to murder our mayor, and to do so even willing to murder a stage load of passengers. If there could be any doubt of their intent, it would be at once removed by knowing of the previous threats made by the gang to murder, not only the Earps, but also Clum, Spicer, Williams, Fitch and Rickabaugh.

It is well known that the Nugget establishment is owned by Hugo Richards of Prescott, who allows the present publisher to have the use of it on condition that they support him as a candidate for Congress.

The Nugget has so far identified itself with the rustlers that it is generally known as the cow-boy organ, and with its support Mr. Richards will be before the people as the cow-boy's candidate. Does Hugo like the platform?

The Nugget may think it is funny, and they are so cunning when they write their witty articles making merry over the pastime and sports of their pretty pets — such as breaking up religious services and making the preacher dance at the mouth of their revolvers, insinuating improper motives to those who oppose them and becoming exceeding hilarious over a race for life made by our mayor to escape being assassinated by them. All these little pleasantries of the cowboys may be exceedingly funny-graphs, may be exceedingly witty, but they will never send Hugo Richards to congress, nor re-elect the present sheriff.

The constant repetition of outrages by this gang of desperadoes known as cow-boys is driving capital, capitalists and enterprise out of the country, and for a journal published in our midst to treat these outrages with levity is an insult to the entire community.

A CITIZEN

214

The attempt on Clum is an effort to silence him as an editor rather than dispose of him as mayor. As mayor, he has appointed the Earps as peace officers but as editor he has aroused the citizens. The cowboys would much rather face the guns of the three Earps and Doc Holliday than have the nearly 10,000 inhabitants of Tombstone join in the fight against lawlessness.

The cowboys do not have a second chance immediately to get Clum; the editor continues on his trip to Washington without returning to Tombstone. The rustlers, though, are not inactive. They can still make another try for the Earps. This time they are more successful as evidenced by this combined news item and editorial.

MIDNIGHT ASSASSINS

U. S. Deputy Marshal Virgil W. Earp Shot in the Back

The Wounds Painful But Not Necessarily Dangerous

THE FACTS SO FAR AS LEARNED

At about 11:30 o'clock last night, U. S. Deputy Marshal Virgil Earp, was proceeding from the Oriental saloon, on the northeast corner of Allen and Fifth streets, to his room at the Cosmopolitan hotel, and when he was about the middle of the crossing of Fifth street, five shots were fired in rapid succession by unknown men, who were standing in the old Palace saloon that is being rebuilt next door above Tasker & Pridham's store, on the southwest corner of the same streets. Immediately after the firing the assassins ran rapidly down Fifth past the Combination shaft, and disappeared in the darkness beyond Tough Nut street.

Two of the shots took effect on Mr. Earp, one badly shattering his left arm, and the other entered his left side, producing a wound the nature of which has not been ascertained at the present writing. Three of the shots went through one of the windows of the Eagle Brewery saloon, on the northwest corner, in range with which Mr. Earp happened to be at the time of the firing. The holes in the windows were at the heights of about four, six and seven feet respectively above the sidewalk; but fortunately none of the inmates of the saloon were injured, the shots impinging harmlessly upon the opposite wall of the room.

215

LATER PARTICULARS

Since the above was written it has been learned that immediately after the shooting three men ran past the ice house on Tough Nut street, and sung out to the man in attendance, who had his door open at the time, "LOCK your door." The same three men were seen by a miner a few moments later making down into the gulch below the Vizina hoisting works. The shots were evidently fired from double barrelled shotguns, loaded with buckshot, and there must have been three men, as five shots were fired in rapid succession. It is simply a miracle that Mr. Earp was not instantly killed, as in the darkness, with the simple aid of a bit of lighted paper the marks of nineteen shot were found on the east side of the Eagle brewery and in the awning posts, three of them passing through the first window on that side of the house.

Mr. Earp walked back into the Oriental and told his brother that he was shot. His friends escorted him to his room in the Cosmopolitan Hotel, and Drs. Matthews and Goodfellow were immediately called in to attend upon him. It was learned before going to press that his left arm received the principal damage, the shot taking effect just above the elbow, producing a longitudinal fracture of the humerus, or bone between the shoulder and elbow. So far as could be learned, the wound in his back is not necessarily dangerous, though painful.

This further proves that there is a band of assassins in our midst, who, having threatened the lives of Judge Spicer, Mayor Clum, Mr. Williams, the Earp brothers and Holliday, have attempted upon two occasions to carry their threats into execution, first upon Mayor Clum and second upon Virgil Earp. The question naturally arises, who will be the next subject? and a further question, how long will our people stand this sort of thing? It is no fault of these damned assassins that several persons were not killed in their dastardly attempts to murder a United States officer last night; for there were many people in the Eagle brewery, over the heads of whom the passing shots flew on their course. A few inches lower and there would have been corpses prostrate upon the floor in place of frightened people wondering what had happened to cause this bombardment.

(Tombstone Epitaph of Dec. 29, 1881)

216

Coupled with the attack on Virgil Earp is a warning to Judge Spicer to leave town — or else. The outlaws haven't forgotten that it was this judge who found the Earps not guilty in the killings at the O. K. corral. The judge, however, doesn't frighten easily and answers his would-be attackers through the columns of the *Epitaph*.

A CHEERFUL LETTER

EDITOR EPITAPH: — On Saturday morning I received the following spirited letter from the postoffice at this place, viz: (*sic*)

(Tombstone, A. T. Dec. 13, 1881)

TO WELLS SPICER: — Sir, if you take my advice you will take you Departure for a more genial Clime. as I don't think this One Healthy for you much longer. As you are liable to get a hole through your coat at any moment If such sons of Bitches as you are Are allowed to dispense Justice in this Territory, the Sooner you Depart from us the better for yourself And the community at large you may make light of this But it is only a matter of time you will get it sooner or later So with those few gentle hints I Will Conclude for the first and Last time.

A MINER

I much regret that the writer of the above did not sign his true name, or at least inform me what mine he works in, for I would really be pleased to cultivate his acquaintance, as I think he would be an amiable companion — when sober.

A close examination of the chirography of the above love letter reveals the fact that it was written with a stub pen, in a back-hand, with the intent to to (*sic*) disguise the handwriting, and must have been written by some one who attended both the spelling and writing school.

As I cannot have the pleasure of a personal interview with the amiable "Miner," will you allow me the privilege of replying to his charming epistle, and say to him that I have concluded not to go, nor would I ever notice his disinterested advice on the subject were it not for the fact that similar threats have been made by others, and that the threats would be carried into execution if they only dared to do it.

Since the daring attempt to murder Mayor Clum and to wantonly kill a stage load of passengers to accomplish it, these little emanations of bravado do not draw forth admiration as would the beauty of summer clouds with silver lining. They are too sombre and surrounded with a deathly black shade of recent transactions — they are bad omens of the future, when viewed in the light of the death glare of the past. This style of threat has been made not only against myself, but at the same time against Mr. Clum and others. The attempt has been made to assassinate Mr. Clum — who will come next?

One and all will ask, from whence do these threats emanate? And each will have his own opinion; I have mine. And now I will try to do justice to the Clanton brothers by saying that they and men outside the city, living on ranches and engaged in raising cattle or other lawful pursuit, as heartily condemn the proceedings as any man in our midst, and that they as honestly denounce all such affairs as any man can. That the real evil exists within the limits of our city.

It is needless to try to turn these matters into ridicule or make them a subject of jest for funny squibs. It is a matter of serious importance to the community.

I am well aware that all this hostility to me is on account of my decision in the Earp case, and for that decision I have been reviled and slandered beyond measure, and that every vile epithet that a foul mouth could utter has been spoken of me, principal among which has been that of corruption and bribery.

It is but just to myself that I should here assert that neither directly nor indirectly was I even approached in the interest of the defendants, nor have I ever received a favor of any kind from them or for them. Not so the prosecution — in the interest of that side even my friends have been interviewed with the hope of influencing me with money, and hence all this talk by them and those who echo their slanders about corruption. And here, too, I wish to publicly proclaim every one who says that I was in any manner improperly influenced is a base and willful liar.

218

Even those who insinuate such to have been the case are only giving a reflex of their own corrupt hearts. "Those who credit crime are those who feel their own hearts weak to unresisted sin."

Memory, not judgment, prompts to thoughts like these,

"An easy faith to win; And tales of broken faith are most readily believed By those who have themselves deceived."

There is a rabble in our city who would like to be thugs, if they had courage; would be proud to be called cowboys, if people would give them that distinction; but as they can be neither, they do the best they can to show how vile they are, and slander, abuse and threaten everybody they dare to. Of all such I say, that whenever they are denouncing me they are lying from a low, wicked and villainous heart; and that when they threaten me they do so because they are low-bred, arrant cowards, and know that "fight is not my racket" — if it was they would not dare to do it.

In conclusion, I will say that I will be here just where they can find me should they want me, and that myself and others who have been threatened will be here long after all the foul and cowardly liars and slanderers have ceased to infest our city . . .

WELLS SPICER.
(*Tombstone Epitaph* of Dec. 18, 1881)

The cowboys do not content themselves with just threats. They manage to murder Morgan Earp while he is playing a game of billiards. Shot through the stomach, he lives less than an hour. So it is not surprising to find an editorial asking:

WHERE ARE WE DRIFTING?

Taking the facts set forth in the report of the grand jury, the letter of Wells Spicer, and the communication that appear in this morning's EPITAPH, a text is presented of "Observer," upon which there is little or no need of comment. The report of the grand jury is based upon facts, therefore incontrovertible. The letter received by

219

Judge Spicer speaks for itself, and as the work of an assassin. The communication from "Observer" is correct in its conclusions, so far as we are able to judge. The very fact that Frank Leslie and Judge Moses were the recipients of an open postal card with the warning to leave denotes that there was no seriousness intended by the sender. That does not lessen the heinousness of the offense, however, and no pains should be spared in ferreting out the miscreant who sent them, and make an example of him or them, there by showing those of his ilk that they will not be permitted to insult and intimidate honest and respectable people in this manner. If there is to be a change for the better in Tombstone there must be entire unanimity of action upon this question. The publication of crimes of this sort is little less heinous than the actual perpetration of them. It is reported that Judge Moses, feeling insecure in his person and possessions, has taken his family and gone with them to California. This, if true, is to be regretted. Our business men ought to have assured him, in unmistakable terms, of their sympathy and support, and should have prevailed upon him to remain. The loss of one or two such men, from such a cause, is more disastrous to the business interest of Tombstone than would be a fire that wiped out one of the best blocks in the city. The attempted assassination of the mayor of Tombstone, the threat of assassination of a commissioner of the United States and justice of the peace, and the warning of two prominent citizens to leave town, in one week, is just a little too much to be borne with patience.

(Tombstone Epitaph of Dec. 18, 1881)

After his return from Washington, Clum continues his campaign. Showing as much courage as when he chased renegade Apaches, Clum writes editorial after editorial condemning the cowboys. Nor does the *Nugget,* alias the "Laughing Hyena," escape his attention.

The Daily Cow-boy across the street foams at the mouth, and gives strong evidence of having a severe attack of the rabies. Its so-called reply to the specific charges made by the EPITAPH as to the different classes of robbery its friends are engaged in are answered by billings-gate, which

220

is universally conceded to be the rogue's argument. They cannot get around the fact that they stand on record as having indorsed the ten-per-cent steal, all the cattle stealing and stage robbing done by their cow-boy friends, the outrages committed by the rustlers, the turning loose of prisoners charged with murder and grand larceny, and other offenses too numerous to mention. They dare not deny that they have virtually indorsed every one of these acts, and as a consequence, answer by making faces at us. We can stand it if they can.

(Weekly Epitaph of Dec. 26, 1881)

The crusade begins to meet with some success. The governor of the Territory asks President Chester A. Arthur for authority to create a special territorial police force to clean up Tombstone. The president even goes so far as to threaten the Territory with martial law and the use of soldiers to quell the ceaseless violence.

Unfortunately, Clum never sees the taming of Tombstone. When the outlaws are unsuccessful in silencing him by threats and bullets, they try other tactics. Clum's two co-editors are approached. Will they sell the paper? Money talks and Editor Clum finds himself outvoted on the question of the sale.

After losing his newspaper, Clum consults with members of the Law and Order League. These men advise him to get out of town. He has done his job by bringing the lawlessness to the nation's attention. Then, too, he is a marked man.

As he leaves town a final attack is made on him. Of his leave-taking from Tombstone, Clum later says: "There were nine of us who were not supposed to get out of Tombstone alive. We received warnings, written in blood. While we paid not too much attention to them, after a few months it became most uncomfortable. They were picking us off one by one. We could never put our hands definitely on those who were doing it. They opened fire on me from both sides of the road, three miles outside of Tombstone, when I left. They shot through my coat, and shot my horse from under me."

Tombstone, though, has not seen the last of this fighting editor. Some fifty years later Clum again enters the town. This time it is to the joyous shouts of citizens, for Tombstone has become a model city in the new state of Arizona. On this tour Clum insists on visiting the office of the still publishing *Tombstone Epitaph*. He sees, too, the ruins that mark the former office of the *Nugget*. The climax of his trip is a sojourn to "Boot Hill," final resting place of Tombstone's "bad men," who once promised that this fighting editor of Arizona wouldn't get out of town alive.

---

1 This will become the U. S. Weather Bureau.

Epilogue

The darkness of time has obscured the names of Arizona's fighting editors, but their accomplishments are now embodied in the hearts of Arizona's great cities. Their living memorials are great metropolises of stone, steel, glass and plastic rising upward to the azure sky.

The law book has long ago replaced the lynch rope. At first glance, the throb and clash of motors, blare of horns, and blinding glare of city lights have erased the last signs of the frontier. Today, however, you will still find the law in isolated parts being administrated by "night riders" — men who ride by moonlight to "remind" the trouble-maker that he must either behave or "git out before sundown tomorrow." But the six-gun has been buried with the vigilante committee and few are the acts of violence.

The early editors' belief in Arizona was finally rewarded. Their dream of statehood became a reality on February 14, 1912. On that day a former waiter in the mining camp of Globe became the first governor of the 48th state. Refusing to ride in a procession, George W. P. Hunt walks the dusty mile to the inaugural platform at the capitol building.

Today, there is a great deal of talk about freedom of the press. This freedom is being as jealously defended now throughout the world as it was over a century ago in a forbidding land called Arizona. Even after World War II and the Korean War have entered the annals of history, courageous newspapermen are imprisoned and even killed while defending the ideas they have put into print.

These men know not the limitation of time or area. One of the latest to follow the tradition established in part by the fighting editors of Arizona is Haroldo Gurgel. In 1953, this crusading Brazilian journalist was assassinated openly on the street after he charged certain local public officials with corruption.

These murderers may have silenced the pen of this newspaperman; but, they could not erase the epitaph written in the journalist's blood at the scene of his death: HERE DIED A JOURNALIST DEFENDING FREEDOM OF THE PRESS.

Bibliography

Allen, Judge S., *Frontier Incidents in Arizona.* Unpublished manuscript in Arizona State Archives, 1938.

Anderson, Alex D., *Silver Country.* New York, G. P. Putnam's & Sons, 1877.

Anonymous, *Rudo Ensayo* Translated by Eusebio Guiteras, American Catholic Historical Society, no date or place of publication given.

Bancroft, Hubert H., *Arizona and New Mexico.* San Francisco, The History Company, 1889.

  History of California. San Francisco, The History Company, 1890.

  Hisory of the North Mexican States and Texas, 1531-1800. San Francisco. A. L. Bancroft & Co., 1884.

Barnes, Will C., *Arizona Place Names.* Tucson, University of Arizona, 1935, Volume VI, Number I of University of Arizona Bulletins.

Bolton, Herbert E., *Kino's Historical Memoir of Pimeria Alta,* two volumes. Arthur H. Clark Co., 1919, Cleveland.

  Padre on Horseback. San Francisco, Sonora Press, 1932.

225

Rim of Christendom. New York, The Macmillan Co., 1936.
"Spanish Explorations in the Southwest," in *The Jesuits in Primeria Alta,* 1502-1706. New York, Charles Scribners' Sons, 1938.
Wider Horizons of American History. New York, D. Appleton-Century Co., 1939.
Bourke, John G., *On the Border with Crook.* London, Sampson, Law, Marston, Searle and Rivington, 1892.
Brown, J. Ross, *A Tour Through Arizona* 1864, reprinted, Tucson, Arizona Silhouettes, 1951.
Brown, Dee, and Schmitt, Martin F., *Fighting Indians of the West.* New York, Charles Scribners' Sons, 1948.
Clum, Woodworth, *Apache Agent.* New York, Houghton Mifflin Co., 1936.

COMPILED WORKS
Arizona, A State Guide, New York, Hastings House, 1940.
A Historical and Biographical Record of the Territory of Arizona. Chicago, McFarland and Poole, 1896.
Arizona and Its Heritage. Tucson, University of Arizona General Bulletin Number 3, 1936.
History of the Arizona Territory. San Francisco, Wallace W. Elliot and Company, 1884.
Men of Achievement in the Great Southwest. Los Angeles, *Los Angeles Times,* 1904.
Men and Women of Arizona, Past and Present. Phoenix, Pioneer Publishing Co., 1940.
What Made Arizona — MEN. Phoenix, Daws Publishing Co., no date.
Cozzens, Samuel W., *The Marvelous Country.* Amherst, N. S. Rogers and Black, 1874.
Dobie, J. Frank, *Coronado's Children.* New York, The Literary Guild of America, 1931.
Dunn, J. P. *Massacres of the Mountains.* New York. Harper & Brothers, 1886.
Dunne, Peter M., S. J. *Pioneer Black Robes on the West Coast.* Los Angeles, University of California,1940.
Farish, Thomas E., *History of Arizona,* eight volumes. Phoenix, State of Arizona, 1915.
Forrest, Earle R., *Arizona's Dark and Bloody Ground.* Caldwell, Idaho, Caxton Printers, Ltd.. 1950.
Hafen, LeRoy R., and Rister, Carl C., *Western America,* second edition. New York, Prentice-Hall, Inc., 1950.
Hamilton, Patrick, *The Resources of Arizona,* third edition. San Francisco, A. L. Bancroft & Co., 1884.
Hammond, J. N., "Pimeria Alta after Kino's Time." New Mexico Historical Review, Volume IV, Number 3.
Hinton, Richard J., *The Hand-Book to Arizona.* San Francisco, Payot, Uphan & Co., 1878.
Horton, Arthur G., *An Economic, Political and Social Survey of Phoenix and the Valley of the Sun, Arizona. 1867-1941.* Tempe, Arizona, Southside Progress, 1941.
James, George W., *Arizona the Wonderland.* Boston, The Page Company, 1917.
Keleher, William A.. *Turmoil in New Mexico, 1846-1868.* Santa Fe, Rydall Press, 1952.
Kelly, George H., *Legislative History of Arizona, 1864-1912.* Phoenix, Arizona, Manufacturing Stationers, Inc. printers, 1926.
226

Lake, Stuart N., *Wyatt Earp, Frontier Marshal*. New York, Houghton Mifflin Company, 1931.

Lockwood, Frank C., *More Arizona Characters*. Tucson, University of Arizona, 1943, General Bulletin Number Six.

Arizona Characters Los Angeles, *Times-Mirror Press*, 1928.

Pioneer Days in Arizona. New York, The Macmillan Co., 1932.

Lumholtz. Carl, *New Trails in Mexico*. New York, Charles Scribner's Sons, 1912.

Luttrel, Estelle, *Newspapers and Periodicals of Arizona 1859-1911*. Tucson, Arizona, University of Arizona, 1949, General Bulletin Number Fifteen.

McClintock, James H., *Arizona the Youngest State*, three volumes. Chicago, S. J. Clarke Publishing Co., 1916.

Mormon Settlements in Arizona. Phoenix, Arizona, Manufacturing Stationers, Inc., printers, 1921.

"Forward Arizona," radio program during 1930-1931. Manuscripts in Arizona State Archives.

McNickle, D'Arcy, *They Came Here First*. Philadelphia, J. B. Lippincott Company, 1949.

Martin, Douglas D., *Tombstone's Epitaph*. Albuquerque, University of New Mexico Press, 1951.

Mowry, Sylvester, *Arizona and Sonora*. New York, Harper and Brothers, 1864.

Myers, John Myers, *The Last Chance*. New York, E. P. Dutton and Co., 1950.

Pattie, James O.. *Personal Narrative of James O. Pattie of Kentucky,* edited by Timothy Flint. Cincinnati, E. H. Flint, 1833.

Pettitt, George A., *Primitive Education in North America*. Los Angeles, University of California Press, 1946.

Pfefferkorn, Ignaz, *Sonora, A Description of the Province,* translated and annotated by Theodore E. Treutlein. Albuquerque, University of New Mexico Press, 1949.

Pumpelly, Raphael, *Across America and Asia*. New York, Leypoldt, 1871.

My Reminiscences. New York, Henry Holt and Company, 1918.

Riegel, Robert E., *America Moves West*. New York, Henry Holt and Co., 1947.

Robinson, Will C., *Story of Arizona*. Phoenix, Berryhill Company, 1919.

Ruxton, George F., *Life in the Far West*. London, William Blackwood and Sons, 2nd edition, no date.

Santee, Ross, *Apache Land*. New York, Charles Scribners' Sons, 1947.

Sloan, Richard E., *History of Arizona*. Phoenix, Record Publishing Co., 1930.

Stephens, H. Morse, and Bolton, Herbert E. "Early Explorations of Father Garces on the Pacific Slope" in *The Pacific Ocean in History*. New York, The Macmillan Company, 1917.

Stratton, R. B., *Captivity of the Oatman Girls*. New York, Carlton & Porter, 1857.

Summerhays, Martha, *Vanished Arizona,* edited by Milo Milton Quaife. Chicago, Lakeside Press, R. R. Donnelly & Sons, 1939.

Sykes, Godfrey, *A Westerly Trend*. Tucson, Arizona, Pioneers' Historical Society, 1944.

Wormington, H. M., *Prehistoric Indians of the Southwest,* second ed. Denver, Denver Museum of Natural History, 1951.

Wyllys, Rufus Kay, *Arizona — The History of a Frontier State*. Phoenix, Hobson & Kerr, 1950.

"Padre Luis Velarde's Relacion of Pimeria" in New Mexico Historical Review, Volume Six, Number Two.

Young, Archer Bryant, *A Social History of Early Globe, Gila County, Arizona*. Unpublished M. A. thesis, University of Colorado, 1939.

227